Marketing Research and Information 2003–2004

Marketing Research and Information 2003–2004

Matthew Housden

AMSTERDAM BOSTON HEIDELBERG LONDON NEW YORK OXFORD
PARIS SAN DIEGO SAN FRANCISCO SINGAPORE SYDNEY TOKYO

Butterworth-Heinemann
An imprint of Elsevier
Linacre House, Jordan Hill, Oxford OX2 8DP
200 Wheeler Road, Burlington MA 01803

First published 2003

British Library Cataloguing in Publication Data
A catalogue record for this book is available from the British Library

ISBN 0 7506 5961 0

Typeset by Integra Software Services Pvt. Ltd, Pondicherry, India
www.integra-india.com
Printed and bound in Italy

Contents

preface welcome to the CIM coursebooks

An introduction from the academic development advisor

In the last two years we have seen some significant changes to the CIM Professional Series initiated by the Chartered Institute of Marketing. The changes have been introduced on a year-on-year basis, with Stage 1 (Certificate) changes implemented last year in 2002, and the Stage 2 (Advanced Certificate in Marketing) being implemented this year. It is anticipated that next year in 2004 the Stage 3 (Postgraduate Diploma) changes will be implemented.

As a result the authoring team, Butterworth-Heinemann and I have aimed to rigorously revise and update the coursebook series to make sure that every title is the best possible study aid and accurately reflects the latest CIM syllabus.

The revisions to the series this year included continued development in the Stage 1 and Postgraduate Diploma Series, and complete re-writes at Stage 2 to align with the radical overhaul of the CIM syllabus. There are a number of new authors and indeed Senior Examiners in the series who have been commissioned for their CIM course teaching and examining experience, as well as their research into specific curriculum-related areas and their wide general knowledge of the latest thinking in marketing.

We are certain that you will find these coursebooks highly beneficial in terms of the content and assessment opportunities and a study tool that will prepare you for both CIM examinations and continuous/integrative assessment opportunities. They will guide you in a logical and structured way through the detail of the syllabus, providing you with the required underpinning knowledge, understanding and application of theory.

The editorial team and authors wish you every success as you embark upon your studies.

Karen Beamish
Academic Development Advisor

How to use these coursebooks

Everyone who has contributed to this series has been careful to structure the books with the exams in mind. Each unit, therefore, covers an essential part of the syllabus. You need to work through the complete coursebook systematically to ensure that you have covered everything you need to know.

This coursebook is divided into units each containing a selection of the following standard elements:

- **Learning objectives** Tell you what you will be expected to know, having read the unit
- **Syllabus references** Outline what part of the syllabus is covered in the module
- **Study guides** Tell you how long the unit is and how long its activities take to do
- **Questions** Are designed to give you practice – they will be similar to those you get in the exam
- **Answers** (at the end of the book) give you a suggested format for answering exam questions. *Remember* there is no such thing as a model answer – you should use these examples only as guidelines
- **Activities** Give you a chance to put what you have learned into practice
- **Debriefings** (at the end of the book) shed light on the methodologies involved in the activities
- **Hints and tips** Are tips from the senior examiner, examiner or author which are designed to help you avoid common mistakes made by previous candidates and give you guidance on improving your knowledge base
- **Insights** Encourage you to contextualize your academic knowledge by reference to real-life experience
- **Key definitions** Highlight and explain the key points relevant to that module
- **Definitions** May be used for words you must know to pass the exam
- **Summaries** Cover what you should have picked up from reading the unit
- **Further study** Provides details of recommended reading in addition to the coursebook.

While you will find that each section of the syllabus has been covered within this text, you might find that the order of some of the topics has been changed. This is because it sometimes makes more sense to put certain topics together when you are studying, even though they might appear in different sections of the syllabus itself. If you are following the reading and other activities, your coverage of the syllabus will be just fine, but don't forget to follow up with trade press reading!

About MarketingOnline

With this year's coursebooks, Butterworth-Heinemann is offering readers free access to MarketingOnline (www.marketingonline.co.uk), our premier online support engine for the CIM marketing courses. On this site you can benefit from:

- Tutorials on key topics every two weeks during the term, comprehensive revision support material and access to revision days from Tactics – the highly acclaimed independent trainer for CIM courses
- Fully customizable electronic versions of the coursebooks – annotate, cut and paste sections of text to create your own tailored learning notes
- Instant access to weblinks related to the coursebooks
- Capacity to search the coursebook online for instant access to definitions and key concepts.

Logging on

Before you can access MarketingOnline you will first need to get a password. Please go to www.marketingonline.co.uk where you will find registration instructions for coursebook purchasers. Once you have got your password, you will need to log on using the onscreen instructions. This will give you access to the various functions outlined below.

Using MarketingOnline

MarketingOnline is broadly divided into four sections which can each be accessed from the front page after you have logged on to the system:

1. **The coursebooks** Buttons corresponding to the three levels of CIM marketing qualification are situated on the home page. Select your level and you will be presented with the four coursebook titles for each module of that level. Click on the desired coursebook to access the full online text (divided up by chapter). On each page of text, you have the option to add an electronic bookmark or annotation by following the onscreen instructions. You can also freely cut and paste text into a blank word document to create your own learning notes.
2. **Revision material** Click on the 'Revision material' link and select the appropriate CIM level and coursebook to access revision material.
3. **Useful links** Click on 'Useful links' to access a list of links to other sites of interest for further reading and research.
4. **Glossary** Click on the 'Glossary' button to access our online dictionary of marketing terms.

If you have specific queries about using MarketingOnline, then you should consult our fully searchable FAQ section – again, this is accessible through the appropriate link on the front page of the site. Please also note that a **full user guide** can be downloaded by clicking on the link on the opening page of the website.

Using this text

The work book is designed to help you study and you should see it as a guidebook rather than a text book. It will shape your reading, guide you through the syllabus, give you exercises and case studies to analyse and will direct you to the best sources of further information. To do this it draws on the same resources to which you have access. What it tries to do is to steer a way through the enormous amount of material that is available to give you a few short cuts. The work book should be used in conjunction with the recommended texts for the module and you should read widely through these texts. Your approach should be to dip into them to extract the key learning from them and then apply this to your own or other organizations.

The layout of the text follows the curriculum to a large extent.

The coursebook at a glance

Unit 1 – Introduction

By the time you have completed this unit you will:

1. Understand the role of Marketing research and Information within the CIM syllabus
2. Understand the layout of this workbook and how to use it effectively
3. Understand the terms that support your learning through the workbook
4. Be aware of the key supporting texts that you will need to look at as part of your programme of study of stage two of the syllabus
5. Understand the role of marketing research and information in business.

Summary

This unit introduces the programme of study you are about to embark on. We look in detail at the CIM curriculum and the importance of understanding the contents of the curriculum and its objectives and assessment policies. This will guide and focus your study on key elements of the course.

We look at each section of the book in detail and introduce the broad concepts that will be explored in more detail in the rest of the work book.

Unit 2 – Information in the knowledge economy

By the end of this unit you will be able to:

1. Outline the development of the information industry
2. Explain the integration of marketing research and database marketing
3. Identify the key drivers behind the growth of the knowledge economy
4. Be able to define key terms including database marketing, marketing research, data mining and data warehousing, Marketing Information Systems (MkIS) and Decision Support Systems (DSS)
5. Understand the nature and extent of the marketing information industry
6. Identify the key organizations involved in the information industry
7. Understand and analyse the role of marketing research and information in decision-making in organizations
8. Place marketing research and database marketing within the context of the marketing information systems and decision support systems
9. Understand the broad ethical dimensions of research and database marketing

10. Understand the principles underpinning legislation and codes of conduct that relate to data protection
11. Be able to outline the 8 principles of the 1998 Data Protection Act
12. Identify the sources for the MRS ICC/ESOMAR and DMA codes of practice
13. Cover syllabus elements 1.1, 1.2, 1.3, 2.5, 3.1, 3.6, 5.4.

Summary

This unit introduces the concepts of marketing and the information that is needed to enable effective management of the marketing function in all organizations. The definition of marketing as the management process responsible for identifying, anticipating and satisfying customer needs profitably means that timely, accurate and pertinent information underpins marketing orientation. We look at the MkIS as the mechanism for delivering this information and explore in detail Marketing Research and the Database as the key components of this system. We look at a number of different definitions of marketing research and database marketing. Marketing research is defined as 'the collection and analysis of data from a sample of individuals or organizations relating to their characteristics, behaviour, attitudes, opinions or possessions. It includes all forms of marketing and social research such as consumer and industrial surveys, psychological investigations, observational and panel studies' (MRS, 1999). We look at this definition in detail and outlined the scope of marketing research within the organization centring on the planning process.

The database is defined as 'A manual or computerized source of data relevant to marketing decision-making about an organization's customers' (Wilson, A., 2003). The database can be enhanced by other data, including geo-demographic and lifestyle data.

We go on to look in detail at the legislative and self regulatory environment within which the industry works. We look at the 8 principles of the Data Protection Act, and the MRS and ICC/ESOMAR codes of practice. We also look at the codes of practice of the Direct Marketing Association and the preference services. The suppression of names of the deceased is also covered.

We also look at the structure of the industry and the nature of the organizations that support the industry in the UK and overseas.

Unit 3 – The marketing database

After completing this unit you will:

1. Be able to define the marketing database
2. Understand the marketing applications supported by the marketing database
3. Understand the management process involved in building, maintaining and enhancing the database
4. Understand and define the concepts of data warehouses and data mining
5. Have completed syllabus elements 2.1, 2.2, 2.3, 2.4, 2.5.

Summary

In this unit, we explore the database and the range of applications it can support.

We examine the processes involved in setting up a database looking at the management issues and the process of capturing, verifying and enhancing data.

We see that there are several types of data and that the data gathered varies from consumer to business-to-business (b2b) markets. We look at the process of gathering data on international customers and see that this raises issues of consistency due to name and address formats.

Data types include:

- Identification data
- Demographic data
- Financial data
- Lifestyle data
- Transactional data.

These fit into four categories:

1. Behavioural data
2. Volunteered data
3. Profile data
4. Attributed data.

We look in detail at the process of setting up a database exploring each of the phases in turn. These are:

- Business review
- Data audit
- Data strategy, specification and verification
- Data verification
- Hardware/software
- Data capture, maintenance and enhancement
- Management issues should the database be run in-house/out-house
- Applications
- Review.

We look at data enhancement through lifestyle and geo-demographic systems.

We look at the process of maintaining data and explored methods of deduplication.

We look at analysis techniques including the use of Online Analytical Processing (OLAP) tools, cluster, regression and Chaid analysis.

Finally, we look at the applications that the database can support; they are described as:

- Planning
- Contacting customers
- Data processing
- Production
- Response handling
- Lead processing
- Campaign management
- Customer research

- Analysis.

The marketing applications of the database are summarized as:

- Find
- Acquire
- Keep
- Cross sell
- Up sell
- Prevent inactivity
- Renew.

Unit 4 – The marketing research process

After completing this unit you will:

1. Be able to identify the stages of a marketing research plan
2. Identify and brief a range of marketing research suppliers
3. Be able to construct a proposal document in response to a marketing research brief
4. Have covered syllabus elements 3.2, 3.3, 3.4, 3.5, 3.6.

Summary

In this unit we look at the research planning process. We see that the definition of the research problem is enabled through internal and exploratory research. The use of research should be justified where possible by the cost of making a poor marketing decision or the profit to be made from a better marketing decision.

The efficient solution of problems through research means that we should start with the cheapest sources of information, that is secondary or desk research. If this does not produce the required information, then we move to primary work. We outline the different types of marketing research and look at qualitative and quantitative work. We see that qualitative work should precede and inform the development of quantitative methodology. We look in detail at the difference between qualitative and quantitative work.

We go on to look in detail at the briefing process and look at each stage in turn.

- Identification details
- Current business position
- Marketing and business objectives should be laid down and distinguished between
- Research objectives
- How the results will be used
- Outline methodology
- Sample details
- Previous research
- Timings
- Budget
- Deliverables
- Terms and conditions
- Key personnel.

We see that the brief is an important document and that the proposal which is delivered by the short-listed agencies, ultimately, will become the contract for the research programme. We look at the process of producing a proposal and how we should select the agency.

- Identification data
- Situation analysis
- Research objectives
- Methodology and rationale
- Sample
- Fieldwork
- Questionnaire/topic guide
- Data handling and processing
- Reporting
- Timetable
- Costs
- CVs of key staff
- Supporting evidence
- Contract details.

Finally, we look at the process of evaluating published work.

Unit 5 – Using secondary research

On completing this unit you will be able:

1. To define secondary marketing research
2. To explain types of secondary data
3. To understand where to find secondary data
4. To understand the limitations and strengths of secondary research
5. To look for data online
6. To understand the applications of secondary research
7. To complete syllabus elements 4.1, 4.2.

Summary

In this unit we look at definitions of secondary or desk research, and at the strengths and limitations of desk research. These are:

Strengths

- It is cheap or free of charge
- It may provide an answer to the problem, this will save time and effort
- It can guide or provide direction for primary work
- It can suggest methodologies for data collection
- It can indicate problems with particular methodologies
- It can provide historic or comparative data to enable longitudinal studies.

Weaknesses

- It is not related to the research question and the temptation may be to force the data to fit the question
- It may not be directly comparable
- Data may be incomplete

- It may not be available
- The data may have been gathered for a particular purpose.

We look at the range of sources that are available to the researcher.

These include:

1. Government data
2. Trade associations
3. Professional institutes
4. Pressure groups
5. Regulatory bodies
6. Financial institutions
7. Company data
8. Online aggregators
9. Directories
10. The trade press
11. National press
12. Specialist companies
13. Syndicated services.

We see that almost anything published on or by companies is capable of yielding useful data on companies, industries and markets.

We also explore secondary data relating to companies' markets on and offline. We explore how search engines and directories work and look at the use of Boolean operators in helping searches on the Internet.

Finally we look at online markets and explore ways of maximizing the effectiveness of searching online.

Unit 6 – Observation research

After completing this unit you will be able to:

1. Define observational research
2. Understand the methods of observational research
3. Understand and define the role of audits in marketing research
4. Understand the application of mystery shopping techniques
5. Identify online observation techniques
6. Outline the ethical issues in observational research
7. Complete syllabus element 4.3.

Summary

In this unit we look at observation research. We look at the types of research.

These are:

- Natural versus contrived
- Visible versus hidden

- Structured versus unstructured
- Mechanized versus human
- Participant versus non participant.

In particular, we look at the audit process and at the key suppliers of audit data in the UK – ACNeilsen and TN Sofres.

We look in depth at the role of mystery shopping in observation research and at the ethical constraints on its use. We see that its main function is:

- To act as a diagnostic tool identifying failings and weak points in service delivery
- To encourage and reward staff
- To assess competitors.

Other purposes of observational research are:

- To improve customer service
- To improve store layout
- To improve staffing levels to ensure reduced waiting time at call centres or at service points
- To generate information to inform reward and recognition schemes
- To monitor time spent on any activity, e.g. TV consumption
- To measure the amount of product consumed
- To look at product combinations
- To explore alternative product uses
- To explore product interaction.

International observational research is also covered.

We look at the mechanical devices used for capturing data both on and off-line. A range of mechanical observation techniques are used in observation research, and these include:

- Psychogalvanometers
- Eye cameras
- Tachistoscopes.

Finally, we look at issues to do with online observation including the use of cookies.

Unit 7 – Qualitative data

After completing this unit you will be able to:

1. Define qualitative data
2. Identify and apply methods for collecting qualitative data
3. Understand the process of analysing qualitative data
4. Understand the techniques of online qualitative research
5. Understand how to use qualitative research to inform marketing decision-making
6. Complete syllabus elements 4.4, 4.5, 4.6.

Summary

In this unit we look at the area of qualitative research. We see that among other definitions, qualitative research can be defined as 'Research that is undertaken using an unstructured research approach with a small number of carefully selected individuals to produced non quantifiable insights into behaviour motivations and attitudes' (Wilson, A., 2003).

We see that the essential characteristics of qualitative research are:

1. It is unquantifiable and it is not representative of larger populations
2. Data collection techniques are unstructured
3. It involves small samples of individuals or groups of people
4. It seeks to reveal opinions, motivations and attitudes.

We look at the various data collection methods that are used in this area including focus groups, depth interviews and projective techniques. We look at the advantages and disadvantages of each technique.

We look in detail about the skills required of the moderator or interviewer.

Moderators should be:

1. Highly qualified and experienced in research, and possibly, psychology
2. Business and marketing aware. They need to be able to translate respondents' feelings into business advantage for their clients
3. Strong communicators, able to relate to a range of people
4. Hard to place regionally in terms of socio-economic class
5. Socially able, relaxed and friendly, but strong enough to control a room of animated, or conversely, disinterested respondents
6. Flexible and quick thinking, with the ability to respond to the unexpected.

The topic guide is a route map and timetable for both group and depth interviews. The guide should break the interview into three distinct phases:

1. The introduction phase
2. The discussive phase
3. The summarizing phase.

We look at the advantages of focus groups:

1. They replicate the dynamic social interactions that occur in the market place
2. They provide rich and detailed knowledge of a subject
3. They are more efficient in terms of time. One focus group can be done in a day. Fourteen depth interviews might take at least two weeks to complete
4. They are cheaper per interviewee than depth interviews
5. They allow interaction with physical stimuli, e.g. products
6. They can involve multiple techniques within the framework of the focus group.

Advantages of depth interviews:

1. They are conducted face to face, and body language can be interpreted

2. Proximity may encourage respondents to reveal more than they might in a remote interview
3. The respondent is the centre of attention and can be probed at length to explore issues that the researcher feels are important. This is the annoying child syndrome with the researcher asking 'why?' (but more subtly) until the issue is explored adequately
4. Group dynamics may prevent individuals expressing themselves particularly over areas that are sensitive, like income
5. Recruitment tends to be easier
6. The logistics are easier, no special rooms are needed
7. They reveal depth of understanding
8. They are flexible. The line of questioning may evolve within the interview and between interviews
9. They can involve a range of techniques.

We explore the use of projective techniques and see that these techniques can be revealing and interesting to administer. Techniques include:

- Sentence completion
- Story completion
- Word association
- Cartoon completion
- Mood boards
- Brand personality or brand CVs
- Brand mapping
- Thematic apperception tests or TAT tests
- Photo sorts
- Role play.

We explore the online applications of qualitative research. There are problems in carrying out qualitative work online. These include:

1. It is often hard to recruit suitable respondents
2. Technical knowledge is required to participate, and a common technical platform is required
3. Interaction is limited and body language cannot be seen
4. It is hard to interpret the meaning of words without the tone of voice and body language
5. It is hard to maintain attention for long periods
6. It is a less creative environment for respondents
7. It is hard to moderate the contribution of all respondents
8. It is hard to establish who exactly is sitting at the terminal.

Finally, we look at the techniques for analysing the data, both off-line and using the computer packages that are available. We see that there are several ways of organizing qualitative data:

1. Tabular: In which data is organized according to certain characteristics or themes
2. Cut and paste: Material is physically cut from transcript and pasted into separate thematic sections
3. Spider diagrams or mind maps: Places the material at the centre of a diagram with responses emanating from the centre
4. Annotation: The researcher colour codes or annotates the transcript to bring together common themes.

Finally, an exercise brings together the various applications discussed in the unit.

Unit 8 – Quantitative data

After completing this unit you will be able to:

1. Define quantitative data
2. Understand the methods for collecting quantitative data
3. Identify online methods for online quantitative data capture
4. Define and describe the use of CAPI, CATI and CAWI
5. Explore the range of applications enabled by quantitative research
6. Complete syllabus elements 4.4, 4.5, 4.6.

Summary

In this unit we look at the methods of collecting survey data for quantitative research.

Quantitative research is defined as 'research that is undertaken using a structured research approach with a sample of the population to produce quantifiable insights into behaviour motivations and attitudes' (Wilson, A., 2003).

We see that data gathering is more structured, and is made from larger samples. This enables quantitative analysis and comparable studies to be carried out.

We look in detail at data collection methods. These include interviewer-administered questionnaires and self completion questionnaires.

Interviewer-administered methods include face-to-face, telephone- and web-based questionnaires. Self completion includes postal, fax, e-mail and web questionnaires.

We see that face-to-face data collection has a number of advantages:

1. There is greater acceptance of the validity of the research if an interviewer can introduce the reasons for the research and show professional membership cards
2. The interview process is more efficient as non eligible respondents can be screened out more effectively
3. They improve response rates as the interviewer can answer questions or help with any difficulty in completing the questionnaire
4. Personal contact creates a sense of obligation and this can be useful with long surveys. This can reduce the incidence of incomplete or unfinished interviews
5. Complexity can be introduced into the survey – for example, the use of show cards or other stimuli material is more easily managed
6. Empathy and encouragement can enable deeper consideration of the questions and ensure accuracy of some claims – for example, gender and age.

There are also some disadvantages:

1. Costs particularly in b2b research may be high, but this must be offset against a higher response rate
2. It can take a considerable amount of time to complete a survey
3. Interviewers may be demotivated and may take short cuts to ensure that their quota of completed survey is made

4. Interview bias is a problem. Bias may affect:

    - Who is interviewed
    - The way questions are asked
    - The way an interviewer responds verbally and visually to an answer
    - The way an answer is recorded

5. Safety of interviewing staff may be an issue in some areas
6. The training and control of field staff is important and adds to costs
7. A dispersed sample geographically, for example regional store mangers, is clearly difficult to administer in this way and other data collection methods might need to be considered.

Face-to-face interviews may be carried out:

- In the home
- In the street
- In the office (executive interviews)
- In other public places.

We look at the personal qualities of good interviewers and at the Interviewer Quality Control Scheme (IQCS) as a means for ensuring quality of field work.

We go on to look at Computer Aided Personal Interviewing (CAPI) and its advantages:

1. Data entry is much simpler
2. There is no print production, so it is cheaper
3. The computer can check for inconsistent replies – for example a respondent has said that he is a non-smoker and later tells an interviewer he smokes on average three cigarettes a week.

Telephone is one of the fastest growing media to collect data. We look at the reasons for this:

1. Changing environment
2. Telephone research mirrors many businesses process and distribution networks
3. Mobile phones and mobile Internet means that research can use a range of methods to reach and stimulate respondents
4. Technology enables very efficient calling procedures.

We look at the advantages and disadvantages of using the telephone:

Advantages:

1. The cost
2. Control
3. It is very good for international or other geographically dispersed samples
4. It is fast
5. It is convenient
6. Third generation mobile phones, mobile Internet and SMS text messaging have extended the capability of the phone as a medium for data capture.

Disadvantages:

1. Lower response rates

    - Respondents find it easier to say 'no' on the telephone

  - They may screen their calls
  - They may be ex-directory
  - They may not engage fully with the interview process and fail to complete the questionnaire

2. Research design is restricted
3. Some social classes have a greater preponderance of ex-directory numbers
4. Access to mobile telephone numbers may be difficult to obtain
5. It is intrusive and may be irritating
6. In certain cases, international access might be a concern
7. Attitudes to the use of telephone in market research may be less positive than in the UK.

We examine Computer Aided Telephone Interviewing (CATI) and its advantages. These are:

- CATI can facilitate the design administration and analysis of telephone interviewing
- Questionnaires can be customized and verbal comments can be recorded
- Inconsistencies can be highlighted and the researcher can probe to correct the inconsistency
- Automated dialling allows for efficient management of the interviewer
- Completely automated telephone interviews are more possible and may be used to capture simple research data, e.g. satisfaction data.

We see that web-based interviews could be interviewer-aided and that the use of CAWI is helping this process.

Self-administered surveys, or surveys that are delivered to the respondents who complete the questionnaire and return them, cover postal, hand delivered, fax and e-mail or web questionnaires.

We look at each in turn discussing the advantages of each.

Postal surveys have several advantages:

1. Cheap
2. It is useful for geographically dispersed and larger samples
3. It reduces interview bias
4. Questionnaires can be piloted and revisions made
5. It is very convenient
6. Longer questionnaires can be delivered and completed effectively
7. They allow respondents to confer and this may be desirable when researching high involvement purchases.

The disadvantages:

1. Response rate may be low
2. Research design is limited
3. They may take time to complete and this can lead to low response
4. The availability of lists to form sample frames
5. There is limited control over the respondent
6. A high incidence of incomplete questionnaires or inconsistent answers may be expected
7. There is potential for bias in responders as those who respond may be those who feel strongly about an issue.

We look briefly at fax and hand delivered surveys, and in more depth at online surveys

Online methods have a number of advantages

1. They are cheap to administer, design, deliver and analyse
2. They are flexible in content
3. They are fast to administer and to report on
4. They have immediate and low cost global reach
5. They can replicate customer behaviour in both consumer and business markets
6. They can be used automatically
7. They are easy to control
8. They can be completed at the respondents' convenience.

There are several disadvantages:

1. Technology may not be supported by all computers
2. The amount of unsolicited e-mails or spam may affect perception of the questionnaire
3. Samples might be difficult to construct
4. It may be hard to validate who has responded
5. People remain suspicious of the Internet and confidentiality needs to be ensured
6. There may be a cost to the respondent especially if the questionnaire takes time to download
7. The ease of use in some organizations has led to very poor 'research' being carried out on an ad hoc basis.

Finally, we look at Omnibus surveys, hall tests and review the use of panel data. Omnibus surveys have the following advantages:

1. Cheap
2. Fast
3. Representative
4. Flexible.

Disadvantages:

1. The sample cannot be changed
2. Questions must be phrased simply
3. Not suitable for opinions or attitudes
4. Question order may affect responses.

Finally, we look at hall tests, simulated test markets, placement and panel data.

Unit 9 – Questionnaire design

After completing this unit you will be able to:

1. Define the questionnaire
2. Understand and outline the questionnaire design process
3. Understand questionnaire formats
4. Understand how to word a questionnaire
5. Understand the issues in question sequencing
6. Outline the role of piloting in the delivery of the questionnaire
7. Outline the use of software packages to enable design

8. Complete syllabus elements 4.4, 4.5.

Summary

In this unit, we look at the process of designing a questionnaire. The questionnaire has four main purposes:

1. It is designed to collect relevant data
2. To remove bias
3. To make data comparable
4. To motivate the respondent.

We look at a process for questionnaire development:

1. Develop question topics
2. Select question and response formats
3. Determine sequence
4. Design layout and appearance
5. Pilot test
6. Undertake the survey.

We look at the process of developing question topics. We explore in depth the types of questions that can be asked which include closed dichotomous questions, closed multiple choice questions, open questions and scale questions. We look in detail at each of these:

1. Likert scales
2. Stapel scales
3. Semantic differentials
4. Intention to buy scales
5. Forced and unforced scales.

We explore the wording of questions and their sequencing. There are a number of rules for the wording and phrasing of questionnaires.

1. Use clear and simple language
2. Avoid ambiguity
3. Avoid two questions in one
4. Avoid leading or loaded questions
5. Avoid assumptions
6. Avoid generalization
7. Avoid negative questions
8. Avoid hypothetical questions.

We look at the design and appearance of the completed questionnaire and the various ways of improving this aspect of questionnaire design. We see that it should be:

1. Laid out effectively in a clear font
2. In a practical format
3. Produced to a high quality with no literals and printed on high quality paper
4. Interesting with a range of question types
5. Coded and interviewer instructions must be clearly distinguished from the questions.

Finally, we look at the importance of the pilot test, a small scale test of the completed questionnaire and a checklist is provided to help judge the quality of the questionnaire.

Unit 10 – Sampling

After completing this unit you will be able to:

1. Define sampling
2. Understand how to construct a sample for a survey
3. Understand and identify the sampling process
4. Understand and apply the statistical basis of sampling
5. Understand and evaluate different sampling methods
6. Understand the concepts of population, census and sample
7. Understand how the sampling frame is constructed
8. Complete syllabus elements 4.6, 5.1.

Summary

In this unit, we explore the process of sampling and looked in detail at the stages involved in the process.

They cover:

- The definition of the population
- The decision to sample or census
- The creation of the sampling frame
- The sampling method.

We look in detail at probability and non probability sampling and the various approaches under each. Probability sampling includes random sampling, systematic sampling, stratified random sampling, cluster sampling and area sampling.

Non probability techniques include convenience sampling, judgement sampling, quota sampling and snowball sampling. We look at the constraints on the choice of sampling method.

The sample size is then discussed. Sample size is determined by financial, managerial and statistical considerations. We look in detail at the statistical basis of establishing sample size.

Finally, we look at the error involved in sampling, and suggested ways of managing error and the process of weighting.

Unit 11 – Quantitative data analysis

After completing this unit you will be able to:

1. Understand the process of data management, entry, editing, coding and cleaning
2. Understand concepts of tabulation and statistical analysis
3. Understand the main techniques of statistical analysis including descriptive statistics, statistical significance and hypotheses testing, the measurement of relationships and multivariate analysis
4. Understand the use of computer packages that can help with the process
5. Cover syllabus elements 4.6, 5.1.

Summary

In this unit, we look at the process of data analysis. We saw that data needs to be entered, coded, edited and cleaned before data analysis can be carried out.

We saw that there are four types of data. These are:

1. Nominal
2. Ordinal
3. Interval
4. Ratio.

The type of analysis that can be carried out is dependent on the type of data that is being analysed.

We look at the process of tabulation. In order to obtain a first look at data, we saw examples of frequency distributions or holecounts and cross tabulation.

We go on to look at the types of analysis that can be carried out looking in detail at the following:

1. Descriptive statistics
2. Statistical significance and hypotheses testing
3. The measurement of relationships
4. Multivariate analysis.

We look in detail at methods under each of these categories.

Unit 12 – Presenting marketing research

After completing this unit you will be able to:

1. Identify the structure for the presentation of a research report
2. Outline the key features of an oral presentation
3. Know how to make the most of a presentation
4. Understand the use of graphical in presentation of data
5. Complete syllabus elements 5.2, 5.3, 5.4.

Summary

This unit looks at the process of delivering results from research. It looks at the structure of a written research report and covers each of these in depth:

1. Title page
2. Contents
3. Executive summary
4. Introduction
5. Situation analysis and problem definition
6. Research methodology and limitations
7. Findings and analysis

8. Conclusions and recommendations
9. Appendices.

We go on to cover the oral presentation of the results and gave tips for presentation success:

1. Introduction
2. Research background and objectives
3. Research methodology
4. Key findings
5. Conclusions and recommendations
6. Questions.

Then, we look at the graphical presentation of the results including:

- Tables
- Bar graphs
- Pie charts and donuts
- Line graphs
- Pictograms.

Finally, we look at common failings in presenting results.

unit 1 introduction

Learning objectives

The Marketing Research and Information module is an element of stage two of the CIM syllabus and a key part of your study for CIM qualifications including the Post Graduate stage three. The gathering, recording and analysis of information relating to marketing opportunities is a key activity in marketing management. Francis Bacon said, 'Knowledge in itself is power'. Anyone working in business today knows that information lies at the heart of good decision-making; this is especially true in marketing. This module provides you with the knowledge and skill to manage marketing information, and the more specialist knowledge to plan, undertake and present the results from market research.

By the time you have completed this unit you will:

- Understand the role of Marketing Research and Information within the CIM syllabus
- Understand the layout of this coursebook and how to use it effectively
- Understand the terms that support your learning through the coursebook
- Be aware of the key supporting texts that you will need to look at as part of your programme of study of stage two of the syllabus
- Understand the role of marketing research and information in business.

Key definitions

MRS The Market Research Society, the society responsible for professional standards in the market research industry in the UK.

ESOMAR The European Society of Market Research linked to WAPOR the World Association of Public and Opinion Research fulfils a similar role to the MRS.

Syllabus The outline of your course.

Aims and objectives The broad educational aims of the course and the more precise learning objectives that deliver the aims.

Statements of marketing practice Link aims and objectives to the practice of marketing.

Study Guide

This unit should take around 3 hours to complete.

Introduction

The Marketing Research and Information module within stage two of the CIM syllabus has five major components. These are:

1. Information and research for decision-making
2. Customer databases
3. Marketing research in context
4. Research methodologies
5. Presenting and evaluating information to develop business advantage.

A brief insight into each of these components appears below. However, you may find it useful to look at the syllabus in detail in your student handbook or at the CIM website, www.cim.co.uk.

Information and research for decision-making

Syllabus elements 1.1–1.4

These elements of the syllabus relate to the role of information in the decision-making process within organizations and the management of marketing. Traditionally, marketers have used the marketing information system (MkIS) and its components to inform the decision-making process. Central to the process was the use of marketing research. Today with the development of customer databases, the marketer has a significant additional weapon in his armoury. We have more information than ever before. And yet companies are still making poor decisions, and still fail to meet their customers' needs effectively and efficiently.

This element of the syllabus explores the background to and the development of, information management and the growth of the 'information-based' economy. It links this to the way in which organizations should determine their marketing information requirements and how information users should specify their needs within the organization in order to drive profitable lasting relationships with customers. It also explores formats and components of the technical systems that are available to marketers to manage information and support decision-making.

Customer databases

Syllabus elements 2.1–2.5

These elements of the syllabus cover the role of marketing databases in the management of Customer Relationship Management (CRM) systems. They look at the process of developing, maintaining and enhancing the customer database. It explores the role of customer and prospect profiling. In an age in which as ever increasing amount of customer data is captured, the syllabus covers the vital role of data warehousing, data marts and data mining. This allows for actionable intelligence to be distilled from the huge amounts of data to which many organizations have access. Finally, this section of the syllabus explores the key area of the relationship of market research with database marketing. It looks at the way research can enhance data that is captured on customers, and presents the two methods working together to produce actionable intelligence. Clive Humby described this process as the T principle. The database provides broad but shallow data about customers. Market research provides narrow but deep information. Below, Figure 1.1 shows how this can work. TGI is a research service run by BMRB. It provides real insight into customers' behaviour and motivation in many markets (more about TGI later). In this example, TGI is run against the internal database and these are linked by common characteristics. This process enhances the data that is held on the database whilst keeping TGI responses anonymous.

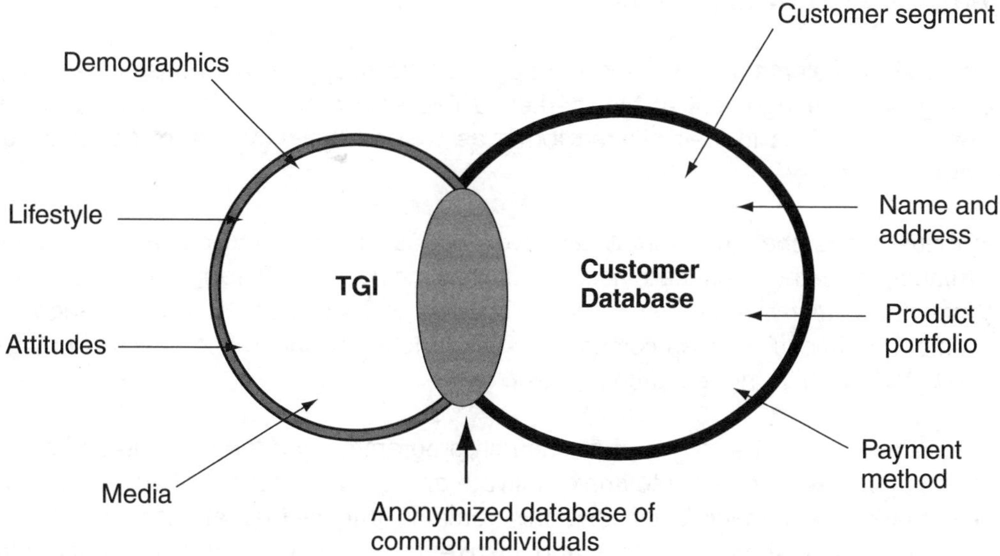

Figure 1.1 The first T process TGI and the database
Source: Clive Humby BMRB

Market research and the database can together, work incredibly effectively in generating advantage for organizations. The use of data from the club card scheme has propelled Tesco into leadership of the highly competitive UK grocery retailing sector. But this has been done not just using data, but through careful analysis of that data and the input from research.

Case history

Tesco

Tesco is an excellent example of a company that is successfully utilizing the tools of marketing research and transactional data to improve its customer focus. The device that Tesco uses to capture transactional data on its customers is Clubcard. Clubcard was set up in 1995 and today over 80 per cent of all transactions are captured. As you can imagine, this is a huge amount of data. In fact over 50 gigabytes of data is captured, including 250 million sales items for 10 million customers in 1100 stores.

Tesco's data analysis company is DunnHumby and it is their job to make sense of the data. In 1995 the data was used to create simple market segmentation models. Today, with enhancement through a range of market research methodologies, Tesco is producing mailings to its Clubcard customers with over 6 million variations. We'll look at Tesco again later.

Source: DunnHumby, 2003.

Marketing research in context

Syllabus elements 3.1–3.6

These syllabus elements cover the nature, size and scope of the industry that supports the provision and management of the marketing research process. This includes the suppliers of research services in their diverse forms as well as the providers of database and other information services.

The industry has changed dramatically over the last decade, and research companies have internationalized and expanded their activities to include the full range of online services and techniques. In many ways, the research industry is always at the leading edge of what is contemporary in business, as companies seek to test new ideas and new technologies in the market place though the research process.

The syllabus covers the stages of a research programme and the procedures and briefing of external agencies. The ability to brief, motivate and get the best out of suppliers is a key part of the marketing manager's job and this remains true in market research. The ability to communicate a research problem and inspire the agency to produce a thoughtful, well structured research plan is crucial to the process of marketing decision-making.

It also outlines the ethical and social responsibilities of the researcher as laid down within the codes of conduct and legislation. More and more data is being captured on customers and research shows that there is a high degree of distrust in the use of data. The recent problems for the industry over the use of the electoral register testifies this. The responsibility for the careful custodianship of customers' data is laid down in law through the 1998 Data Protection Act and through a number of codes of conduct that relate to data protection and the responsibilities of companies to individuals. Failure to comply with these codes of conduct and self-regulation has serious implications for the future of data-driven marketing. Failure to comply with legislation is of course even more serious!

Research methodologies

Syllabus elements 4.1–4.6

These elements of the syllabus deal with the marketing research task and the methods that support the research process. They cover the range of methods and techniques that underpin good research design. The design of marketing research methodologies is a complex task and it draws on techniques that have been tested in other subject areas; in psychology and the social sciences and particularly in statistics. Many students are worried about the numeracy skills required to complete this course. You do need to be numerate – after all, figures are the raw material of the business world. However, the key thing in marketing research is to know the right questions to ask and to understand what the statistics do to data. Statistics enable decisions to be made that reduce the risk to the business and are an invaluable tool in the process of effective marketing.

The syllabus also looks at the role of secondary or desk research in research both on- and off-line. Secondary data is data that has been published elsewhere. Current techniques draw heavily on the Internet and this has changed this aspect of research beyond recognition. We still need to be able to distinguish good from poor data and the workbook gives a range of techniques that you can use to determine this.

The syllabus distinguishes between and define both qualitative and quantitative research and the range of techniques that are used to gather this information. Finally, the syllabus explores the fascinating area of questionnaire and topic guide design and delivery, and the statistical techniques that support research design and analysis.

Presenting and evaluating information to develop business advantage

Syllabus elements 5.1–5.3

These final syllabus elements cover the evaluation and presentation of research data and conclusions. The syllabus covers the statistical basis of the analysis of quantitative research data. They also cover the range of techniques that are used in the analysis of qualitative data. Finally, the syllabus covers the production of written research reports and oral presentations of the results.

Understanding aims and objectives of marketing research and information, and achieving your learning outcomes

Having reviewed the CIM syllabus for this module you can see that the syllabus is broken down into six levels.

- Aims and objectives
- Related statements of marketing practice
- Knowledge and skills requirements
- Related skills for marketers
- Assessment
- Support materials.

It is important to understand the role of each of these in informing your learning on the module. As a student on CIM courses, you are, of course, learning to be a marketing professional and also to study more effectively. As the marketer has a range of tools at his disposal to deliver effective marketing, the learner has a range of tools to help him study more effectively. Understanding the syllabus and the terms that marketing educators use will help you use this manual more effectively, and help your progress towards success on CIM courses.

Aims and objectives

The aims and objectives are the broad objectives for the module as a whole. They explain clearly what the module is designed to achieve and, most important, give you a clear idea of the broad areas of study and what you will be learning.

You can see that the key aims and objectives of the marketing research and information module are to 'provide participants with both the knowledge and skills to manage marketing information, and the more specialist knowledge and skills required to plan, undertake and present results from market research' (CIM, 2003).

Related statements of marketing practice

These statements link the syllabus to the tasks of the marketing professional. They link with other statements that are included in the design of other modules within stage two and three of the syllabus. By the time you complete the syllabus, you will have shown that you possess the skills that sustain the marketing manager in today's business environment. The statements have been developed by the CIM in consultation with senior marketers.

As you can see, the key statements that apply to this module are:

- The evaluation of information requirements, the management of research projects and the marketing information system
- The evaluation and presentation of information for business advantage
- The ability to contribute information and ideas to the strategy process.

Learning outcomes and knowledge and skills requirements

Learning outcomes are developed to narrow and focus the aims of the programme around specific subject areas. They are interesting for you as the assessment is designed against the outcomes. If you understand the learning outcomes of the module then you have a clear idea of what the examiners will be looking for in your assessment. They are also linked to the knowledge and skills requirements, which describe the main content of the course. Some learning outcomes are delivered through the same knowledge and skills requirements.

Table 1.1 Learning outcomes and knowledge and skills requirements

Learning outcomes	Knowledge and skills requirements	
Identify appropriate marketing information and market research requirements for business decision-making	1.1	Demonstrate a broad appreciation of the need for information in marketing and its role in the overall marketing process
	1.2	Explain the concept of knowledge management and its importance in the knowledge-based economy
	1.3	Explain how organizations determine their marketing information requirements and the key elements of user specifications for information
	1.4	Demonstrate an understanding of marketing management support systems and their different formats and components

Plan for and manage the acquisition, storage, retrieval and reporting of information on the organization's market and customers	2.1	Demonstrate an understanding of the application, the role in CRM and the benefits of customer databases
	2.2	Describe the process for setting up a marketing database
	2.3	Explain how organizations profile customers and prospects
	2.4	Explain the principles of data warehouses, data marts and data mining
	2.5	Explain the relationship between database marketing and marketing research
Explain the process involved in purchasing market research and the development of effective client supplier relationships	3.1	Describe the nature and structure of the market research industry
	3.2	Explain the stages of the market research process
	3.3	Describe the procedures for selecting a market research supplier
	3.4	Explain the ethical and social responsibilities inherent in the market research task
Write a research brief to meet the requirements of an organization to support a specific plan or business decision	3.5	Identify information requirements to support a specific business decision in an organization and develop a research brief to meet the requirements
Develop a research proposal to fulfil a given research brief	3.6	Develop a research proposal to fulfil a given research brief
Evaluate the appropriateness of different qualitative and quantitative research methodologies to meet different research situations	4.1	Explain the uses, benefits and limitations of secondary data
	4.2	Recognize the key sources of primary and secondary data
	4.3	Describe and compare the various procedures for observing behaviour
Design and plan a research programme	4.4	Describe and compare the various methods for collecting qualitative and quantitative data
	4.5	Explain the theory and processes involved in sampling
Design a questionnaire and topic guide	4.6	Design a questionnaire and discussion guide to meet a project's research objectives
Interpret quantitative and qualitative data, and present coherent and appropriate recommendations that lead to effective marketing and business decisions	5.1	Demonstrate an ability to use techniques for analysing qualitative and quantitative data
	5.2	Write a research report aimed at supporting marketing decisions
	5.3	Plan and design an oral presentation of market research reports
Critically evaluate the outcomes and quality of a research project	5.4	Plan and design an oral presentation of market research reports

Source: CIM module two syllabus

Assessment

There are two types of assessment that you may encounter. The first is the traditional written exam and the second is a work-based project. Whatever you choose, the content of the assessment will reflect the content of the learning outcomes, and knowledge and skills requirement. It is really important that when you revise for the exams that you cover the entire syllabus. Questions may relate to detailed elements of the curriculum but the entire syllabus will be used to inform the examination. It is important that you also include a range of well-worked examples that allow you to illustrate your answers and bring them to life. Remember the CIM course is giving you a licence to practise marketing, and the use of examples in the right context shows that you understand how the theory can be applied in a business context.

The exam will be practical in nature. Questions will ask you to solve a problem or prepare a briefing document, write a plan or evaluate between different techniques. It will ask you to use the theory to deliver solutions to particular situations and show that you understand how to apply the theory in a variety of business contexts.

Preparation for the exam is really important and the CIM will support you in this task. www.cim.co.uk provides a range of exam guidelines, tips and examples. You should practise writing against the clock. It is really hard work to write freehand for any length of time. Particularly as most of us now rarely write freehand.

Recommended resource materials

These are listed in the syllabus and in the curriculum information section of this text. They will form the background reading for the course as a whole. This workbook reflects the resources that are recommended, and adds to them with other books, websites, examples and case studies. The secret is to read widely and keep careful notes.

Activity 1.1

The use of a portfolio of cases derived from your reading of the trade press and other materials is recommended. This is a valuable practice throughout your career. Your reading of the trade press is vital to keep up to speed with current practice. As a minimum for this module you should include Marketing and Marketing week, Campaign, Precision Marketing and Direct Response and Research, the magazine of the Market Research Society. It should go without saying that you also keep up to date with the general business press including the Financial Times, The Economist and the Wall Street Journal. It is important that you keep a file of a range of material that relates to marketing research, database marketing and CRM, at home and in international markets.

You may choose to access these resources online at www.mad.co.uk, www.ft.com, www.economist.com and www.wsj.com

There are a range of websites that report on the marketing research and information sector and these are listed in the curriculum information section.

Summary

This unit introduced the programme of study you are about to embark on. We looked in detail at the CIM curriculum and saw the importance of understanding the contents of the curriculum and its objectives and assessment policies. This will guide and focus your study on key elements of the course.

We looked at each section of the book in detail and introduced the broad concepts that will be explored in more detail in the rest of the coursebook.

Further study

Go to the CIM website at www.cim.co.uk and familiarize yourself with the material that is available to you.

Hints and Tips

Take a look at the following sites www.mrs.org and www.esomar.nl. They are packed with useful material.

Bibliography

CIM (2003). *Syllabus for stage two,* CIM, pp. 19.

unit 2 information in the knowledge economy

Learning objectives

By the end of this unit you will be able to:

- Outline the development of the information industry
- Explain the integration of marketing research and database marketing
- Identify the key drivers behind the growth of the knowledge economy
- Be able to define key terms including database marketing, marketing research, data mining and data warehousing, Marketing Information Systems (MkIS) and Decision Support Systems (DSS)
- Understand the nature and extent of the marketing information industry
- Identify the key organizations involved in the information industry
- Understand and analyse the role of marketing research and information in decision-making in organizations
- Place marketing research and database marketing within the context of the MRIS and DSS
- Understand the broad ethical dimensions of research and database marketing
- Understand the principles underpinning legislation and codes of conduct that relate to data protection
- Be able to outline the 8 principles of the 1998 Data Protection Act
- Identify the sources for the MRS, ICC/ESOMAR and DMA codes of Practice
- Cover syllabus elements 1.1, 1.2, 1.3, 2.5, 3.1, 3.6, 5.4 .

Key definitions

Marketing Marketing is the management process responsible for identifying, anticipating and satisfying customer requirements profitably (CIM, 2003).

Marketing research The collection, analysis and communication of information undertaken to assist decision-making in marketing (Wilson, A., 2003).

The marketing database A manual or computerized source of data relevant to marketing decision-making about an organization's customers (Wilson, A., 2003).

Data mining The process of extracting hidden and actionable information from large databases (Antinou, T., 1997).

Data warehouse A database whose records contain information aggregated from multiple locations on a customer basis.

Data mart A cut down version of a data warehouse, containing only that data deemed useful for analysis and reporting purposes.

Data capture The process and system for gathering and recording data on customers.

ESOMAR European Society for Opinion and Market Research.

Study Guide

This unit should take you around 3 hours to complete. You should supplement your reading of the unit with at least 3 hours' activity around the unit including reading relevant sections of the recommended texts and reviewing the trade press to begin your case study and clippings portfolio.

Introduction

As we have already heard from Francis Bacon, 'Knowledge itself is power' (Bacon, F., 1597). Bacon was referring to power in a political context and was writing at a time when knowledge was an exclusive product. We all know, however, the value of good information in our day-to-day lives. Today the problem is not accessing information but analysing this to produce intelligence upon which we can act. We also know the value of information in our business lives; the information that allows you to pre-empt a competitor's sales promotion campaign; the customer insight that allows for a direct mail piece to land on the door step just as the consumer is deciding whether or not to buy, or the research that allows your website to have greater impact. Peter Chisnall takes Bacon's idea and applies it in a business context. In his classic text on marketing research, he described good information as 'the raw material used by management in deciding a company's policy and day to day operations' (Chisnall, P., 2001) .

He is right. Without pertinent, reliable, accurate and timely information, decision-making would be impossible. Management decisions would be made in a vacuum. Without information and intelligent analysis of the data, the organization is disconnected from its markets, suppliers, people, customers and future.

One more time, what is marketing?

The starting point for this coursebook has to be the definition of marketing. Can you remember it?

Activity 2.1

See if you can remember the CIM definition of marketing. If you can't remember the whole thing, try to write a paraphrased version. You may be able to remember other definitions. What are the differences? What are the similarities? You may need to visit your notes for the planning module.

Let's have a look at the CIM definition in detail.

Marketing is a management process. We will not dwell too long on this. It is enough to say that marketing is about getting things done through and with people. We need to work with a range of colleagues, suppliers and intermediaries to deliver satisfaction to our customers.

'*Customers*' is an interesting word. They are the only reason businesses exist. It is easy to say marketing is about customers but even this simple word has multiple meaning in the marketing context. Are we talking about current customers, lapsed customers, future customers, profitable customers, best customers or key account customers? The list is as long as the number of segmentation variables we can use.

Of equal interest to us are the next few words.

Marketing is about identifying customer needs. This sounds straightforward. Let's think about this in more detail.

Activity 2.2

I buy mineral water. What need am I fulfilling?

Write down as many as you can think of.

It may help you to think about the context in which a person may buy water. Think hard, you should have at least 6 points.

The next part of the definition is concerned with the anticipation of customer needs. This task is even harder. Forecasting has been described as trying to tell someone where to steer a car by looking through the rear window. Think about the pace of development of new technology. Gordon Moore of Intel Corporation, the computer chip manufacturer, has said that the processing power of computers will double every 18 months and the price will halve. This has become known as Moore's Law. He was right and wrong. The pace of change has been faster. Those companies that are at the forefront of the IT revolution have found it very hard to anticipate customer needs as the customers themselves have found it hard to understand the pace of change and how this might affect their buying patterns.

The IT revolution and the airlines

In the mid 1990s, airlines were respecifying their fleets. The lead-time for commissioning and delivery of new planes is significant. Airlines asked their business customers what changes they would like to see. Some said more legroom, some said better food and more choice of films. Some said that they would like to telephone from the plane. Only a few mentioned at-seat power jacks for their laptops. This meant that many of the new planes that came on line in the late 1990s and early 2000 did not allow business executives to run laptops other than on the laptop's battery.

It is not always enough simply to ask your customers what they want. The questions have to be asked in the right way. We will look at this in detail later on.

Some markets change quickly, others evolve but they always change. As Hugh Davidson says 'tomorrow's standards are always higher' (Davidson, H., 1997). The information strategy of the organization must be set up to ensure that these changes can be anticipated, monitored and acted upon. Risk can never be eliminated from business decision-making. The key thing is to manage and, where possible, reduce the levels of risk to which the organization is subject to within acceptable levels relative to required return on shareholders' investments.

The next part of the definition is concerned with customer satisfaction. This has been an area of growth in marketing over the last 10 years as concepts of relationship marketing and Customer Relationship Management (CRM) have become popularized and applied in businesses. The measurement of lifetime value and work on loyalty (notably by Frederick Reichheld in his book The Loyalty Effect (Reichheld, F., 2001)), has shifted the emphasis from one of sales and new business to customer retention and repeat business. A corollary of this has been a focus on customer satisfaction. The idea is that satisfied customers stay loyal, and loyal customers are more profitable. Well again research shows that this is not always the case. Customers may be satisfied but still leave. They may be enticed away by better offers or products or may no longer have a need for our products or services. They may seek variety or new experiences. Jones and Sasser's work published in the Harvard Business Review (Jones, T. and Sasser, W., 1995) confirms that satisfied customers do defect.

So establishing levels of satisfaction is not enough. The organization must ensure that the underlying attitudes and behaviours are revealed. If customers do defect, then the organization needs to ensure that the reasons for leaving are established and changes are made if appropriate.

Finally, the definition talks about profit. The reason we are in business. Simple – well not really. The development of the marketing database that captures data on the buying behaviour of customers means that we can begin to see that some customers are more profitable than others. We can see that the Pareto Effect which states that 20 per cent of customers account for around 80 per cent of profit is generally true. Indeed in many businesses less than 20 per cent of customers account for more than 80 per cent of profits. So if under Henry Ford all customers were created equal, we now can prove that some customers are more equal than others.

P and O and Elsie Mader

P and O ran a competition to establish who had been on P and O cruises the longest. The winner was Elsie Mader. She had been cruising with P and O so many times that her total time aboard came to more than 10 years.

Source: IDM Course Material

Companies are using this information to work out which customers they need to retain, and by profiling existing highly profitable customers they can more easily identify the type of customer they wish to recruit. For P and O this would be more Elsie Maders! More controversially some companies are using this transactional data to deselect or 'sack' customers who are unprofitable.

Another aspect of profit is deciding when to take profit. Companies using direct response techniques know that many customers are acquired at a loss. The relationship with customers only makes sense from a business perspective over time.

Direct insurance

The average cost of acquiring a customer in the insurance market has been estimated as £120. If the premium is £200, it is clear that this does not allow for very much profit to be made on a one-off transaction. This is why as soon as you buy insurance products you will receive mailings for extended cover, other insurance products, or other financial services products.

So the definition of marketing is not as straightforward as perhaps it first appeared. At the centre of all the elements of the definition is the need for information and research, analysis and insight that allow for a depth of understanding and marketing decisions made at reduced risk.

This applies to all organizations whether they be in business-to-consumer (b2c) markets, in business-to-business (b2b) markets, in fund-raising or in government or not-for-profit markets. At the heart of all successful enterprises is managed information. This may come from marketing research or from the customer database but as Alan Wilson points out in the module's core text, it is integration that is important.

'Integrated information is critical to effective decision-making. Marketing information sources can be as though of separate jigsaw pieces; only when they are connected does the whole picture become clear. Taking decisions by looking at each of the pieces individually is not only inefficient but is likely to result in wrong assumptions and decisions being made' (Wilson, A., 2003).

The marketing information system (MkIS)

The MkIS is the system that organizations use to put information at the heart of the decision-making process.

The MkIS defined by Kotler 'consists of people equipment and procedures to gather, sort, analyse, evaluate and distribute timely and accurate information to marketing decision makers' (Kotler, P. et al., 1999).

The typical MkIS consists of four elements:

The marketing research system – This is the backbone of the marketing information system. However the MkIS also contains other elements. These are:

The marketing intelligence system – This refers to the published data existing in the market place. It may include published research reports, government statistics or the national or trade press. We will look at this in detail when we examine secondary research.

The decision-support system – The decision-support system contains the tools needed to make sense of data; it may include statistical packages and the intranet with a range of tools and information designed to help marketers make decisions.

Internal records – These include sales records, accounts records, details on past communications and the results of previously commissioned marketing research.

These last elements are often now consolidated within the marketing database. Let's look at the two mainstays of the MkIS in turn, starting with marketing research.

What is marketing research?

Let's start with a few definitions, Alan Wilson in the course text defines marketing research as, 'The collection, analysis and communication of information undertaken to assist decision-making in marketing' (Wilson, A., 2003). This picks-up on the essential characteristics of marketing research, i.e. the gathering and analysis of information to inform decisions. This decision-making aspect is important. Marketing research should enable decision-making. Some authors would argue that a decision MUST result from the marketing research process, and in practice this is most often the case, even if the decision is to do nothing!

Activity 2.3

On page 4 of Wilson's book he identifies four characteristics of marketing research. Go to page 4 and write them down in your notes. These will underpin your study of the discipline.

There are a number of other definitions and we need to look at these. Perhaps the most important from the UK perspective is that of the Market Research Society (MRS). The MRS is the professional body overseeing professional standards in the Marketing Research industry in the UK (more about them later).

Marketing research is defined by the Market Research Society as 'the collection and analysis of data from a sample of individuals or organizations relating to their characteristics, behaviour, attitudes, opinions or possessions. It includes all forms of marketing and social research such as consumer and industrial surveys, psychological investigations, observational and panel studies' (MRS, 1999).

As you can see and as you might expect, it is much more technical. It covers techniques and sector applications. Don't worry now if you do not understand terms like 'sample', or 'observational and panel studies'. You will by the time you finish the coursebook!

The American Marketing Association's early definition sounds like Alan Wilson's.

In the past, the American Marketing Association defined research as the 'Systematic gathering, recording and analysing of data relating to problems in the marketing of goods and services' (American Marketing Association, 1961). They changed this to the definition; below and why do you think they did?

The word 'problems' causes some difficulties. Marketing research is also about identifying opportunities for growth in business. They changed this to the following definition; in place for some time now; notice they included opportunities this time.

'Marketing research is the function that links the consumer, customer and public to the marketer through information – information used to identify and define marketing opportunities and problems; generate, refine and evaluate marketing actions; monitor marketing performance; and improve understanding of marketing as a process. Marketing research specifies the information required to address these issues, designs the method for collecting information, manages and implements the data collection process, analyses the results, and communicates the findings and their implications (American Marketing Association, 2003).

How about the CIM? They too have their own definitions. This is taken from the website. www.cim.co.uk has a useful glossary of Marketing terms. You should add this to your 'Favourites' list.

The CIM defines marketing research as 'The gathering and analysis of data relating to market places or customers; any research which leads to more market knowledge and better-informed decision-making' (CIM, 2003).

You may have noticed by now that the definitions refer to marketing and market research almost interchangeably. The distinction is not important. Market research has come to be seen as a subset of marketing research. Market research refers to research on markets whereas marketing research covers the broad scope of marketing activity.

The database

The other elements of the MkIS are often incorporated within the marketing database. Alan Wilson defines the marketing database as 'A manual or computerized source of data relevant to marketing decision-making about an organization's customers' (Wilson, A., 2003).

There are a few things about this definition that need to be explained.

The database does not have to be computer-based. It can be kept on hard copy. However, access to database technology is very easy and cheap. Even the cheapest and simplest software is capable of storing a significant number of records. Microsoft Access is perfectly serviceable for many businesses.

While the definition limits itself to 'customers' other definitions spell out the fact that the database will collect data about past and potential customers as well as current customers. De Tienne and Thompson use the following definition of database marketing:

'The process of systematically collecting in electronic or optical form data about past, current and/or potential customers, maintaining the integrity of the data by continually monitoring customer purchases and/or by inquiring about changing status and using the data to formulate marketing strategy and foster personalized relationships with customers' (De Tienne, K. and Thompson, J., 1996).

The IDM defines the marketing database as 'a comprehensive collection of inter-related customer and/or prospect data that allows the timely accurate retrieval use or manipulation of that data to support the marketing objectives of the enterprise'. (Downer, G., 2002).

Wilson says that the database differs from an accounting system in that the data must be relevant to marketing decision-making. This is a subtle but important difference. Clearly the accounting system may reveal very interesting information to the marketer. It may contain details of what the customer has bought and when, and the frequency of purchase. We will see later that this information is important to successful database marketing. However, it is important that the data fed into the marketing database is relevant to marketing decisions now and in the future. It costs money to store and process data and in this information age it is easy to have too much data.

Wilson (Wilson, A., 2003) suggests that marketers develop customer databases for four reasons:

1. To personalize marketing communications
2. To improve customer service
3. To understand customer behaviour
4. To assess the effectiveness of the organization's marketing and service activities.

The motivation for setting up databases is quite broad. Let's look in detail at the uses of marketing information.

Information and the scope of marketing research

So what is marketing information used for? The clue is in definitions in the section above. But let's try and be more specific.

Activity 2.4

Think about the marketing process. How does marketing information help this process? Write as many things as you can. Use your textbooks when you run out of ideas. We'll resolve this question in the activity debrief.

The marketing research and database industry

The information industry has changed dramatically over the last twenty years inline with changes in business generally. The business has internationalized, and the major organizations that supply research and database services to the market are amongst the largest organizations in marketing services.

The industry has embraced new technology and whilst it is still possible to carry out research without the use of a computer, much of the drudgery has been taken out of the process. The emergence of the Internet as a major channel and communications medium has meant that online research and research about online marketing is perhaps the fastest growing area. In 2001 according to ESOMAR, US$15.9 billion was spent on marketing research worldwide; of this, US$1.7 billion was spent in the UK.

	Turnover* 2001		% Distribution	% Increase 2001/000	
	US$ million	Euros million		US$	Euros
World total	15 890	17 756	100	2.8	5.8
Europe	6316	7058	40	4	7.1
EU 15	5842	6528	37	4.2	7.3
North America	6577	7349	41	3.3	6.3
USA	6159	6882	39	4	7.1
Central/S. America	775	866	5	3.3	6.4
Asia Pacific	2027	2265	13	(−4.8)	(−2.0)
Japan	1070	1196	7	(−11.3)	(−8.6)
M. East and Africa	195	218	1	n/a	n/a

* Based on average exchange rates: 2000: 1 EURO = $US 0.9213; 2001: 1 EURO = $US 0.8949. (Source: IMF International Financial Statistics May 2002)

NB: The estimates are not adjusted for inflation.

Figure 2.1 Worldwide expenditure on marketing research 2001
Source: ESOMAR

Who carries out research?

Research and database information can be produced internally or externally and the management task can be carried out in-house or externally.

Alan Wilson (Wilson, A., 2003) identifies the types of organizations that exist to provide information and research services to the companies. These include:

List brokers – These are suppliers of lists of contacts for marketing purposes. They may include names and addresses, telephone numbers and e-mail addresses. Details of list owners and types are held by the DMA in the UK. You can see these at www.dma.org.uk.

Full service agencies – These are agencies that provide a full range of research services, e.g. TN Sofres.

Specialist service agencies – These are those that specialize in certain types of research, for example international research or online research.

Field agencies – Specialize in the delivery of fieldwork and the administration of questionnaires.

Data analysis companies – As the name suggests these specialize in the analysis of data.

Consultants – These are independent consultants who may offer a range of services.

Other suppliers into the industry include database bureaux who may host an external database for a company.

Leading global research companies

Rank 2001	2000	Organization	Headquarters	Parent country	No. of countries with subsidiaries/branch offices[1]	Research only full time employees*	Global research revenues[2] (US$ millions)	% change from 2000	Revenues from outside home country[3] (US$ in millions)	% of global revenues from outside home country
1	–	NU N.Y.	Haarlem	Netherlands	81	31,919	2,400.0	9.1	2,400.0	100.0
2	2	IMS Health Inc	Westport Conn.	USA	74	5,400	1,171.0	3.6	702.0	60.0
3	–	WPP Plc.	London	UK	62	6,285	1,008.9	8.1	673.8	68.9
	3	The Kantar Group	Fairfield, CT	UK	62	6,070	962.2	9.1	663.2	69.9
	–	Icon Board Navigation	Nuremberg Ger.	UK	6	215	44.6	9.3	10.4	23.2
4	4	Taylor Nelson Sofres Plc	London	UK	41	8,685	813.2	8.1	639.2	78.6
5	5	Information Resources Inc.	Chicago, Ill.	USA	20	4,000	555.9	4.7	135.5	24.4
6	8	GfK Group	Nuremberg	Germany	48	4,750	479.8	6.1	296.9	61.9
7	7	NFO World Group Inc.	Greenwich Conn.	USA	40	9,500	452.9	–3.7	289.9	64.0
8	9	Ipsos Group S.A.	Paris	France	28	3,382	429.9	8.2	355.3	82.7
9	–	NOP World	London	UK	7	1,748	324.7	4.2	171.7	52.9
	11	NOP World	London	UK	7	1,300	249.9	6.0	159.1	64.2
	20	Roper Starch Worldwide	New York, N.Y.	USA	2	448	748	–17.4	12.6	16.9
10	10	Westat Inc.	Rockville Md	USA	1	1,576	285.8	8.1	0.0	0.0
11	12	Synovate	London	UK	43	2,500	266.5	1.1	258.4	97.0
12	13	Arbitron Inc	New York, N.Y.	USA	2	800	227.5	9.1	7.9	3.5
13	15	Maritz Research	St. Louis,	USA	5	830	181.7	3.8	55.8	30.7
14	14	Video Research Ltd*	Tokyo	Japan	3	368	162.2	5.0	1.6	1.0
15	17	Opinion Research Corp.	Princeton, N.J.	USA	8	1,700	133.6	2.3	42.2	31.6
16	19	J.D Power and Associates	Agoura Hills, Calif.	USA	5	600	128.0	23.1	18.7	14.5
17	18	INTAGE Inc.*	Tokyo	Japan	2	304	108.5	1.0	3.7	3.4

18	16	The NPD Group Inc.	Port Washington, N.Y.	USA	11	720	101.7	16.9	13.0	12.7
19	21	Jupiter Media Metrix Inc.	New York, N.Y.	USA	7	480	858.8	−22.6	17.2	20.0
20	22	Dentsu Research Inc.	Tokyo	Japan	1	96	79.4	30.7	0.2	0.3
21	24	Harrtls Inter-active Inc.	Rochester, N.Y.	USA	4	940	75.4	−1.2	10.5	13.9
22	–	Abt Associates Inc.	Cambridge Mass.	USA	3	329	62.8	17.0	34.1	15.0
23	–	Sample Institut. GMbH & Co KG	Moln	Germany	5	323	59.2	17.0	34.1	57.8
24	23	BOPE Group	Rio de Janeiro	Brazil	13	1,307	56.1	22.5	19.6	33.2
25	25	MORPACE Int Inc.	Farmington Hills, Mich.	USA	3	309	48.3	−9.2	15.9	32.9
26	–	Nikkel Research Inc.	Tokyo	Japan	4	180	48.3	1.4	2.4	5.0
			Total			**88,951**	**$9.743.9**	**6.3%**	**$6.178.8**	**63.3%**

1. Includes countries which have subsidiaries with an equity interest or branch offices, or both.
2. Total revenues that include nonresearch activities for some companies are significantly higher. This information is given in the individual company profiles.
3. Rate of growth from year to year has been adjusted so as not to include revenue gains or losses from acquisitions or divestments. *See company profiles for explanation. Rate of growth is based on home country currency.*
4. For VNU, includes some non-research employees.

* For fiscal year ending March 2002.

Figure 2.2 Leading global research companies 2001
Source: ESOMAR

These companies are carrying out a variety of research techniques. The table below shows the split between techniques. Don't worry if you don't understand all the terms – you will by the end of this book!

Type of research	**%**
Face-to-face interviews	32.9
Telephone interviews	19.5
Discussion groups	8.8
Consumer panels	8.3
Postal/self completion	8.0
Hall/central location test	7.7
Retail audits	4.5
In-depth interviews	3.6
Street interviews	2.0
Observation	0.3
Web/Internet interview	0.2

Figure 2.3 Per cent research turnover by method 2002
Source: BMRA (2002).

Professional bodies and Institutes

There are a range of professional bodies that support the profession in the UK. These are divided between the Professional Institutes and the Professional Associations. The main difference is that the institutes support the individuals in the industry while the association supports the industry in the economy.

In the UK, the Institutes that support the market researcher and information professional include:

The CIM – www.cim.co.uk

The MRS – www.mrs.org.uk

The IDM – www.theidm.com

The associations that support marketing research and information industry include:

The British Market Research Organisation (BMRA) – www.bmra.org.uk

The Direct Marketing Association (DMA) – www.dma.org.uk

These national institutes and associations are linked to regional and world representative bodies. For example, the MRS is linked to ESOMAR or the World Association of Opinion and Marketing Research Professionals (WAPOR). The origins of ESOMAR were in Europe. It was founded in 1948 as the European Society for Opinion and Marketing Research. Its links with WAPOR mean it represents over 4000 members in 100 countries.

ESOMAR can be found at www.esomar.nl and WAPOR at www.unl.edu/WAPOR. Both sites are well worth visiting. The DMA is linked to FEDMA, the Federation of European Direct Marketing. FEDMA can be found at www.fedma.org.

Most of the national bodies have a links page through to their international counterparts.

Activity 2.5

Go to the MRS website www.mrs.org.uk and look at The Research Buyer's Guide. This will give you a clear picture of the types of services that its members provide.

Do the same at the Direct Marketing Association's site at www.dma.org.uk.

Ethics, regulation and codes of practice in market research

The 'data' industry has grown rapidly as the technology that is available to capture, store, analyse and exchange data has improved. The amount of data held on individuals is incredible and this raises many issues. The data has value. It has personal and possibly material value to the individual, and commercial value to the company that has acquired the data. It also has a range of costs that are associated with its capture and storage. It is therefore important that companies manage the data effectively and do not betray the trust placed in them by individuals who may have given up very sensitive information. The amount of data captured will only increase. 3G mobile phones can capture location information of users and this can be used to target customers with messages for local retail stores.

Wilson (Wilson, A., 2003) points out that ethics in market research are the moral guidelines that govern the conduct of behaviour in the marketing research industry. He says that the industry is dependent on:

- *Goodwill of respondents* They have to be willing to carry out research and give up information
- *Trust* Underpins all relationships in the industry. Respondents have to trust researchers to handle their data in an ethical manner; clients trust researchers to carry out research properly
- *Professionalism* Data must be used in a professional manner
- *Confidentiality* Data must be kept confidential and anonymous, and not disclosed to third parties.

The right to privacy is enshrined in the Human Rights Act.

Data protection

The UK has had data protection legislation since 1984. The current Data Protection Act which was passed in 1998 and came into force in 2000, was introduced in response to the 1995 European Union Directive on Data Protection. The Act regulates 'processing' of data; this covers data on any living person and there are separate rules for sensitive data, e.g. health, sexuality, religion, disabilities, etc. If you collect data on Halal meals then your data falls in this separate, more sensitive category.

The guiding principles in the Act are transparency and consent. Individuals must have a clear understanding of why their data is being captured and what it will be used for, and they must consent to its use and be given the opportunity to opt out of any later use of this data.

Opt-out is the standard at the moment. However, this is changing, and the latest rules seem to be asking people to actively opt in to future use of their data. This is almost certain to become the standard and it is good practice now to ask individuals to actively opt in to the future use of their data.

There are three key terms to understand in the Act:

1. *Data controller* Is the collector of data.
2. *Data processor* Is the processor of the data. For example, Sainsbury is the collector of Nectar card data and Loyalty Marketing Group is the processor.
3. *The data subject* Is the individual on whom information is collected.

Every UK business that processes data must register with the Data Protection Registrar; this can be done online at www.dpr.gov.uk. It costs £70 for 2 years, as part of the process you must identify all uses to which the data will be put.

The current Act has 8 key principles:

1st Principle Where a company/organization processes data it must be done fairly and lawfully. Overarching principle means that information about the organization gathering information must be given and consent from data subjects must be obtained. Information must be given about the identity of the processor, the use to which the information will be put and all else that is relevant.

Exemptions do exist, for example, when data is collected and used in pursuit of a contract. For example, Amazon could use your name and address to send you a book. Other exemptions refer to data that is needed to ensure the well being of the subject, e.g. health records may be accessed in accidents and emergency situations. It is always best to check with legal counsel to understand these exemptions in detail.

2nd Principle Data must be obtained only for specific and lawful purposes, and shall not be further processed in a manner incompatible with that purpose.

3rd Principle Personal data must be adequate, relevant and not excessive in relation to the purposes for which it is processed.

4th Principle Personal data must be accurate and where necessary up to date, with every reasonable step taken to ensure this.

5th Principle Personal data should not be kept for longer than is necessary.

6th Principle Personal data shall be processed in accordance with the data subjects' rights. These include:

- Right to access – if an individual pays £10 within 30 days, a copy of the data held should be provided
- Right to prevent data being used for direct marketing – direct marketing is communication by any means of advertising or marketing material communicated to particular individuals. Individuals can write and materials must not be sent
- Right to prevent decisions being made on automated processing, e.g. automated decision on credit
- Right to prevent processing that may cause damage or distress.

7th Principle The data must be kept secure against accidental loss, destruction or damage. The data controller, i.e. the collector of the data must have a written contract with the data processor who may process data on behalf of the controller guaranteeing security. There must be appropriate technical and organizational procedures to ensure this and preventing any unauthorized or unlawful processing of data.

8th Principle Overseas transfer of data, should not be outside the European Economic Area (EEA), EU plus Norway, Iceland and Liechtenstein, unless consent is given. If data is exported, it must be to countries approved by the information commissioner. Hungary, Switzerland, New Zealand and Canada are the only ones that qualify at present. The US has set up a system called safe harbour (sic). Under the safe harbour system US companies can self-certify as complying with EEA data rule. In the US, 175 companies have signed up.

Penalties for non-compliance or contravention of the Act are fines of £5000 or more and damages.

Exemptions also exist for data processed for marketing research. Personal data for research can be reprocessed and data relating to longitudinal studies may be kept. Once data is anonymized, it can be kept indefinitely, and once personal identifiers are removed, subjects do not have the right to access data.

The advice is to take advice, enormous damage may be done through the negative publicity surrounding breaches of the Data Protection Act.

There are a number of other relevant Acts but the Data Protection Act is the most onerous. You may need to consider the Telecommunications (Data Protection and Privacy) Regulations 1999 which covers telephone marketing and the opt-out via the Telephone Preference Service (TPS). It also covers opt-out via the Fax Preference Service (FPS). These are the responsibility of the Director General of Telecommunications. There are codes of practice that relate to list and database practice; these amongst many other things say that lists should be run against the latest Mail Preference Service (MPS) suppression files. They should comply with the Data Protection Act. They should not use selections from a database that are more than 6 months old. If data is to be used for a significantly different purpose than originally intended, then consumers must be informed.

Codes of practice

These are self-regulatory codes developed by the professional bodies responsible for the regulation of the industry. These are not legally binding but do represent good practice, and members of the professional bodies must comply with the code of conduct. The ICC/ESOMAR code of practice is fully compatible with the MRS code of conduct which is available at www.mrs.org.uk. You should download this and add it to your study materials.

ICC/ESOMAR code of marketing and social research practice

General

B1 Marketing research must always be carried out objectively and in accordance with established scientific principles.

B2 Marketing research must always conform to the national and international legislation which applies in those countries involved in a given research project.

The rights of respondents

B3 Respondents' cooperation in a marketing research project is entirely voluntary at all stages. They must not be misled when being asked for cooperation.

B4 Respondents' anonymity must be strictly preserved. If the respondent, on request from the researcher, has given permission for data to be passed on in a form which allows that respondent to be identified personally:

a. the respondent must first have been told to whom the information would be supplied and the purposes for which it will be used, and also
b. the researcher must ensure that the information will not be used for any non-research purpose and that the recipient of the information has agreed to conform to the requirements of the Code.

B5 The researcher must take all reasonable precautions to ensure that respondents are in no way directly harmed or adversely affected as a result of their participation in a marketing research project.

B6 The researcher must take special care when interviewing children and young people. The informed consent of the parent or responsible adult must first be obtained for interviews with children.

B7 Respondents must be told (normally at the beginning of the interview) if observation techniques or recording equipment are used, except where these are used in a public place. If a respondent so wishes, the record or relevant section of it must be destroyed or deleted. Respondents' anonymity must not be infringed by the use of such methods.

B8 Respondents must be enabled to check without difficulty the identity and bonafides of the Researcher.

The professional responsibilities of researchers

B9 Researchers must not, whether knowingly or negligently, act in any way which could bring discredit on the marketing research profession or lead to a loss of public confidence in it.

B10 Researchers must not make false claims about their skills and experience or about those of their organization.

B11 Researchers must not unjustifiably criticize or disparage other researchers.

B12 Researchers must always strive to design research which is cost-efficient and of adequate quality, and then to carry this out to the specification agreed with the client.

B13 Researchers must ensure the security of all research records in their possession.

B14 Researchers must not knowingly allow the dissemination of conclusions from a marketing research project which are not adequately supported by the data. They must always be prepared to make available the technical information necessary to assess the validity of any published findings.

B15 When acting in their capacity as researchers the latter must not undertake any non-research activities, for example database marketing involving data about individuals which will be used for direct marketing and promotional activities. Any such non-research activities must always, in the way they are organized and carried out, be clearly differentiated from marketing research activities.

Mutual rights and responsibilities of researchers and clients

B16 These rights and responsibilities will normally be governed by a written contract between the researcher and the client. The parties may amend the provisions of rules B19–B23 below if they have agreed this in writing beforehand; but the other requirements of this Code may not be altered in this way. Marketing research must also always be conducted according to the principles of fair competition, as generally understood and accepted.

B17 The researcher must inform the client if the work to be carried out for that client is to be combined or syndicated in the same project with work for other clients but must not disclose the identity of such clients without their permission.

B18 The researcher must inform the client as soon as possible in advance when any part of the work for that client is to be subcontracted outside the researcher's own organization (including the use of any outside consultants). On request, the client must be told the identity of any such subcontractor.

B19 The client does not have the right, without prior agreement between the parties involved, to exclusive use of the researcher's services or those of his organization, whether in whole or in part. In carrying out work for different clients, however, the researcher must endeavour to avoid possible clashes of interest between the services provided to those clients.

B20 The following records remain the property of the client and must not be disclosed by the researcher to any third party without the client's permission:

a. marketing research briefs, specifications and other information provided by the client;
b. the research data and findings from a marketing research project (except in the case of syndicated or multi-client projects or services where the same data are available to more than one client).

The client has, however, no right to know the names or addresses of respondents unless the latter's explicit permission for this has first been obtained by the researcher (this particular requirement cannot be altered under Rule B16).

B21 Unless it is specifically agreed to the contrary, the following records remain the property of the researcher:

a. marketing research proposals and cost quotations (unless these have been paid for by the client). They must not be disclosed by the client to any third party, other than to a consultant working for the client on that project (with the exception of any consultant working also for a competitor of the researcher). In particular, they must not be used by the client to influence research proposals or cost quotations from other researchers.
b. the contents of a report in the case of syndicated research and/or multi-client projects or services where the same data are available to more than one client and where it is clearly understood that the resulting reports are available for general purchase or subscription. The client may not disclose the findings of such research to any third party (other than his own consultants and advisors for use in connection with his business) without the permission of the researcher.
c. all other research records prepared by the researcher (with the exception in the case of non-syndicated projects of the report to the Client, and also the research design and questionnaire where the costs of developing these are covered by the charges paid by the client).

B22 The researcher must conform to current agreed professional practice relating to the keeping of such records for an appropriate period of time after the end of the project. On request, the researcher must supply the client with duplicate copies of such records provided that such duplicates do not breach anonymity and confidentiality requirements (Rule B4); that the request is made within the agreed time limit for keeping the records; and that the client pays the reasonable costs of providing the duplicates.

B23 The researcher must not disclose the identity of the client (provided there is no legal obligation to do so) or any confidential information about the latter's business, to any third party without the client's permission.

B24 The researcher must, on request, allow the client to arrange for checks on the quality of fieldwork and data preparation provided that the client pays any additional costs involved in this. Any such checks must conform to the requirements of Rule B4.

B25 The researcher must provide the client with all appropriate technical details of any research project carried out for that client.

B26 When reporting on the results of a marketing research project, the researcher must make a clear distinction between the findings as such, the researcher's interpretation of these and any recommendations based on them.

B27 Where any of the findings of a research project are published by the client, the latter has a responsibility to ensure that these are not misleading. The researcher must be consulted and agree in advance the form and content of publication, and must take action to correct any misleading statements about the research and its findings.

B28 Researchers must not allow their names to be used in connection with any research project as an assurance that the latter has been carried out in conformity with this Code unless they are confident that the project has in all respects met the Code's requirements.

B29 Researchers must ensure that clients are aware of the existence of this Code and of the need to comply with its requirements.

The MRS also publishes a range of guidelines on aspects of marketing research. The current list is as follows:

Market research guidelines

Best practice in Mystery Customer Research (also see new revised draft)

Free Prize Draws Guidance Note

Guidance Note: How to Apply the MRS *Code of Conduct* in Employee Research

Guidelines for Research Among Children and Young People

Internet Research Interim Guidance Note

Qualitative Research Guidelines (also see new revised draft)

Quantitative Data Collection Guidelines

Questionnaire Design Guidelines

The Responsibilities of Interviewers

Legislative guidelines

A Basic Guide to the Data Protection Act 1998

The Data Protection Act 1998 and Market Research: Guidance for MRS Members

Market Research Processes and the Data Protection Act (DPA) 1998

Draft guidelines

Code of practice for conducting Market Research in town centres

Draft Business to Business Guidelines

Draft Guidelines for collecting data for mixed or non-market research purposes

Draft Mystery Shopping Guidelines

Draft Observational Research Guidelines

Draft Public Opinion Research Guidelines

Draft Qualitative Research Guidelines

Source: MRS

These should be reviewed at the MRS website.

The DMA code of practice

The DMA code of conduct is available at www.dma.org.uk. There are a range of codes that relate, for example, to SMS marketing and marketing to children. You should review these as part of your study.

The preference services

Preference services are suppression lists that enable consumers to stop receiving marketing communications via various media. Consumers register on the service, and companies must run and deduplicate their files against the suppression list. Information on these is available from the Direct Marketing Association at ww.dma.org.uk. The e-mail preference service is a new service that is run out of Direct Marketing Association in the US.

Preference services cover Telephone, Mail (there is a separate category for households expecting a baby), Fax and E-mail.

The Mailing Preference Service allows you to register your wish not to receive unsolicited direct mail.

Baby MPS is a service which allows parents who have suffered a miscarriage or bereavement of a baby in the first weeks of life to register their wish not to receive baby-related mailings.

The Telephone Preference Services allows you to register your home phone number not to receive unsolicited sales and marketing calls.

The Fax Preference Service allows you to register your home or business fax number not to receive unsolicited sales and marketing faxes.

The E-mail Preference Service is a global service managed by the DMA in the States which allows you to register your e-mail address so as not to receive unsolicited sales and marketing e-mail messages.

Figure 2.4 DMA Services
Source: www.dma.org.uk

Direct Marketing Authority

- The Direct Marketing Authority acts as the final arbiter on complaints referred to it by the DMA governance secretariat.

List Warranty Register

- The List Warranty Register (LWR) was set up in June 1994. This initiative, inspired by the DMA Data Council, is designed to make compliance with the industry codes of practice easier for both DMA and Non-DMA members alike. It is a free service paid for by the industry.

  The LWR is a central database of list owner and user warranties. It helps to eliminate paperwork within the industry by negating the requirement for list owners and users to supply separate warranties every time a list is rented. It promotes best practice within the list industry and helps to raise standards for the benefit of the industry and the consumer. The warranty is an assurance that the data has been collected lawfully, is up to date and complies with relevant Codes of Practice. It should not be taken as a guarantee of responsiveness.

  If you would like to check whether a list owner or list user has a current warranty, e-mail your query to lwr@dma.org.uk.

  TPS, MPS, FPA, EPS

Source: DMA

Deceased suppressions

There are a range of services that enable companies to remove the names of the deceased from their lists. These include the Bereavement Register, the Deceased Register and Mortascreen.

Information on these is available at www.dma.org.uk.

Summary

This unit has introduced the concepts of marketing and the information that is needed to enable effective management of the marketing function in all organizations. The definition of marketing as the management process responsible for identifying, anticipating and satisfying customer needs profitably means that timely accurate and pertinent information underpins marketing orientation. We looked at the MkIS as the mechanism for delivering this information, and in detail explored Marketing Research and the Database as the key components of this system. We looked at a number of different definitions of marketing research and database marketing. Marketing research was defined as 'the collection and analysis of data from a sample of individuals or organizations relating to their characteristics, behaviour, attitudes, opinions or possessions. It includes all forms of marketing and social research such as consumer and industrial surveys, psychological investigations, observational and panel studies' (MRS, 1999). We looked at this definition in detail and outlined the scope of marketing research within the organization, centring on the planning process.

The database was defined as 'A manual or computerized source of data relevant to marketing decision-making about an organization's customers' (Wilson, A., 2003). We saw that the database can be enhanced by other data, including geo-demographic and lifestyle data.

We went on to look in detail at the legislative and self regulatory environment within which the industry works. We looked at the 8 principles of the Data Protection Act and the MRS and ICC/ESOMAR codes of practice. We also looked at the codes of practice of the Direct Marketing Association and the preference services. The suppression of deceased names was also covered.

We also looked at the structure of the industry and the nature of the organizations that support the industry in the UK and overseas.

Further study

Question 1

You are the marketing manger for a major supplier of computer hardware, mainly to the consumer market. The company has a database of 350,000 active customers. The company wishes to enter the small office/home office sector. You have been given the job of researching and contributing to the development of the marketing plan for this new venture. The board feels that their investment on the database should be adequate to inform the development process.

Write a report to the board outlining the following:

- How the database and marketing research will work together to help the marketing planning process?
- In order to convince the board, illustrate your report with examples from other industries.

Bibliography

American Marketing Association (1961). *Report of the Definitions Committee.* Chicago: AMA. Quoted in Chisnall P. *Marketing Research* 6th edition. McGraw Hill, 2001

American Marketing Association (2003). www.marketingpower.com/live/content.php?Item_ID=4620.

Bacon, F. (1597). *Religious Meditations,* Chapter: Of Heresies.

Bennett, P. (1995). *Dictionary of Marketing Terms 2nd edition.* American Marketing Association.

Chisnall, P. (2001). *Marketing research 6th edition.* McGraw Hill.

CIM (2003). www.cim.co.uk.

Crouch, S. and Housden, M. (2003). *Marketing research for managers* 3rd edition. Butterworth-Heinemann.

Davidson, H. (1997). *Even More Offensive Marketing,* Penguin.

De Tienne, K. and Thompson, J. (1996). *Database Marketing and Organizational Learning Theory: Towards and research Agenda, Journal of Consumer Marketing,* **13**(5).

Downer, G. (2002). *The Interactive and Direct Marketing Guide,* The IDM.

Experian (2003). www.micromarketing-online.com.

Jones, T. and Sasser, W. (1995). *Why Satisfied Customers Defect, Harvard Business Review.*

Kotler, P. et al. (1999). *Principles of Marketing 2nd European edition.* Prentice Hall Europe.

MRS (1999). *Code of Conduct,* MRS.

Reichheld, F. (2001). *The Loyalty Effect: The Hidden Force Behind Growth Profits and Lasting Value,* Harvard Business School Press.

Wilson, A. (2003). *Marketing research: an integrated approach,* FT Prentice Hall.

unit 3 the marketing database

Learning objectives

After completing this unit you will:

- Be able to define the marketing database
- Understand the marketing applications supported by the marketing database
- Understand the management process involved in building, maintaining and enhancing the database
- Understand and define the concepts of data warehouses and data mining
- Have completed syllabus elements 2.1, 2.2, 2.3, 2.4, 2.5.

Key definitions

Behavioural data Data that is derived directly from the behaviour of the customer.

Volunteered data Data that is given up by the customer through for example, registering on a website.

Profile data Data that is obtained by linking the database with other sources of information.

Attributed data Data that is extrapolated from the results of market research.

Golden fields The key information elements of the database that must be completed and maintained for good database marketing.

Lifestyle data Lifestyle companies collect information on customers' lifestyles. The data is assembled from various sources; guarantee cards filled in, in return for an extended warranty; questionnaires inserted in magazines or mailed to previous respondents; competition entry forms and so on (Thomas, B. and Housden, M., 2003).

Geo-demographics Companies supply a system of categorizing the country into a number of different demographic types. Each postcode in the country is assigned one of these types. This means that each customer on your database can be matched to a demographic type. When this is done across all of your customer records, a demographic profile emerges (Thomas, B. and Housden, M., 2003).

Data capture Information taken on to a computer system.

Deduplication System of removing names and addresses which appear in a list more than once.

OLAP On Line Analytical Processing.

Study Guide

This unit should take you around 3 hours. You should add another 3 hours for supplementary reading and case studies.

The marketing database

We defined the marketing database in Unit 1. Can you remember any of the definitions?

We had three. The course text book by Alan Wilson defines the database as 'A manual or computerized source of data relevant to marketing decision-making about an organization's customers' (Wilson, A., 2003).

De Tienne and Thompson use the following definition of database marketing:

'the process of systematically collecting in electronic or optical form data about past, current and/or potential customers, maintaining the integrity of the data by continually monitoring customer purchases and/or by inquiring about changing status and using the data to formulate marketing strategy and foster personalized relationships with customers' (De Tienne, K. and Thompson, J., 1996).

The IDM defines the marketing database as 'a comprehensive collection of inter-related customer and/or prospect data that allows the timely, accurate, retrieval, use or manipulation of that data to support the marketing objectives of the enterprise' (Downer, G., 2002).

Activity 3.1

We have three definitions. What are the common characteristics that link them?

Alan Wilson (Wilson, A., 2003) identifies four types of customer data:

1. *Behavioural data* – This is derived directly from the behaviour of the customer.

2. *Volunteered data* – Data that is given up by the customer through – for example, registering on a website.

3. *Profile data* – This data is obtained by linking our database with other sources of information. They are linked by commonly held data – for example name, address or postcode. For example Mosaic (see below).

4. *Attributed data* – This is data that is extrapolated from the results of market research. Although held anonymously, the results of research on a small sample of the database can be flagged against the entire database. For example, a survey that looked at attitudes by age group could be used to group all customers into a relevant segment.

What does this mean in practice? We have all heard of information overload. So in that case what data should a database contain? Clearly there will be a difference between business-to-consumer (b2c) and business-to-business (b2b) markets.

Activity 3.2

The list below presents six categories of data that might be collected. Try to flesh out the list. Under each heading write as many types of information that you may need to inform marketing decisions. What are the implications for b2b markets?

- Identification data
- Demographic data
- Financial data
- Lifestyle data
- Transactional data
- Other data.

Complete the debrief before proceeding.

Geo-demographic and lifestyle profiling

Geo-demographic and lifestyle profiling is a useful addition to the marketers' armoury. Once we have data in the 'Golden' fields, they can be enhanced through overlaying bought in data. Data can be bought from, for example, Experian who runs the Mosaic system, CACI who runs ACORN and Claritas who runs a number of lifestyle overlays.

Dunn and Bradstreet offers profiling and other services in the b2b market.

Activity 3.3

Visit the following websites:

- www.experian.com
- www.claritas.co.uk
- www.caci.co.uk
- www.dnb.com.

Review the services that these companies offer and add them to your favourites list.

Lifestyle classification works normally on researched lists. Claritas, for example, collects data from the warranty registration cards for domestic appliances filled in by new customers. Geodemographics works on the idea that 'birds of a feather flock together' and that customers who share postcodes will share behavioural characteristics.

You can see this with the Mosaic classifications below. Mosaic divides households in the country into 12 groups and 52 types. The Mosaic classification is based in large part on census data but also includes other data sources. These are:

- Electoral registers, where available
- Data from the Lord Chancellor's office
- Companies house data
- Retail data
- Land registry
- Driving and vehicle licensing authority.

The Mosaic system's 12 groups are as follows:

A1: High income families

B2: Suburban semis

C3: Blue collar owners

D4: Low rise council

E5: Council flats

F6: Victorian low status

G7: Town houses and flats

H8: Stylish singles

I9: Independent elders

J10: Mortgaged families

K11: Country dwellers

L12: Institutional areas

The census happens every ten years in the UK. In the past, census data was gathered from what are called Enumeration Districts of about 150 households and then translated into postcode areas. The 2001 data is presented in what are called output areas and is postcode based. It is this data that the Mosaic system now uses. Other geo-demographic systems work in a similar way. For example ACORN is shown below.

ACORN categories	**% house holds**	**Socio-economic group**
A Thriving	19.0	
B Expanding	10.4	
C Rising	9.0	
D Settling	24.5	
E Aspiring	13.9	
F Striving	23.2	
ACORN groups		
A1 Wealthy achievers, suburban areas	14.0	
A2 Affluent greys, rural communities	2.2	
A3 Prosperous pensioners, retirement areas	2.8	
B4 Affluent executives, family areas	3.4	
B5 Well-off workers, family areas	7.0	
C6 Affluent urbanites, town and city areas	2.5	
C7 Prosperous professionals, metropolitan areas	2.5	
C8 Better-off executives, inner city areas	4.0	
D9 Comfortable middle agers, mature home owning areas	13.7	
D10 Skilled workers, home owning areas	10.8	
E11 New home owners, mature communities	9.9	
E12 White collar workers, better-off multi-ethnic areas	4.0	
F13 Older people, less prosperous areas	4.4	
F14 Council estate residents, better-off homes	10.9	
F15 Council estate residents, high unemployment	3.6	
F16 Council estate residents, greatest hardship	2.4	
F17 People in multi-ethnic, low income areas	1.8	
ACORN neighbourhood types		
A1 1.1 Wealthy suburbs, large detached houses	2.2	AB
A1 1.2 Villages with wealthy commuters	2.8	AB
A1 1.3 Mature affluent home-owning areas	2.7	ABC1
A1 1.4 Affluent suburbs, older families	3.4	ABC1
A1 1.5 Mature, well-off suburbs	2.9	ABC1
A2 2.6 Agricultural villages, home-based workers	1.5	ABC2D

ACORN categories		% house holds	Socio-economic group
A2 2.7	Holiday retreats, older people, home-based workers	0.7	ABC2D
A3 3.8	Home-owning areas, well-off older residents	1.5	ABC1
A3 3.9	Private flats, elderly people	1.3	ABC1
B4 4.10	Affluent working families with mortgages	1.8	ABC1
B4 4.11	Affluent working couples with mortgages, new homes	1.3	ABC1
B4 4.12	Transient work-forces, living at their place of work	0.3 –	
B5 5.13	Home-owning family areas	2.5	ABC1
B5 5.14	Home-owning family areas, older children	2.6	C1C2
B5 5.15	Families with mortgages, younger children	1.9	C1C2
C6 6.16	Well-off town and city areas	1.1	AB
C6 6.17	Flats and mortgages, singles and young working couples	0.9	ABC1
C6 6.18	Furnished flats and bedsits, younger single people	0.5	ABC1
C7 7.19	Apartments, young professional singles and couples	1.4	ABC1
C7 7.20	Gentrified multi-ethnic areas	1.1	ABC1
C8 8.21	Prosperous enclaves, highly qualified executives	0.9	ABC1
C8 8.22	Academic centres, students and young professionals	0.6	ABC1
C8 8.23	Affluent city centre areas, tenements and flats	0.7	ABC1
C8 8.24	Partially gentrified, multi-ethnic areas	0.8	ABC1
C8 8.25	Converted flats and bedsits, single people	1.0 –	
D9 9.26	Mature established home-owning areas	3.4	ABC1
D9 9.27	Rural areas, mixed occupation	3.4 –	C1
D9 9.28	Established home-owning areas	3.9	
D9 9.29	Home-owning areas, council tenants, retired people	3.0	ABC1

ACORN categories		% house holds	Socio-economic group
D10 10.30	Established home-owning areas, skilled workers	4.3	C2
D10 10.31	Home owners in older properties, younger workers	3.2	C1C2
D10 10.32	Home-owning areas with skilled workers	3.3	C2DE
E11 11.33	Council areas, some new home owners	3.7	C2DE
E11 11.34	Mature home-owning areas, skilled workers	3.3	C2DE
E11 11.35	Low-rise estates, older workers, new home owners	2.9	C2DE
E12 12.36	Home-owning multi-ethnic areas, young families	1.0	C1
E12 12.37	Multi-occupied town centres, mixed occupations	2.0 –	
E12 12.38	Multi-ethnic areas, white collar workers	1.0	C1
F13 13.39	Home owners, small council flats, single pensioners	2.3	C2DE
F13 13.40	Council areas, older people, health problems	2.1	C2DE
F14 14.41	Better-off council areas, new home owners	2.0	C2DE
F14 14.42	Council areas, young families, some new home owners	2.7	C2DE
F14 14.43	Council areas, young families, many lone parents	1.6	C2DE
F14 14.44	Multi-occupied terraces, multi-ethnic areas	0.7	C2DE
F14 14.45	Low-rise council housing, less well-off families	1.8	C2DE
F14 14.46	Council areas, residents with health problems	2.1	C2DE
F15 15.47	Estates with high unemployment	1.3	DE
F15 15.48	Council flats, elderly people, health problems	1.1	C2DE
F15 15.49	Council flats, very high unemployment, singles	1.2	DE
F16 16.50	Council areas, high unemployment, lone parents	1.5	DE
F16 16.51	Council flats, greatest hardship, many lone parents	0.9	DE
F17 17.52	Multi-ethnic, large families, overcrowding	0.5	DE
F17 17.53	Multi-ethnic, severe unemployment, lone parents	1.0	DE
F17 17.54	Multi-ethnic, high unemployment, overcrowding	0.3	DE

Figure 3.1 ACORN classifications
Source: ACORN

Variations of the ACORN system have been introduced to serve the classification needs of specific markets. These include:

- Investor ACORN
- Change ACORN
- Scottish ACORN
- Financial ACORN.

Examples of two of the Mosaic classifications can be seen below. Whilst there are some weaknesses in the approach, you can see that in certain markets the use of this data would be very helpful.

Mosaic Group: A High income families

Mosaic Level: A1 Clever capitalists

Clever capitalists make very high use of financial services and tend to have high value savings and loans.

They are enthusiastic patrons of the Arts. Foreign holidays will often be spent in owned accommodation. Long-haul holidays are supplemented by winter skiing trips and off-season short breaks.

Here you will find the heaviest readership of *The Financial Times*, foreign language newspapers and business magazines such as *The Economist*. Television viewing is very light and, other than listening to Radio 4 on the way to work or late at night, few people are heavy radio listeners.

Clever capitalists eat out a lot in smart restaurants and clubs; at home they patronize Waitrose and Marks & Spencer.

Luxury or exotic cars are often hidden behind imposing gates and protected by sophisticated alarms. These neighbourhoods are good for specialist bathroom equipment, saunas and, sometimes, swimming pools.

Mosaic group: E Council flats

Mosaic level: E22 Flats for the aged

Flats for the aged have very little requirements for sophisticated financial products. No one needs a mortgage and there is little demand for credit.

One of the principal leisure activity of flats for the aged is bingo. Many people read, knit and play cards. Few spend much time gardening or on home decorating.

This group is a low consumer of media; few can afford cable or satellite and many go without a daily newspaper. The Mirror and The News of the World are more commonly read here than by any other type.

Flats for the aged rely on daily food shopping, primarily from local stores, and are happy to cook from basic ingredients. Many are the beneficiaries of Meals on Wheels.

People of this type spend very little on consumer durables other than special products for the infirm or elderly (Experian, 2003).

Mosaic also works at a European level and has a number of other targeting tools that the marketer can use.

Case Study

Bang & Olufsen and Micromarketing

Bang & Olufsen is one of the world's leading premium audio visual and telecoms product retailers. Operating throughout most major international markets, the company's innovative products place great emphasis on design, originality and sound quality. It is essential, however, for an organization like Bang & Olufsen to continually seek effective methods of refining its marketing and store-planning activities in order to maintain a clear competitive lead. These marketing requirements led the company to conceive an international development project that used the latest micro-marketing analysis tools to establish two main levels of intelligence:

- A greater understanding of target customer profiles
- Improved intelligence on the relative value and potential of existing and prospective store locations.

As the first stage in this international project, Experian was asked to undertake a test exercise in the UK, covering a number of key stages. An in-depth analysis of the existing customer base identified dominant target customer types using *MOSAIC* and defined catchment areas. Areas of high likely demand were identified, along with an appraisal of catchment overlaps, providing an understanding of the best areas in which to site new stores. Catchment areas, customer data and demand models were input into Experian's *Micromarketer* software along with *Site Quality Indicators (SQI's)*. *SQI's* are derived from data about each specific retail site, including the quality of its location within a retail centre, the proximity of major attractors such as department stores, as well as transport, access and parking factors. This meant that each potential Bang & Olufsen store site could be evaluated with a new level of precision.

Key differences are already evident between the different country markets. For instance, the longer distances which the UK customers are prepared to travel to a Bang & Olufsen store vary little between a concession in a major city centre store and a destination store in a small market town. In other words, these stores operate uninfluenced by the normal shopper flow. In contrast, however, some French and Spanish city centre outlets have been revealed to attract as much as 50 per cent of their customers from a mere 1 kilometre radius. Finally, further enhancements are also taking place in the UK. Now that refined key target profiles have been established centrally, Experian's CD-based electoral roll selection tool, *Prospect Locator*, is now being used to target local mailings around each store, combining these profiles with the additional strength of local knowledge and market intelligence (Experian, 2003).

Thomas (Thomas, B. and Housden, M., 2003) suggests a general rule as to the hierarchy of data held on the database:

1. *Your own customer data* – most powerful as it relates to your customers and their existing relationship with you
2. *Lifestyle data* – as it relates to individuals by name and address
3. *Demographic data* – dealing as it does with the characteristics of neighbourhoods rather than households.

The process of setting up a marketing database

The process of setting up a database is complex and demanding. A staged planning approach is outlined below.

- Business review
- Data audit
- Data strategy, specification and verification
- Data verification
- Hardware/software
- Data capture, maintenance and enhancement
- Management issues should the database be run in-house/out-house
- Applications
- Review.

We will look at each of these stages in turn.

Business review

It is important that the overall mission and objectives are reviewed in order to inform the process of establishing the database. It could be that a database is not required to fulfil the mission of the business or that the cost of a particular database design or hardware is too great. All business decisions should begin with an understanding of the strategic direction of the business. The database decision is no exception. We must ask:

- How will data help the business achieve its business and marketing objectives?
- Where will the business be in 10 years' time?
- What media, information and technology changes will need to be built into the system?
- What segments will the data support now and in the future?
- What business processes will the database support?
- How will the database be accessed?
- Is the database open to customers through the Internet?

The data audit

Carrying out an in-depth data audit is the next stage of the process. We need to establish the following:

- What information requirements does the organization have now and in the future?
- Where is this information held currently?
- What unnecessary information is currently held?
- How is this information currently used?
- How will it be used in future?
- Which departments and individuals need access to this information?
- If information is not available, where does it come from?
- Who will enter the data and ensure that is accurate and complete?
- What applications will this information support?
- How does the proposed system integrate with existing information management systems?
- Data strategy, specification and verification.

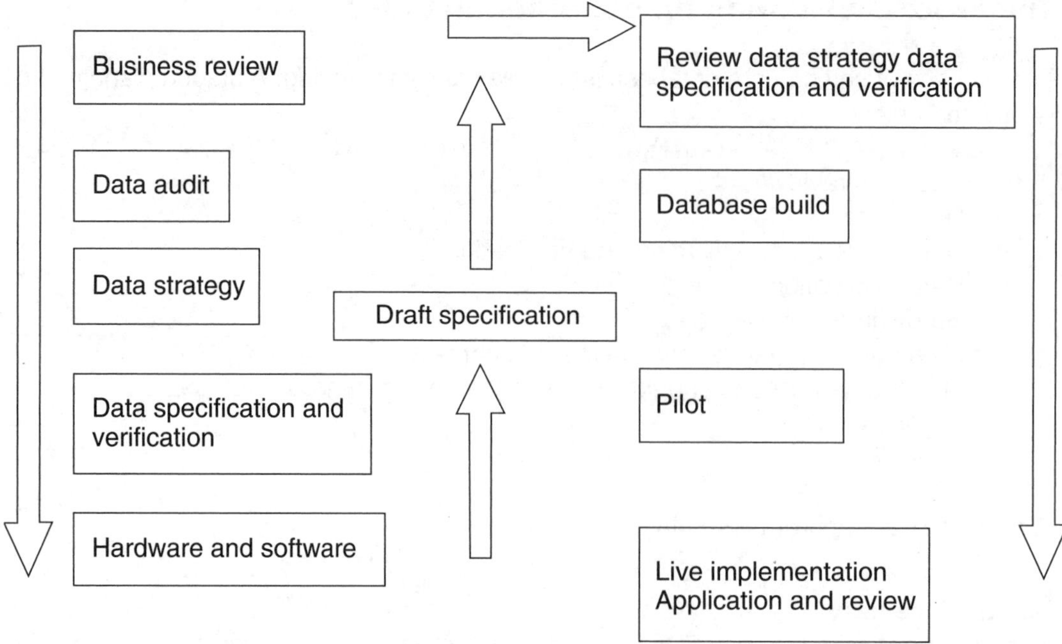

Figure 3.2 The database development process

The review of strategy and the data audit should result in a long-term strategy for data within the organization. This should be capable of evolution and development over time as the markets served by the organization and the organization itself changes.

The strategy should specify the information that is required by the organization outlining where the information is available and what additional data is to be acquired and managed.

It should determine the following:

- Who and what departments are able to use and update data held on the database?
- How will the data be kept up to date and who is responsible for this?
- What data verification rules will be put in place to ensure quality and completeness?
- What analysis systems will the database support?

Activity 3.4

Where will this data come from? Think about the ways that your company or a company of your choice may capture data on its customers. Write down as many data sources as you can.

Data needs to be kept up to date. This is a legal obligation under the 1998 Data Protection Act but is also vital for good practice in database marketing. Information has a life. It is estimated that professional marketers change their job every 18 months to 3 years. The lapse rates for trade press titles such as *Marketing* and *Marketing Week* are around 25–30 per cent. In the consumer market, data expires almost as quickly.

- People move house. About 10 per cent of households move house each year. The Royal Mail keeps a list of movers called the National Change of Address File (NCOA). The Postal Address File (PAF) will also help. This is a list of all 26.5 million addresses in the UK and is regularly updated.
- They die. It is dreadful to send mailings to dead people; it is ethically unacceptable and causes distress for families that have recently suffered bereavement. There are a number of services that help the marketer avoid this, e.g. The Bereavement Register and Mortascreen. These services allow companies to remove the deceased from their lists. The Deceased Register is a service based on cards completed at the Register Office and is supported by the Information Commissioner and Local Government. For further details go to the DMA website or the Royal Mail website.
- They are enticed away by the competition, by better, more relevant or cheaper offers.
- They leave due to poor marketing.
- They move out of the market, Club 18–30 has a clear target market!
- Their lifestyle changes, they marry or have children, or simply stop drinking or smoking or go on a diet
- Their financial circumstances change, they trade up or trade down

Telegraphing your renewal date

If you have taken out a subscription deal with the Daily Telegraph, you will have to decide at the end of your subscription period whether you wish to continue with the arrangement. The Telegraph knows from its database records when this decision will have to be made and they will mail you beforehand.

They will remind you what a great newspaper you read and restate the benefits of taking out a further subscription. The marketing database enables them to time these communications so that they are highly relevant to the individual recipients.

The Telegraph will not stop at simply sending you a simple reminder. They will also carry out anti-attrition studies. This is an important area – having gone to the considerable time and expense of recruiting a customer, one does not want to lose them through lack of understanding of their needs. Many companies fail to carry on these simple procedures. Research from the Swedish Post Office shows that 65 per cent of customers leave because of a lack of contact from the company. This has been confirmed in another study by McGraw Hill (Thomas, B. and Housden, M., 2003).

Procter and Gamble

Nappy talk

Proctor and Gamble market the Huggies brand of nappies. P and G has around two and a half years to sell the estimated 4,500 nappies that the average child uses in this time. They try to ensure that every nappy used is a Huggies nappy. This involves a range of broad-scale communications and a series of data-driven targeted direct marketing communications. The Huggies Mother and

Baby Club recruits members through the Bounty list, a list of expecting mothers that is compiled through responses to take ones and other media distributed to pregnant women. The women sign up for a range of free samples including Huggies nappies that are delivered after the delivery of the child. A series of targeted communications is also delivered to the family covering the period from the date of birth to potty training. Amongst these is a series of publications that provide information on care and other elements of child rearing. These include free samples and coupons. The publications are seen as valuable in themselves. They cover the following:

Step 1 Pregnancy

Step 2 Birth and early days

Step 3 Reaching out to the world

Step 4 Sitting up

Step 5 Crawling everywhere

Step 6 First steps

Step 7 Toddler days

The publications deepen and strengthen the relationship between customers and the brand at a crucial time of life and the trust developed during this time sustains other brands in the P and G family.

Data verification

Data verification is important. A regular review of the data is important. Data fields should be reviewed to check that they are up to date and that they hold the data they are supposed to hold. We need to check if the data is usable and if not determine what we have to do to make use of the data? We also need to check that we do not hold duplicate data.

Deduplication

Deduplication is an important part of the process of verifying data. Duplication of records may occur for a number of reasons, including keystroke error or other data entry problems, or simply the fact that volunteered information is not provided in a consistent way.

We may have two addresses with slightly different names:

e.g. Lewis K 128 Greene St SL6 8TY 12/8/62

or Lewes Keith 128 Greene Ave SL6 8PY 12/8/62.

These may be different people or the same person. Deduplication ensures that we do not send multiple mailings or make repeat contacts in other ways. There are a number of software solutions that allow for deduplication of records. These packages can be set to different degrees of sensitivity and may be based on the number of matched characters and/or numbers or a string of digits or may allocate a weighting depending on the character of the data that is being assessed.

The two types of system are deterministic decision tables or probabilistic linking.

Deterministic decision tables evaluate data fields for degree of match and a letter grade is assigned, the grades form a match pattern which is looked up in a table to determine if a pair matches or not

Lewis	K	128	Greene St		SL6 8TY	12/8/62
Lewes	Keith	128	Greene Ave		SL6 8PY	12/8/62
B	B	A	B	D	B	A = BBABDBA
+5	+2	+3	+4	−1	+7	+9 = +29

Probabilistic linkages evaluate fields for degree of match and a weight is assigned that represents the informational content contributed by those values. The weights are summed to derive a total score that measures the reliability of the match.

The deduplication strategy will be determined by the cost of holding duplicate data and the cost of deduplicating this data and can be set for under or over kill.

Reference tables may be used to help the verification of data. Wilson (Wilson, A., 2003) gives examples of reference tables for titles, job description, brands, models of car, etc. These are crucial for the maintenance of data quality as they reduce errors.

Formatting will be used to ensure that data is entered consistently, that it fits the fields and is presented in consistent style. International databases have a range of issues around salutations, titles, address and post code formats.

Hardware and software

There are a range of vendors in the market. There are dozens of questions that need to be asked. The key questions are:

- Mainframe or PC
- Cost and time
- Integration with existing systems
- Scalability
- Do we have in-house expertise?
- Support offered
- Analysis systems support
- Maintenance costs
- Data capture, maintenance and enhancement
- Management issues – should the database be run in-house/out-of-house.

In-house or out-of-house

Database bureaux will host your database for your organization.

In-house operation has advantages and disadvantages:

Disadvantages

- Cost of hardware and consultancy may be significant
- Speed of development can be slow
- Service standards may be lower than those from an out-of-house provider

- Skills in IT and strategy may be weak
- Specialist processing skills may not be readily available.

Advantages

- Strategic orientation of the business should be assured
- Integration and access is manageable
- Greater control and ownership
- Cost may be lower.

Database bureaux have the following advantages

- Skills and systems are developed and tested
- No fixed costs. You pay for what you get
- Speed. Resources can be allocated to ensure prompt delivery and penalty clauses can be built in
- Performance guarantees can be built into the contract.

Often there is migration from the bureau into the organization. This means that learning can take place at lower risk. The usual approach is outlined below:

- Set-up at the bureau
- Sort out data issues
- Set-up updates and enhancements
- Develop internally
- Run the two in parallel
- Import.

Applications

As we saw with the Tesco example, a huge amount of data may be captured by organizations. The key thing is to be able to analyse the data.

How it all works

Thomas and Housden put it simply in their book Direct Marketing in Practice (Thomas, B. and Housden, M., 2003):

Remember the marketing database is a series of tables. These can cover a huge range of data:

A list of names and addresses

A list of transactions

A list of suppliers/delivery methods and so on

A list of promotion codes

A list of customers who have been mailed, and their responses or any logical collection of data.

For instance, it would not be logical to store details of every transaction against every customer, in the same table. Some customers may have dozens of transactions, others only one. To avoid large areas of wasted space, transactions are stored in a separate table, with a link between the customer's name and address and the transaction.

Having assembled the data, records have to be selected for a particular mailing campaign. This is done by a process of raising queries. For instance, if we wished to mail customers who had spent more than £500 in the past 6 months we would:

Tell the computer to identify all transactions of £500 or more between the dates XX and YY

Link these transactions to the name and address table

Get a count of how many names and addresses have been identified

If and when required, extract the related names and addresses for use in the promotion.

Using queries in this way enables us to model campaigns and identify whether our selection parameters have been appropriate. If the count shows we have only 50 customers who fit the category (spent £500 within last 6 months), we may wish to broaden the parameters.

We could extend the period to 12 months and/or reduce the qualifying total to £250. This would produce a larger number of prospects. The exact process used depends on the software being used. PC software is generally more user-friendly and allows the marketer to access the data directly. This makes modelling campaigns easier and quicker than was the case with mainframes and IT departments.

Data mining

Is the process of analysing the database or the data warehouse to extract meaningful and actionable information. Antinou defines it as 'the process of extracting hidden and actionable information for large databases' (Antinou, T., 1997). Data mining software can help this process. The process of analysis includes the process of statistical analysis of data or simple counts. It also includes a range of tools to help analyse the database. These are known as online analytical processing or OLAP.

OLAP tools establish an analysis universe for and allow for queries to be made of data. For example, counts of the number of people of a certain age who bought a particular product. These tools allow us to drill into the database to analyse sub-samples in detail. This sample may be removed from the database and analysed off-line.

Other analysis techniques

Regression identifies the nature of a relationship. Regression analysis scores individuals according to their characteristics.

For example, buyers of a certain product may have certain other characteristics:

- They may live in certain areas
- Have certain income levels
- Have a certain number of children.

By applying this to all records and scoring those records, we can predict those with the highest scores have a greater tendency to buy. We will look at regression later in the coursebook.

Cluster analysis Groups customers according to their general characteristics. This can be used to create segments from the database.

Chaid analysis Is used to break down the customer base into segments based on certain key variables. It is used to target subgroups on the data base more effectively. Thomas and Housden (Thomas, B. and Housden, M., 2003) give a good example of how this works.

In order to understand the workings of CHAID let's consider an example of a bank wishing to sell ISA's. At present, 8 per cent of customers have an ISA and they wish to increase this to 10 per cent. The CHAID model is fed, say 30,000 customer records containing data on:

Number of ISA's

Household income

Size of mortgage

Years as a customer

and so on

The CHAID software considers all of the given variables and determines which is the most important in this case.

Let's say it establishes that the most significant factor is 'years as a customer'. It further subdivides this factor into, say: less than 1 year with the bank; 1 to 5 years as a customer; more than 5 years. It may then identify something like the following:

Less than 1 year as a customer – only 3 per cent have an ISA

1 to 5 years – 8 per cent have an ISA

More than 5 years – 12 per cent have an ISA

The CHAID model then moves on to the next stage which is to take each of these three segments and considers the next most significant variable in each instance.

It may ascertain that in the most loyal customer segment (more than 5 years with the bank) the next best discriminator is mortgage size. People in this segment with mortgages of more than £100,000 may have a 14 per cent take-up of ISA's.

By breaking down each segment into its significant variables, a number of potentially good sub-segments may emerge.

How can the data be used?

The data can be used in a number of ways. The case below presents an outline of how the database works in financial services.

The database and financial services

The financial services sector is a heavy-user of database analysis. Amongst others, a major bank has used their database in the following ways:

i. To manage the branch network
   1. Identifying the most profitable branches
   2. Staff appraisal, monitoring, reward and recognition
   3. To identify staff training needs
   4. To manage branch location.

ii. To acquire new customers
   1. Through profiling of good, existing customers and using this
   2. To plan for the acquisition of new customers.

iii. To increase profitability of existing customers
   1. Reducing the cost of marketing
   2. Improved targeting
   3. Personalizing marketing communications
   4. Reduce attrition.

iv. Developing new products

v. Developing new market segments.

Planning Defining objectives, segmentation studies, targeting, campign management analysis costs and return on investement

Contacting customers Which medium or combination of media is the most effective and efficient, at what time?

Data processing Counts and reports to aid planning

Production Production of lists and labels for address management; producing lists for follow-up activities; merging letter copy and addresses

Response handling Recording responses to promotional mailings via unique tracking codes

Lead processing Tracking enquiries through 'to sale' and 'after sales'

Campaign management Customer paperwork and reports to help manage promotions

Customer research Information from questionnaires may be added to records to make the future planning process more effective

Analysis Pre-determined reports and other analysis

Marketing applications of the database can be summed up as:

- Finding
- Acquiring
- Keeping
- Cross selling additional products
- Up-selling higher value products
- Prevent inactivity
- Renewing.

Customers!!

Summary

In this unit, we have looked at the database and the range of applications it can support.

We have explored the processes involved in setting up a database looking at the management issues and the process of capturing, verifying and enhancing data.

We saw that there were several types of data and that the data gathered varies from consumer to b2b markets. We looked at the process of gathering data on international customers and saw that this raises issues of consistency due to name and address formats.

Data types include:

- Identification data
- Demographic data
- Financial data
- Lifestyle data
- Transactional data.

These fit into four categories:

1. Behavioural data
2. Volunteered data
3. Profile data
4. Attributed data.

We looked in detail at the process of setting up a database exploring each of the phases in turn. These were:

- Business review
- Data audit
- Data strategy, specification and verification
- Data verification
- Hardware/software
- Data capture, maintenance and enhancement
- Management issues: should the database be run in-house/out-of-house
- Applications
- Review.

We looked at data enhancement through lifestyle and geo-demographic systems.

We looked at the process of maintaining data and explored methods of deduplication.

We looked at analysis techniques including the use of OLAP tools, cluster regression and Chaid analysis.

Finally, we looked at the applications that the database can support. We saw that they could be described as:

- Planning
- Contacting customers
- Data processing
- Production
- Response handling
- Lead processing
- Campaign management
- Customer research
- Analysis.

The marketing applications of the database were summed as:

- Find
- Acquire
- Keep
- Cross sell
- Up sell
- Prevent inactivity
- Renew.

Further study

Question 2

You have been appointed as marketing manager for the Drama Factory, a small regional arts and entertainments venue. You want to develop a marketing database to facilitate the marketing of the centre, but need to convince the trustees of the centre of its value in order to receive funding.

Write a report for the trustees outlining the process involved in establishing a database for marketing.

- How will external suppliers help this process?
- What applications will the database facilitate?

Hints and Tips

Thomas and Housden's book *Direct Marketing in Practice* contains a very useful and accessible chapter on database and its applications.

Bibliography

Antinou, T. (1997). Drilling or Mining? Handling and Analysis of Data between now and the Year 2000, *Marketing and Research Today,* **May**, pp. 115–120.

Thomas, B. and Housden, M. (2003). *Direct Marketing in Practice,* Butterworth-Heinemann.

Wilson, A. (2003). *Marketing research: an integrated approach,* FT Prentice Hall.

unit 4 the marketing research process

Learning objectives

After completing this unit you will:

- Be able to identify the stages of a marketing research plan
- Identify and brief a range of marketing research suppliers
- Be able to construct a proposal document in response to a marketing research brief
- Have covered syllabus elements 3.2, 3.3, 3.4, 3.5, 3.6.

Key definitions

The marketing research brief Description of a research problem used to inform potential suppliers of solutions.

The proposal A written and often an oral response to the research brief.

Qualitative research An unstructured research approach using a small number of selected individuals to produce non quantifiable insights into attitudes, behaviour, emotions and motivations.

Quantitative research A structured research approach using a sample of the population designed to produce quantifiable data.

Primary research Is research carried out to meet a specific objective. It is new to the research world.

Secondary research Published research or research carried out for some other purpose.

Desk research The collation of existing research results and data from published secondary sources for a different purpose (MRS, 2003).

Experimental research Research measuring causality or the changing of one variable to observe the effect on another whilst other extraneous variables are kept constant.

Coding The process of allocating codes to responses collected during fieldwork facilitating analysis of data (MRS, 2003).

Editing Checking raw data for consistency, coherence and completeness before coding.

Exploratory research Research intended to develop initial ideas or insights and to provide direction for any further research (Wilson, A., 2003).

Fieldwork The collection of primary data from external sources by means of surveys, observation and experiment (MRS, 2003).

Group discussions/focus groups A number of respondents gathered together to generate ideas through the discussion of, and reaction to, specific stimuli. Under the steerage of a moderator, focus groups are often used in exploratory work or when the subject matter involves social activities, habits and status (MRS, 2003).

Pilot The pre-testing of a research design on a small scale prior to full roll out.

Longitudinal research Data collection over time to examine trends.

Causal research Research that examines whether one variable causes or determines the value of another variable (Wilson, A., 2003).

Descriptive research Research studies that describe what's happening in a market without potentially explaining why it is happening (Wilson, A., 2003).

Observation research A non-verbal means of obtaining primary data as an alternative or complement to questioning (MRS, 2003).

Study Guide

This unit should take around 3 hours to complete.

Introduction

We now move on to the discipline of marketing research. In this unit we explore the process of planning research and briefing researchers to carry out the process. This will be an important part of your course. The senior examiner in a recent briefing to tutors told them to focus on the process of developing research briefs, responding to those briefs through the presentation of the proposal and then presenting the final report. This activity represents the day-to-day management of the research function in business and you may expect it to form an important part of your assessment in this module.

The brief is very important. Even if the research is to be carried out in-house, a briefing document is required. It provides a fixed reference that all parties involved should sign off. For the commissioner of the research, it provides 'bullet proof' evidence that a certain date or budget was agreed on. In complex research studies, it keeps all parties on track and can help the process of project management.

In this unit we will also look at the research planning process in detail. This will be important for you as it provides the framework for the next few sections of the workbook. We will introduce concepts here that will be explored in more detail in later units.

The planning process is one of the frameworks you will need to learn for the exam. Other structures that will be covered in this unit are the briefing document – this too will be useful to learn.

The marketing research plan

The planning process for marketing is important. Research costs money and takes time, and a planned approach to the process can save both.

1. Review the business situation
2. Define the marketing issue or problem
3. Carry out exploratory research
4. Previous research
5. Internal research
6. Redefine the problem
7. Brief issued
8. Agency selected
9. Research design
10. Desk research
11. Primary research
    a. Qualitative
    b. Quantitative
12. Pilot
13. Fieldwork
14. Data input coding and editing
15. Data analysis
16. Results
17. Findings and recommendations
18. Report/presentation
19. Decision.

Figure 4.1 The marketing research plan

The process may appear complicated but the degree of complexity is dependent on the nature of the research task. Research problems may be solved at the exploratory or internal research phase and a decision result from a simple database enquiry. For example, 'how many of our customers were repeat buyers last year?' Other problems may demand more complex solutions and may involve the use of multiple external partners to deliver. Let's look at each stage of the process.

Review the business situation

We start the process with a review of the current business position. Restating the values and mission of the business, and identifying markets served and our unique selling proposition helps to focus the research process on the broader goals of the business. It may help to state the marketing objectives of the business and summarize the current marketing plan, which should provide the underpinning for all activity.

Marketing decisions need to be made in response to a constantly changing business environment and research may be needed to inform these decisions.

Activity 4.1

You are a marketing manager for a major whisky manufacturer. Whisky sales are stagnant and you are looking at the success of spirits-based drinks like Reef and Breezer. You have been asked to look at the development of a whisky-based drink to target a younger market. What information would you need to carry out this project?

The review of the business environment is an ongoing process and research requirements may reflect the dynamic nature of this environment – for example customers' reaction to a competitor's new product. Or, it may reflect the planned development of the business as expressed in the marketing plan – for example, the international launch of a product range. The process of environmental scanning may be the responsibility of the research department and the issue of sector or competitive briefings either face to face or through a corporate intranet may be part of this process. The vital thing is that the key decision makers are kept informed of changes and are able to make intelligent decisions. The business case needs to be established as resources within the marketing function are always under pressure. We need to ensure that the research proposed is fully informed by the business situation and that the relative costs and benefits are weighed up before going ahead.

Defining the issues or problem

Defining the problem, despite appearances is not easy. Problems can generally be solved in many ways. The problem definition needs to reflect the organization's resources, or be expressed in a way that clearly identifies the opportunity that is being looked at.

Sometimes, a view of the problem for a pressured executive may not actually be the real issue. The research company that is asked to review marketing communications activity may find that there are particular political issues with the current agency or that the brand is poorly managed or that the pricing strategy is wrong. Very often we have to carry out informal or exploratory research to identify and define the research question we are trying to answer. Poor research questions or problem definition can lead to expensive and unnecessary work being carried out.

Research problems

Being able to define a problem in an appropriate way is very important. Often managers appear to want the answer to the meaning of life by 5.00p.m. Understanding the business to be able to isolate and define a problem is a skill that comes with experience. For example, the ill-informed manager may say 'why are our sales falling?' while the experienced manager might say 'what are the perceptions of our service standards against our key competitors?' He has already limited the research to a narrow problem area and researchers have a much clearer idea of the purpose to which the research will be put. It may be that the researcher has to carry out this refining and defining process but it can be helped by good communication and understanding at this stage.

Carry out exploratory research

This stage, as outlined above, is designed to clarify the research problem. It is largely informal and may involve a range of techniques. It should involve discussions with those who are involved with the problem and its solution. It may involve a review of the trade press and simple scanning of internal documents and resources. The aim is to inform the process and to become 'immersed' in the problem and its potential solutions. Even at this stage the researcher may be thinking ahead about methods that could be used to deliver the information required. The key thing is to uncover the real purpose of the research and, possibly, the constraints in terms of time and budget that may affect the process.

We also need, at this stage, to think about the value of the research. There is little point in spending more on research than the profit to be gained by making a right decision, or the cost of making a wrong decision. Remember research will not eliminate risk entirely but may reduce it to acceptable levels. An understanding of the commercial constraints of carrying out research may be gained through intuition or experience but it can also be worked out more scientifically.

If research is required to justify packaging redesign, then we can estimate the improved sales of such a move and offset the cost of research against this. This objective and task approach to setting research budgets is the best way of managing research budgets. However it is not always possible to carry out this process accurately.

If the cost of a research project to determine between two product flavours was £25,000, and the research-based launch generated incremental profits of £40,000, then clearly, the research is worthwhile. It should always be possible to estimate the likely impact on a project if it is done with or without research and this can help in determining whether the research should be done and the extent of that research.

Previous research

As part of this process, previously carried out research should be reviewed to see if the problem has been dealt with elsewhere. It may be that the solution lies on work that has been done in other departments. For example, work to improve the navigation of the website may have been done in the IT department. Access to previously commissioned work may be through the intranet or through the company library. Or it may be that individual managers have commissioned research which has not been distributed widely through the organizations.

Visiting a major Belgian food manufacturer, a market research executive noticed the same research report on the bookshelves of three separate senior managers. This report cost US$10,000 and the company had effectively wasted US$20,000.

Internal research

Internal research will involve the use of the MkIS and the database. It may be that the problem, as we said, can be solved at this stage. Whatever, it is worth spending time now on internal records to, maybe, solve the problem or help to define it.

For example, a problem that involves finding out the average age of a company's existing customers may be solved through a simple interrogation of the customer database.

Redefine the problem

The output of this stage is a clear statement of the research problem that is agreed by all parties. After this, a brief can be written.

The marketing research brief, short listing and proposal

These sections are covered more in detail below. However, a brief should be written for all projects even if the research is to be carried out in-house. The proposal written to the brief will become the contract for the research when it is accepted, and is equally important.

Research design

In this part of the process, we start thinking about the type of research methods we might employ to solve the particular problem we have identified. At this stage, we will introduce the terms. Later we will drill down into more detail.

Wilson identifies three types of marketing research these are:

1. Exploratory
2. Conclusive – descriptive research
3. Conclusive – causal research.

Whilst Wilson tells us that these are not mutually exclusive, they represent a research continuum from purely descriptive to purely causal.

Activity 4.2

Using your text books write down definitions for the three types of research.

Desk research

Desk or secondary research is information that has already been gathered for some other purpose. It may be held within the organization or by other organizations. It is called desk research because it is usually accessible from a desk via the intranet or online or in hard copy. This is dealt with in detail in the next section. In the research plan, desk research is carried out before primary research. This is because it is generally cheaper. It may solve the problem without any need for expensive primary work.

Primary research

Primary research is research carried out to meet a specific objective. It is 'new to the world research'. Primary research is the common currency of marketing research. It is what most of us have come across either through telephone research, or face-to-face interviews or increasingly through online research.

Primary research may be based on observation, may be qualitative or quantitative.

Observation research is data gathered by observing behaviour. No questions are asked of participants.

The MRS defines observational research as (MRS, 2003):

Definition

A non-verbal means of obtaining primary data as an alternative or complement to questioning.

Qualitative research describes research that cannot be quantified or subjected to quantitative analysis. It typically uses small sample sizes and is designed to produce a depth of understanding, context and insight. It helps to uncover the motivation behind the behaviour rather than to identify the behaviour itself. It seeks to get under the skin of respondents, uncovering their deeper feelings. It is essentially subjective but it is a highly developed and important research methodology.

The MRS defines qualitative research as (MRS, 2003):

Definition

A body of research techniques which seeks insights through loosely structured, mainly verbal data rather than measurements. Analysis is interpretative, subjective, impressionistic and diagnostic.

Quantitative research

Quantitative is the opposite of qualitative in that it is statistically verifiable. It provides answers to the questions 'who' and 'how many' rather than the depth of insight as to why. It uses a structured approach to problem-solving using a sample of the population to make statistically-based assumptions about the behaviour of the population as a whole.

The MRS defines quantitative research as (MRS, 2003):

Definition

Research which seeks to make measurements as distinct from qualitative research.

Questionnaire design

Both qualitative and quantitative work require some form of data collection. In qualitative work, this usually involves the creation of a topic guide, which helps the researcher to ensure that all the areas intended to be covered have been dealt with. The data capture mechanism is usually an electronic recording either digitally or via an audio or videotape.

Quantitative research is usually gathered and recorded via a questionnaire. This can be delivered via a number of different media including face-to-face, telephone, mail or online.

The pilot

All primary research should be piloted or tested to see that the data collection methods are sound. This may be difficult with some forms of qualitative work but a basic runthrough is very important. Pilots will help with the structure and sequencing of questions and may identify areas of questioning that have not been considered. It ensures that the data collection device is effective and efficient.

Fieldwork

Fieldwork is the generic term given to the collection of primary data. It may cover the collection of observational, quantitative and qualitative data. The administration of a major quantitative study may involve serious logistical considerations whilst qualitative work may involve highly qualified and skilled researchers. The management of fieldwork is often given to specialist field managers or fieldwork agencies. The process is very important as the failure to adhere to methodology at this stage may compromise the entire project.

Data input, coding and editing

Data that is gathered from respondents must be recorded and edited to produce a data set that is capable of being analysed. In qualitative work, this may mean producing a transcript of the interview. In quantitative work, it means creating a data set that the computer can work with. This is covered in detail in Unit II where questions have been asked that allow for a number of different answers (open questions). All potential responses must be given a different code to enable analysis. Data is checked for completeness and consistency, and if there are significant problems the respondent may be called back to check details. Often today, data is input straight into the computer via systems known as CATI, CAPI and CAWI.

These are:

- Computer-aided telephone interviewing
- Computer-aided personal interviewing
- Computer-aided web interviewing.

Data analysis

Data is analysed via the computer to produce a range of results. This process is covered in detail in Unit 2.

Results, findings and recommendations

A marketing decision should result from the results of the research. Results should be presented clearly in a way that focuses on the problem to be solved. It is easy with today's statistical packages to produce hundreds of tables to a high degree of statistical sophistication. Results must be presented in a way that is accessible to the audience and that presents clearly the solution to the problem posed.

Report/presentation

Presentation of the results will usually be in the form of a written report and this may be supported by an oral presentation. The data will need to be presented but this should be in the appendices. The body of the report remains solutions-focused.

Decision

The output should be marketing decisions that are made at reduced risk and a feedback loop should exist to the business situation.

The marketing research brief

We will now look more in detail at the marketing research brief. The briefing document is perhaps the most important stage of the research process. As the old aphorism states 'be careful what you ask for, you may get it'. A tight brief is vital to the management of the marketing research process. It provides a focus for discussion and a guiding hand through the project. Many companies see the briefing process as part of an almost gladiatorial trial of strength where a brief is issued, limited information is given, and the resulting proposals are torn to bits in the arena of the pitch. The justification is that ideas are tested in the heat of the moment and that if an agency cannot justify an approach under fire, they are unlikely to be effective. The lack of detail is seen as allowing the agency to interpret and explore ideas. Some research briefs are given on one side of a page of A4. This may be sufficient but is almost certainly inadequate for complex multifacetted research tasks. Equally some companies go the other way, even specifying the colour and weight of paper for the final presentation. This maybe overkill.

On the other side, some agencies receive a brief as Drayton Bird says 'rather like a baby bird waiting to be fed by its mother, passively, humbly and gratefully' (Bird, D., 2003).

Both approaches are wrong. The best marketing solutions come through cooperation and active involvement. Agencies need the right information in order to be able to produce a suitable proposal. If there are issues over confidentiality, then, confidentiality agreements can be signed before the brief is issued. Members of the MRS are obliged to comply with the code of conduct that ensures client confidentiality. But the agency needs the tools to do the job – in this case, information.

The development of the brief should be a team activity. The structure is outlined below:

- *Identification details* These should include the title, date, contact names and details.
- *Current business position* This should detail the nature and scope of the business, key markets served, key competitors and future direction.
- *Marketing and business objectives* should be laid down and distinguished between.
- *Research objectives*, will almost certainly differ from marketing objectives but are informed by them. For example, the marketing objectives may be to enter a new market while the research objectives may be to identify the product attributes that appeal most to potential customers.
- *How the results will be used* The overall purpose and context for the research needs to be specified. How will the research be used and what other decisions might it inform in the future.
- *Outline methodology* This is a difficult area but in discussing the problem, research methods may have been discussed. Certainly, where there is expertise in the briefing team the research methodology may have been discussed in detail. There is no danger in allowing the proposing agency to have access to these views. Certainly the brief should include details on whether a qualitative or quantitative approach is required. Also outline question areas could be given.
- *Sample details* The details of the group of interest should be indicated. If the sample is to include businesses over a certain size, then the agency should be told to avoid them wasting their time.
- *Previous research* Previously-commissioned work that is relevant to the current study may be outlined or made available to the agency pitching for the business.
- *Timings* It is important that a detailed timetable of activity is included. This should cover time for questions, and details of the formal date and time for the presentation to take place if this is required.
- *Budget* A tricky area but generally it is advisable to give some indication of the budget that is available for the project.
- *Deliverables* How will the results be presented and when. Will there be a formal debriefing presentation? How many copies of reports will be needed?
- *Terms and conditions*, confidentiality, etc.
- *Key personnel names* and details of all key staff involved in the project.

Briefing: This is a cut-down brief presented to ensure client confidentiality

Usage and attitudes in the ambient ready meals market (ARMs)

Purpose of the research to establish usage and attitudes to the consumption of ambient ready meals in the domestic UK market

Background to the company

Description of the company

Ownership, turnover, brands, ambient ready meal brands

Market's size and market share data, trend's volume and value's competition

Background to the problem

Falling retail share, seek to stabilize market share through refined mix

Research objectives

Why are ARMs bought?

When are they used?

Who prepares them?

On what occasions?

Perception of quality relative to other RM categories

To competitors

Attitudes to price

Attitudes to advertising

Methods

Qualitative

Focus groups in key target audiences

Quantitative

Around 1500 housewives, representative of UK households. Quota sample

Question areas built out of the qualitative study

Brands bought, brands recognized, consumption occasion, attitudes to ARMs and other RM categories

We would like your advice on this aspect of research design and implementation

Timing

Proposal: 2 April

Presentation: Week commencing 12 April

Commission: 4 May

Report: Early July

Budget

In the region of £15,000

Report to

Brand manager

Marketing research manager

Marketing director.

Short listing

Once the brief is written and agreed, it should be sent to a short list of agencies. The short list generally should be no longer than four. Occasionally, more than four agencies are asked to pitch. It is courteous to let the agencies know how many other companies they are up against. It is unlikely if they value their work that they will refuse to pitch. Generally four agencies should be adequate. The MRS code of conduct covers the client–agency relationship and it recommends that four agencies are used. It also covers the issue of ownership of the work, which can be significant, put into the proposal.

'A10 Clients should not normally invite more than four agencies to tender in writing for a project. If they do so, they should disclose how many invitations to tender they are seeking.

A11 Unless paid for by the client, a specification for a project drawn-up by one research agency is the property of that agency and may not be passed on to another agency without the permission of the originating research agency' (MRS, 2003).

The short list can be drawn up in a number of ways.

Activity 4.3

How would you go about choosing a research agency? With your fellow CIM delegates or on your own brainstorm the methods of selecting an agency.

The proposal

The proposal should be presented in a written format and on time. A formal presentation may accompany the proposal. The proposal should be seen before any formal face-to-face presentation in order for it to be assessed and questions framed. These questions may be sent to the agency before the formal meeting.

Identification data

Key contact details, title and date.

Situation analysis

An outline of the current business position.

Research objectives

A clear statement of the purposes of the research.

Methodology and rationale

Crouch and Housden (Crouch, S. and Housden, M., 2003) suggest that the following questions should be answered:

- Why use the sample selection procedure indicated?
- Why use the size of sample indicated?
- Why the personal interview technique rather than group discussion?
- Why a 20-minute questionnaire and not a 30-minute questionnaire?
- Why are open-ended questions requiring expensive coding and analysis being included in a large-scale quantitative survey?
- Why is a written report or verbal presentation included, or why not?
- Why the timetable indicated?
- Why is the cost indicated?

Sample

A precise definition of the sample to be selected and a justification of this.

Fieldwork

What data collection methods are proposed?

Questionnaire/topic guide

It is unreasonable to expect a final questionnaire but an indication of what the agency expects to see in the questionnaire should be provided.

Data handling and processing

How will data be captured, edited, coded and analysed? What tables will be provided? How will the data be presented?

Reporting

What is included in the cost?

Timetable

A full detailed timetable of research activity and key milestones.

Costs

What is included? Is VAT included? How long is the quote valid? Terms of business and payment schedule.

CVs of key staff

Are the people who are presenting the people you will be dealing with? What is their experience? What professional memberships do they have?

Supporting evidence

Is the agency a member of professional bodies? Are references provided?

Contract details: the proposal will generally form the contract on acceptance.

Figure 4.2 The proposal: an outline structure

Selecting the agency

So how do we finally select the agency?

Wilson (Wilson, A., 2003) identifies a check list of seven points:

1. The agency's ability to understand the brief and translate it into a comprehensive proposal
2. The compatibility of agency and client teams. Can we work with them?
3. The evidence of innovation in the proposal. Has the agency added value?
4. Evidence of understanding of the market and the problem facing the organization
5. Sound methodology
6. Meeting budget and time scales
7. Relevant experience.

To this we can add relevant professional body memberships.

Evaluating other research reports

It will often be the case that a manager is presented with a research report and asked to apply its findings when he or she was not personally responsible for commissioning the research programme. In this case, the research must be assessed for its quality before its findings can be used with confidence. The following checklist can be used to judge research quality when only the report is available for assessment.

Evaluating existing research

A scheme for judging research quality

1. **What were the objectives of the research?**

   Are they appropriate to the problem to which the findings are now to be applied?

2. **What method was used to collect the information?**

   Is it appropriate to the information needed?

3. **Who was asked the questions?**

   Is the sample definition appropriate?

4. **How many people were asked?**

   Is the sample size adequate?

5. **What were the actual questions?**

   Check the copy of the questionnaire in the technical appendix. Do they seem to be good questions – well framed and appropriate to the objectives?

6. **Who did the fieldwork?**

   Is there a basis for judging the quality of the fieldwork? Were professional interviewers used? What checking procedures were used?

7. **When was the fieldwork carried out?**

   Was the timing sufficiently recent for the results still to hold? Was the time of year/time of day appropriate?

8. **Are the tabulations comprehensible?**

   Are they legible, with clear headings, and indexed?

9. **Would further cross-tabulations produce useful information?**

   Are these possible?

10. **Is the report in a logical order and readable?**

    Does it make sense?

11. **Is there a meaningful summary?**

    Is it easy to grasp the main points being made?

12. **Are there conclusions? (if appropriate)**

    Are they supported by the data?

13. **Did the research meet its objectives, and if not, why not?**

    Does this invalidate the research?

Figure 4.3 A scheme for judging research quality
Source: Crouch and Housden 2003

Summary

In this unit we looked at the research planning process. We saw that the definition of the research problem is enabled through internal and exploratory research. The use of research should be justified where possible by the cost of making a poor marketing decision or the profit to be made from a better marketing decision.

We saw that the efficient solution of problems through research means that we should start with the cheapest sources of information, that is secondary or desk research. If this does not produce the required information, then we move to primary work. We outlined the different types of marketing research and looked at qualitative and quantitative work. We saw that qualitative work should precede and inform the development of quantitative methodology. We looked in detail at the difference between qualitative and quantitative work.

We went on to look in detail at the briefing process and looked at each stage in turn.

- Identification details
- Current business position
- Marketing and business objectives should be laid down and distinguished between
- Research objectives
- How the results will be used
- Outline methodology
- Sample details
- Previous research
- Timings
- Budget
- Deliverables
- Terms and conditions
- Key personnel.

We saw that the brief was an important document and that the proposal which is delivered by the short-listed agencies, ultimately, will become the contract for the research programme. We looked at the process of producing a proposal and how we should select the agency.

- Identification data
- Situation analysis
- Research objectives
- Methodology and rationale

- Sample
- Fieldwork
- Questionnaire/topic guide
- Data handling and processing
- Reporting
- Timetable
- Costs
- CVs of key staff
- Supporting evidence
- Contract details.

Finally, we looked at the process of evaluating published work.

Further study

Question 3

You are the marketing manager for a company marketing china collectibles. You wish to establish an online service for your products. You wish to recruit a research agency to evaluate the potential of this market. Write a briefing document for the project. Explain how you would choose a short list of agencies to pitch for you business and how you would go about selecting the company to do the work.

Bibliography

Crouch, S. and Housden, M. (2003). *Marketing research for managers* 3rd edition, Butterworth-Heinemann.

Drayton Bird (2003). www.draytonbird.com.

MRS (2003). www.mrs.org.uk.

Wilson, A. (2003). *Marketing research: an integrated approach*, FT Prentice Hall.

unit 5 using secondary research

Learning objectives

On completing this unit you will be able:

- To define secondary marketing research
- To explain types of secondary data
- To understand where to find secondary data
- To understand the limitations and strengths of secondary research
- To look for data online
- To understand the applications of secondary research
- To complete syllabus elements 4.1, 4.2.

Key definitions

External data Data that is held by external organizations.

Internet A network of computers.

World Wide Web An internet protocol supervised by the world wide web consortium at www.w3.org.

Intranet A closed private company network based on web technology.

Extranet A process that shares information from internal source with selected external organizations.

Search engines Internet-based tools for searching for Uniform Resource Location (URL) or web addresses.

Newsgroups Web-based bulletin board services.

Chat rooms Locations on the Internet enabling web-based text or video-based real time interaction.

ISP Internet service provider.

Study Guide

This unit should take you around 3 hours to complete. You will need to explore online services so make sure that you have access to the Internet. You should allow another 2 hours to complete the tasks set for you.

Introduction

Secondary desk research is an important part of the researcher's armoury. In the last unit, we saw that the key goal of marketing research is to provide effective solutions efficiently. The use of desk research can ensure this. In the planning process, it precedes primary work. This is because it generally can be acquired at lower cost and can be obtained far more quickly. The key thing for the researcher is knowing where and how to look, and how to judge the quality of this work. In the IT age, there are a vast range of sources available to the researcher; some are more reliable than others.

What is secondary or desk research?

The MRS defines desk research as 'The collation of existing research results and data from published secondary sources for a specific, often unrelated, project' (MRS, 2003).

Crouch and Housden (Crouch, S. and Housden, M., 2003) define secondary desk research as 'data that has already been published by someone else, at some other time period, usually for some other reason than the present researcher has in mind. The researcher is therefore a secondary user of already existing data which can be obtained and worked on at a desk'.

Alan Wilson (Wilson, A., 2003) defines secondary data as 'Information that has previously been gathered for some purpose other than the current research project. The data is available either free or at a cost and can be delivered electronically by computer or in printed hard copy format'.

There are two broad classifications of secondary data – internal and external.

We dealt with internal data in Unit 2 on the database. In this unit we will explore external data.

The definitions raise issues about the nature of secondary data.

Activity 5.1

Reflect on the definitions of secondary research. What problems do you think the researcher may experience in using secondary data?

The strengths and weaknesses of secondary data

Strengths

- It is cheap or free of charge. Costs vary but very often a full report on markets or market sectors can be put together very quickly and cheaply
- It may provide an answer to the problem – this will save enormous time and effort
- It can guide or provide direction for primary work
- It can suggest methodologies for data collection
- It can indicate problems with particular methodologies
- It can provide historic or comparative data to enable longitudinal studies.

The weaknesses of secondary data

- It is not related to the research question and the temptation may be to force the data to fit the question.
- It may not be directly comparable. This is particularly the case in international markets where markets may be defined differently. For example, data on the low-alcohol drinks market varies from market to market as definitions of 'low' alcohol change.
- Data may be incomplete. For example, the cross channel trade in drinks and tobacco is significant but not included in official statistics. Data may relate to certain markets – for example, data on food markets may relate to the retail trade rather than to the retail and catering markets, or vice versa. Pan national studies will certainly find this. In many countries a significant amount of the retail trade is made through street markets. This is very hard to quantify. In this case it may be possible to weight data or use other techniques to complete the data set.
- It may not be available. It may be that there are certain markets that are not adequately covered – for example, in Europe, data on the Belgian or Dutch market is often hard to obtain as these are relatively small markets within the EU.
- The data may have been gathered for a particular purpose. Production statistics in certain markets are unreliable. Data may be presented to portray a company or government in a more favourable light. We see this in the UK with the ongoing debate of how unemployment figures should be presented. Information that is reviewed without access to the methodology should be viewed with suspicion and other data sources should be brought in to confirm the data under review.
- Data for international markets may be more expensive and unreliable.
- Data for international markets may be in a foreign language. Translating costs in business markets are very expensive.

Monitor your Euro market

A major research company was commissioned by a leading American food manufacturer to research the market for its products in the European Union. The starting point of the research design was to buy secondary research from Euromonitor. The report provided market data on all 15 EU countries, including market size, trends, market segmentation data, brand shares, brief profiles of the leading players in the sector retail and distribution analysis, and some basic consumer research. At around £7,500 the report gave executives very good background data and a short cut through the research problem.

Evaluating secondary data

When looking at published research reports, the user should ask the following questions:

- Who published the study? Was it a national government? Was it a trade association? What is the nature of the organization? Is the publisher of the data the same as the organization that collected the data?
- For what purpose? Is the study designed to sell a service? Is it designed to counter negative publicity? Is it designed to generate publicity?
- When was the data gathered? Is it relevant?
- How was the data collected? Was the data capture mechanism reliable? Was it a self-selecting sample?
- Who collected the data? Are they independent? Are they trained? Are they members of a professional body? What sample was used?
- How reliable is the data?
- Is raw data presented?
- Can I replicate the study? Is the methodology included? Can I test the data for accuracy?
- Is the data comparable?

Sources of secondary data

There is a vast range of source of secondary data, and the emergence of the Internet as a key information consolidator and provider has increased the availability of information to the desk researcher. It has increased access to previously remote information, for example data held in libraries overseas, and it has increased the ability to distribute this information. We will look later at online sources and methodology.

Data on markets and organizations can be obtained from many different sources. An able researcher will be flexible and innovative in their approach to information searches, and the most unlikely sources can reveal important information. For example, the publications of the HR department in a certain company told a researcher about the staffing levels at particular factories in India which had been classified as confidential by the corporate affairs and marketing departments.

List of sources

One of the best aids to secondary researchers are lists of sources. The specialists in this area are Euromonitor and Croners.

Euromonitor publishes a range of information directories.

These include the following:

- World Directory of Business Information Libraries
- World Database of Business Information Sources on the Internet
- International Marketing Data and Statistics
- World Directory of Marketing Information Sources
- World Marketing Data and Statistics on the Internet
- China: A Directory and Source Book
- Eastern Europe: A Directory and Source Book
- World Directory of Business Information Websites
- World Directory of Non Official Statistical Sources
- Latin America: A Directory and Source Book.

Euromonitor also publishes Findex 2002: The World Wide Directory of Market Research, Reports, Studies and Surveys. This is a list of over 8,400 market research studies covering twelve product sectors including a broad description of contents, price and contact details.

Try looking at the Euromonitor website at www.euromonitor.com.

Other companies providing this service include:

- Market Search Directory is a list of 20,000 market research reports from 700 research companies. World wide details at www.marketsearch-dir.com
- Croners Executive Companion and Croners Office Companion includes a list of business information services. The service is available on- and off-line. Details are at www.croner.co.uk
- www.web.idirect.com: A listing of online sources of business information
- www.europa.eu.int: Is a listing of information sources in the European Union.

Governments

Governments publish vast quantities of data about the economy and society. Much of this data forms the basis of commercial services, provided at some cost by research firms. For example the geo-demographic profiling services draw heavily on census data. These publications are very cheap and it is always worth checking to see what is available. Certain governments are making this data available online. The US government is exceptional and the UK government's e-government initiative is slowly opening up data sources to online enquiry. A good example of this is the trade partners' website which can be found at the following address:

www.tradepartners.gov.uk

Other sources can be identified through the following sites:

www.ukonline.gov.uk

www.statistics.gov.uk

UK online is a general guide to government online services whilst www.statistics.gov.uk is the website of National Statistics, the statistical service of the UK government.

There is also a statistical service for the European Union and this provides comparative data across all member countries.

These can be found at:

www.europe.org.uk

www.europa.eu.int/comm/eurostat/

The United Nations statistical service is at:

www.un.org.

Other national governments have their own statistical services and these can normally be accessed online.

Activity 5.2

Visit www.statistics.gov.uk and spend 30 minutes surfing through the site. Add it to your favourites. Try to identify publications that may be useful for your business.

Trade organizations

Trade organizations is a broad category of information providers that include:

- Trade associations
- The trade press
- Professional institutes
- Chambers of commerce
- Regulatory bodies and pressure groups.

Trade associations

These exist for almost every industrial sector. Some publish amazing details on their members' activities. Associations such as the British Market Research Association publish annual reviews of the Market Research industry for its members. A directory of trade associations is published by CBD and this identifies trade associations with contact details and details of activities. These can be found at www.cbdresearch.com.

Trade press

Trade press is invaluable as a source of up-to-date information on markets and companies. Almost every trade is represented, and titles like Pig Farmer Weekly, Tunnels and Tunnelling, Wood Based Panelling International, The Grocer, Advertising Age and Off Licence News give an indication of the range of sources that are available. The journalists quickly become experts in their field and they too are worth contacting. Details of trade titles can be found in the advertisers annual.

Web address: www.hollis–pr.co.uk.

For international press, Willings Press Guide is an alternative source both on- and off-line. Online they are at www.willings press.com.

Professional institutes

These institutes generally represent individuals within the profession and some provide excellent data on their industries.

The CIM is a good example. It has a wide range of information on its website and supports members through its knowledge centre and library in Cookham. Hopefully, you have already used the website. It is at www.cim.co.uk.

Chambers of commerce

These can be very helpful for organizations, particularly in overseas markets, where commitment to the Chambers' mission is sometimes greater than in the UK.

The British Chambers of Commerce website is at www.chamberonline.co.uk.

The world organization is the The World Chambers Federation and their web address is at www.iccwbo.org.

Regulatory bodies and pressure groups

The activities of organizations like the Financial Services Authority, the Advertising Standards Authority and Oftel generate information on the sectors they cover.

Look at the Advertising Standards Authority website at www.asa.org.uk.

Pressure groups like Greenpeace or Action on Smoking and Health (ASH) can provide data on the industries they monitor and causes they represent. www.ash.org.uk. has a statistical report on smoking and smoking behaviour.

Trade unions and other member organizations can provide useful data. For example, the Salmon and Trout Association covers the market for fly fishing through its activities aimed at preserving habitat and stocks.

Financial data

The activities of investment houses and stock brokers produce regular reports on the activities of their target companies. The briefings that inform these reports often contain useful market and strategic data that can be extremely revealing.

The press

The Financial Times and Wall Street Journal are required reading for marketing professionals, and their services include online archives. Other national and local press can be accessed for relevant data.

The FT and Wall Street Journal are at:

www.ft.com

www.wsj.com.

Specialist services

Information about companies

The best source of information in the UK is Companies House; all companies over a certain size are obliged by law to lodge financial and other information at Companies House. The companies house website also has a range of links to international disclosure of company data.

Companies House is found online at www.companies-house.gov.uk.

Other organizations provide information on companies. Services such as Dunn and Bradstreet and Kompass are excellent commercial sources of company information.

Information on markets

There are hundreds of companies providing secondary or published data on markets.

A full list can be accessed at the MRS website: www.mrs.org.

Some of the more important providers include:

ACNeilsen

Neilsen provides data on media and advertising spend and a range of data to industry.

www.acneilsen.co.uk.

BMRB

Is a leading UK research agency that provides the Target Group Index (TGI). TGI is a valuable resource to marketers and allows customer data to be enhanced in a number of ways. It also provides a useful insight into diverse markets.

Activity 5.3

Go to www.bmrb-tgi.co.uk. Follow the links and find out as much as you can about TGI.

After your session, you should be able to answer the following questions:

- What is TGI?
- What sample is used?
- How is data captured?
- What implications does this have for my business?

Many companies exist to provide services to industry in the area of secondary research.

Syndicated research services

Companies like Mintel, Euromonitor, and Frost and Sullivan provide what are known as syndicated or multi-client studies on a huge range of markets. These are published market research studies that are available to anybody who wishes to buy them. Prices range from a few hundred to many thousands of pounds depending on the complexity of the report and number of markets covered.

Typically, reports will cover:

- Market size, structure and trends
- Import, export and production data
- Key players' competitive profiles including financial data
- Market share data
- Advertising and marketing communications spend.

Details can be found at the following websites:

- www.mintel.com
- www.euromonitor.com
- www.frost.com.

Online aggregators

The development of the Internet and its diverse capabilities has lead to the emergence of a new breed of information providers who aggregate or bring together information from diverse sources and allow access on a subscription basis or for a one off payment.

Examples include general services like Hoovers, Profound, and Lexis Nexis and specialist services like the World Advertising Research Centre (WARC) or MAD which covers the UK marketing press. These may contain translations from a range of international publications.

www.mad.co.uk

www.profound.com

www.hoovers.com

www.lexis-nexis.com

www.warc.com.

Information on online markets

There is a great deal of information on the Internet on online markets. Not all of it is reliable. The government, as indicated above, is often the most reliable source and there are more reputable suppliers in the market. The best sources for online research are often based in the USA. But there are a range of other useful suppliers.

Activity 5.4

Look at some or all of the following websites. They have been shown to be useful sources of research or data on the online sector.

- www.nua.com
- www.teleconomy.com
- www.forrester.com
- www.siebel.com
- www.3.gartner.com
- www.broadvision.com
- www.uk.jupitermmxi.com
- www.accenture.com
- www.pwcglobal.com
- www.bcg.com
- www.idc.com
- www.bitpipe.com
- www.iabuk.net
- www.ovum.com

- www.it-analysis.com
- www.gzigaweb.com.

Evaluate them against the following criteria:

- Name of company
- Business sector:
    - Research company, hardware supplier, software supplier, consultancy, trade association
- Quality of data
- Range of data
- Credibility
- Recency
- Geographic scope
- Sector coverage
- Cost
- Data collection method.

Follow the links and add them to your favourites list.

Other sources include:

- CRM technology companies
- Management consultancy
- IT consultants.

Searching online

Online research is the fastest growing area of research today and the area of secondary research is no different. The problem is that with such a huge array of sources available, where do we start looking.

If you know the Uniform Resource Locator (URL or web address), then you can go online via your Internet Service Provider (ISP) and go directly to the site. From this site a series of links may be following or 'surfed' and this process can yield useful information. If you do not know the URL or your search is more general, then the starting point is the use of search engines or directories.

Definition

Search engines – Search engines use 'spiders' or 'robots' to go out and search the web and create a database of sites which is then matched against the search terms or keywords entered by the browser in the search engine.

Some examples of search engines include:

- Alta Vista www.altavista.com
- Google www.google.com
- Hotbot www.hotbot.lycos.com
- Infoseek www.infoseek.go.com
- Northern Light www.northernlight.com

Activity 5.5

Try searching for marketing research using at least two different search engines. What are the differences? Try using the advanced search options to narrow the search to qualitative research.

Definition

Directories – Directories are compiled lists or indexes of websites that are reviewed and often rated by compilers. This can remove the randomness of searches through engines which may be an advantage in the early stages of exploratory research. It is possible to pay web directory compilers to ensure that a site occurs early in the list of sites presented as the result of a search.

Source: Crouch and Housden (Crouch, S. and Housden, M., 2003).

Examples of subject directories include:

- LookSmart www.looksmart.com
- Lycos www.lycos.com
- Yahoo www.yahoo.com.

Activity 5.6

Try exercise five using the directories. What differences do you notice?

Searching Online

Successful online searching will be achieved if the search terms are carefully defined. We saw how this process works in Unit three. Careful phrasing of the search term and creative use of Boolean operators can help.

Boolean operators are usually found in the advance search section in the search engine or directory.

Boolean logic operators help the browser search the web.

The simplest of these are the words 'and' or '+', 'not' or '–' and 'or'. Others may allow the use of what are known as proximity operators, such as 'followed by' or 'near'. These can help refine search terms and produce more relevant results.

For example, MRS 'and' UK 'not' USA would refine search terms on this term.

Other engines may have advanced search facilities which employ Boolean operators in a more user-friendly format.

The use of Google's advance search feature can reduce the number of results for any search term to far more manageable and relevant numbers.

There are directories of search engines at www.searchability.com and www.virtualfree-sites.com.

Newsgroups and discussion forums

Newsgroups exist for almost every topic under the sun, including marketing research. Newsgroups can be useful sources of information and also for establishing opinions on products and services. Some companies monitor newsgroups for research purposes and some seed newsgroups with product information and recommendations. This is a dubious practice if it is not done transparently and if uncovered can lead to the user being barred from the service.

Most search engines allow groups to be searched for. Try www.groups.google.com.

Summary

In this unit we looked at definitions of secondary research, and looked at the strengths and limitations of research. These were:

Strengths

- It is cheap or free of charge
- It may provide an answer to the problem, this will save enormous time and effort
- It can guide or provide direction for primary work
- It can suggest methodologies for data collection
- It can indicate problems with particular methodologies
- It can provide historic or comparative data to enable longitudinal studies.

Weaknesses

- It is not related to the research question and the temptation may be to force the data to fit the question
- It may not be directly comparable

- Data may be incomplete
- It may not be available
- The data may have been gathered for a particular purpose.

We looked at the range of sources that are available to the researcher.

These included:

- Government data
- Trade associations
- Professional institutes
- Pressure groups
- Regulatory bodies
- Financial institutions
- Company data
- Online aggregators
- Directories
- The trade press
- National press
- Specialist companies
- Syndicated services.

We saw that almost anything published on or by companies is capable of yielding useful data on companies, industries and markets.

We also explored secondary data relating to companies' markets and online markets. We explored how search engines and directories work and the use of Boolean operators in helping searches on the Internet.

Finally we looked at the online market and explored ways of maximizing the effectiveness of searching online.

Further study

Both Wilson (Wilson, A., 2003) and Crouch and Housden (Crouch, S. and Housden, M., 2003) have significant resources outlined in the relevant chapters. You should scan these chapters and add relevant websites to your list of favourites.

Hints and Tips

Question 4

You are working for a small Midlands-based manufacturer of components for the motor industry. Your sales manager has identified a potential new market in the Czech Republic. The company cannot afford to carry out marketing research without establishing the nature of the demand for the product.

You have been asked to produce a preliminary market report from secondary data. There is no syndicated study available. What are the advantages and disadvantages of this approach? How can the disadvantages be overcome?

Bibliography

Crouch, S. and Housden, M. (2003). *Marketing research for managers* 3rd edition. Butterworth-Heinemann.

MRS (2003). www.mrs.org.

National Statistics (2003). www.statistics.gov.uk.

Wilson, A. (2003). *Marketing research: an integrated approach*, FT Prentice Hall.

unit 6 observation research

Learning objectives

After completing this unit you will be able to:

- Define observational research
- Understand the methods of observational research
- Understand and define the role of audits in marketing research
- Understand the application of mystery shopping techniques
- Identify online observation techniques
- Outline the ethical issues in observational research
- Complete syllabus element 4.3.

Key definition

Observation A non-verbal means of obtaining primary data as an alternative or complement to questioning (MRS, 2003).

Panels A permanent representative sample maintained by a market research agency from which information is obtained on more than one occasion either for continuous research or for ad hoc projects (MRS, 2003).

Audit The measurement of product volume and value through the distribution network audit may be wholesale, retail or consumer.

Mystery shopping The use of individuals trained to observe, experience and measure the customer service process, by acting as a prospective customer and undertaking a series of pre-determined tasks (MRS, 1997).

Peoplemeter The mechanical device used by BARB to collect data on TV audiences in the UK.

EPOS Electronic Point Of Sale equipment.

Cookies A file stored on your hard drive used to identify your computer and other information including preferences to another remote computer.

Ethnographic research Observation involving total immersion in the life of the subject.

Study Guide

This unit should take you around 3 hours to complete.

Introduction

Observation research is one of the fastest growing areas of marketing research. Techniques such as mystery shopping and audits are growing in popularity as the need to ensure customer satisfaction is growing and the technical ability to monitor individuals' behaviour expands. Our online behaviour can be tracked even to the extent of being able to trace the search terms used to access a particular website. The use of CCTV and video means that the average UK consumer is caught on camera many times a day. This of course raises ethical considerations that we discussed earlier. Observation is however a tried and tested technique in marketing research.

Definitions of observation research

The MRS defines observation as 'A non-verbal means of obtaining primary data as an alternative or complement to questioning' (MRS, 2003).

Wilson defines it as 'a data gathering approach where information in the behaviour of people, objects and organizations is collected without any questions being asked of the participant' (Wilson, A., 2003).

Observation strengths

Observation has several strengths:

- It is not dependent on the respondents' memory. It records exactly what has happened, not what the respondent believes has happened.

Smoke and mirrors

In surveys of smoking behaviour, respondents have been shown to under-report the number of cigarettes they smoke by up to 100 per cent. The same applies to alcohol units. Very often GPs will write cigarettes smoked as 10/20; 10 being the reported number, 20 the more likely figure.

- The potential for bias in research is reduced as the researcher is the witness of behaviour rather than actively asking for information – the way an interviewer asks for information can influence responses
- Mechanical recording of observed behaviour may reduce the incidence of reporting errors
- Observation does not rely on the verbal skills of a respondent to describe the behaviour
- Observation measures what has happened, not what respondents say that they will do in a certain situation
- Observation can counter the high refusal rates in some markets
- Observation can be used to monitor behaviour preceding an action. For example, picking up and looking at competing products before making a final decision
- Observation does not interfere with the respondents' day-to-day life. It is their activity that is of interest. They do not have to fill in diaries or complete questionnaires.

Disadvantages of observation techniques

There are some disadvantages:

- Observation does not measure the reasons for certain behaviour. It cannot uncover motivation or attitudes
- Observation cannot measure the likelihood of repeat behaviour
- Only public behaviour can be assessed. Private behaviour is very difficult to research in this way although efforts have been made to manage this process.

Categories of observation research

Wilson (2003) identifies five different categories of observation research. These are:

1. Natural versus contrived
2. Visible versus hidden
3. Structured versus unstructured
4. Mechanized versus human
5. Participant versus non-participant.

Natural	Contrived
Rather like David Attenborough and mountain gorillas, customers are observed in their natural state	The researcher sets up an observation situation
Respondents may be observed going around a supermarket, browsing a website, etc.	This may be a supermarket fixture set up in a room or children playing with new toys with the researcher present
They are not aware that they are being observed	Customers are aware that they are being observed
Visible	**Hidden**
Customers are aware that observation is taking place because they can see the recording equipment	Respondents know that they are being observed but cannot see the observer or recording equipment
Structured	**Unstructured**
Observers keep a tally or count of certain behaviours	Observers record or make notes on all aspects of the observed behaviour
Mechanical	**Human**
The installation of equipment to measure behaviour	More appropriate for complex behaviour involving multiple interactions
Participant	**Non participant**
The observer participates in the observed behaviour, for example, in mystery shopping	The behaviour is observed remotely

Telephone man

Observational research by Abbott Meade Vickers for British Telecommunications informed an advertising strategy that aimed to get men spending more time using the telephone. Observation found that men spent less time on the telephone, generally stood whilst talking on the phone and passed the phone to their partner when family or social events were being discussed.

The campaign that was developed from this involved a student ringing home, the phone was answered by her father who said 'I'll fetch your mother'. The student said 'I phoned to talk to you'. A surprised father then enjoys his chat with his daughter. The strap line 'it's good to talk' followed.

Observation methodologies

There are a range of observational techniques that are used throughout the research industry. Many of these take advantage of new technology.

Audits and scanner-based observation

An audit measures product movement and consumption through the value chain.

There are three types of audit – wholesale, retail and home.

The use of Electronic Point of Sale (EPOS) and hand-held scanning devices has changed this sector of the market significantly over the last 10 years.

Audits have been in place for some time, but the process of carrying them out was far more time consuming than it is today. Researchers used to do stock counts looking at stock delivered into retail stores, stock out and stock remaining. This would give a clear idea of retail sales in the period under consideration. Companies still carry out this work in smaller stores to verify wastage and stock loss through theft, but the use of EPOS technology has significantly reduced the amount of time taken to produce results. Companies like ACNeilsen and TN Sofres are significant players in this market.

Activity 6.1

Visit www.acnielsen.co.uk and www.tnsofres.com/superpanel. Review the information that is available on the services that ACNielsen and TN Sofres offer to the market. At the ACNielsen site you should review the retail measurement services and consumer panel services, particularly Homescan.

In the past, home audit methodology has included the keeping of written diary records. Respondents keep a diary of behaviour. These are still used in markets or by companies where scanning technology is not available, and to measure behaviour that is not capable of being scanned, e.g. meal times and number of people eating together.

Home audits can also involve waste bin audits. Though not a pleasant task, this allows researchers to evaluate product consumption or usage rate in the home.

The use of observation equipment in stores can produce data on other areas of the shopper's behaviour, for example the route around the store, or the way that a consumer browses a retail fixture.

Audit data can produce a huge range of analysis, and the services of ACNeilsen and TN Sofres provide the raw material for the marketing management of the retail and grocery marketing sector.

These data include

- Market share
- Brand share
- Brand loyalty
- Category loyalty
- Retail sector analysis
- Retail share
- Retail price checks
- Average basket
- Sales promotion responses, etc.

The services are available internationally and most European markets are covered. Some European markets remain harder to audit through traditional means, and statistical weightings are used to produce a full picture of retail sales. Other markets can be audited but the use of scanning technology may mean that more low-tech solutions are needed to carry out the task.

For example, in Indonesia sales of cigarettes are made from kiosks that may sell 1–2 cigarettes from a pack at a time. This is hard to measure!

Media measurement

The measurement of media is a key element of observation research. The most important of these in the UK is the Broadcaster's Audience Research Board (BARB). BARB provides the measurement service for television viewing in the UK. In early 2003 the contract for TV-viewing measurement was changed. This new contract is due to run for 5–8 years. The old panel which was set up in 1991was replaced with a new panel recruited from scratch over the last 2 years. The main change is to increase the size of the panel from 4,300 homes to 5,100 homes. This reflects the changes in the media landscape in the UK. In 1983, there were only three TV channels in the UK; today there are hundreds. The old sample was not large enough to ensure robust data on smaller TV audiences.

Other changes to the panel design were reported by BARB to include:

- Removal of demographic disproportionality. The undersampling of downmarket audiences has ended and the entire panel is now proportionate to the population.
- Improved geographic representation. Regional panels will be represented more closely to their proportion of the UK population. London, for example, has 20 per cent of the UK population, but under the old BARB system had only 12 per cent of panel homes. Under the new system it will have 17 per cent of panel homes.
- Revised panel controls (the aspects against which the panel is recruited to ensure it is representative – such as age, social class, etc.). Multi-channel television homes will be recruited with a greater level of panel controls than on the previous system.
- A more detailed weighting scheme to introduce a greater level of representativeness to the reporting sample.
- An increased annual Establishment Survey (the source of population estimates and penetration figures on which panel controls are based) of 50,000 interviews to provide more robust estimates, particularly by platform.
- Updated metering equipment that is non-intrusive, upgradeable and therefore future-proofed.

Source: BARB

BARB: Watching you watching them

Television measurement service

The measurement service provides television audience data on a minute-by-minute basis for channels received within the UK. These data are available for reporting nationally as well as at the ITV and BBC at the regional level.

Viewing estimates are obtained from panels of television owning households representing the viewing behaviour of the 24+ million households within the UK. The panels are selected to be representative of each ITV and BBC region.

Panel homes are selected via a multi-stage stratified and unclustered sample design. This ensures that the panel is fully representative of households across the whole of the UK. Each panel is maintained against a range of individual and household characteristics (panel controls). As the estimates for the large majority of the panel controls are not available from Census data, it is necessary to conduct surveys (Establishment Survey) to obtain this information.

The Establishment Survey is a random probability survey carried out on a continuous basis involving some 50,000 interviews per year. The nature of this survey ensures that any changes within the characteristics of the population can be identified. Panel controls can therefore be updated and panel household representation, adjusted to ensure representativeness, is maintained. In addition to being the prime source of television population information, the Establishment Survey also generates a pool of potential recruits from which panel member homes are recruited. Each of the panel member households have all their television receiving equipment (sets, video cassette recorders, set-top box decoders, etc.) electronically monitored by a 'peoplemeter' monitoring system. This system automatically identifies and records the channel to which each television set is tuned when switched on and all viewing involving a VCR (recording, playback, viewing through the VCR, etc.). In addition, the metering system incorporates the capability to 'fingerprint' videotapes during recording sessions and to subsequently identify such recorded material when played back (time-shifted viewing).

All permanent household residents and guests declare their presence in a room whilst a television set is on by pressing an allocated button on a handset. The metering system monitors all registrations made by each individual.

Throughout each day, the meter system stores all the viewing undertaken by the entire household. Each night the panel household is contacted by the processing centre by telephone to collect the stored data. This procedure is carried out on every home each day to produce 'overnight' television viewing data.

Source: www.barb.co.uk

Other media are audited in different ways – some are based on observation, some on other research methods.

In the UK, the measurement of poster sites is carried out though observation. Video cameras are used to measure the number of full faces looking at a poster. This data is used to help the media sales people.

A really useful site that discusses the full range of media research services is www.zenith-media.com. The A to Z listing covers the full range of research services for media.

Activity 6.2

Go to www.zenithmedia.com and find out the following:

1. What is the name of the poster research organization in the UK?
2. List three Internet audience research businesses.
3. What is the NRS?
4. What is the ABC?

Other observation techniques

Ethnography

Ethnography is a research technique that has been used in the social sciences for some time and is increasingly used in marketing. Ethnographic research involves total immersion in the life of the subject and researchers may spend a considerable amount of time with the subject of the research. Results may be recorded or written down post experience. The research may look at family interaction with a product or brand and may be looking for depth of insight to inform market positioning.

Football crazy

Ethnographic research has been used by researchers looking at the problem of football hooliganism in the UK. Researchers travel with known hooligans and later record their experiences. As you might imagine, other research techniques would be impossible to use to research this behaviour.

This research has informed government policy and policing tactics.

Researchers at the Football Research Unit at Liverpool John Moore's University have joked that there is no football hooligan problem in the UK. It is, in fact, completely made up of ethnographic researchers posing as hooligans.

The big question is, 'Who did eat all the pies?'

Mechanical observation

A range of mechanical observation techniques are used in observation research which include:

Psychogalvanometers
This measures the respondents' reaction to a message. It uses the same techniques as a lie detector, measuring the electrical resistance of the skin. The amount of sweat on the skin increases during arousal and it is this that is measured. It is most often used for pre-testing advertising and copy.

Puplimeters
Puplimeters measure the same responses through a measurement of pupil dilation.

Eye cameras

Eye cameras are used to track the movement of the eye around an object, maybe a piece of creative or a retail fixture. This method has been used on websites' research to explore the navigation of sites and may be combined with a mechanical record of key strokes or mouse movement.

Tachistoscopes

Reveal the test material in micro second bursts. The respondents' ability to recall detail is measured. It is believed to predict advertising effectiveness amongst other uses.

Mystery shopping

Mystery shopping is defined by the MRS as 'The use of individuals trained to observe, experience and measure the customer service process, by acting as a prospective customer and undertaking a series of pre-determined tasks' (MRS, 1997).

This may be done by companies assessing the activities of competitors in the market or by companies assessing the performance of their own sales staff.

Wilson (Wilson, A., 2003) identifies three main purposes for mystery shopping:

1. To act as a diagnostic tool identifying failings and weak points in service delivery
2. To encourage and reward staff
3. To assess competitors.

Mystery shoppers should present facts rather than opinions and these may include the shopping environment as well as interactions between the researcher and staff. This is designed to reduce researcher bias. There needs to be careful recruitment of mystery shoppers as staff may become familiar with them, and age, gender and appearance of shoppers may affect the experience. Also, the shopper needs to fall within the target market. The shopper needs to be natural and to make the experience as close to life as possible. Some mystery shopping has involved the use of hidden cameras. Training is also very important and data capture and recording needs to be carefully considered. Analysis of the data can be highly subjective and a formal structure for analysis might be needed to ensure the valid comparison of results between retail outlets – the use of some form of recording equipment may help this task.

This dealer bites

Mystery shopping is used extensively in the car market. The brand advertising of the leading car companies is ultimately reinforced or compromised by the sales people staffing the room. One mystery shopper described the experience of entering the sales show room as like 'being thrown into a shark-filled pool'.

Online observation

We have already mentioned the use of observation techniques in designing websites. However, the characteristics of the Internet allow for a lot of data to be captured through remote observation. The use of cookies allows the website owner to identify repeat visits.

A cookie is a text file placed on the browser's computer that allows the browser's computer to be identified on subsequent visits. A cookie may contain the computer's address or the details of a customer registration. This means that when the customer logs on, a personalized greeting can be made or passwords provided. Cookies cannot extract information.

Most online retailers use this system, e.g. Amazon will drive content to particular customers based on their previous behaviour. Browser behaviour through the site can also be captured and used. This has been used to tailor-make print brochures based on customers' browsing behaviour through the site. We can track where browsers have come from and where they go to after leaving the site.

Ethics in observation research

There are clearly significant ethical considerations in the use of observation research. The basic rule is that if observation is to take place in a situation in which behaviour could not usually be observed, then permission should be asked. The MRS code of conduct has specific sections on Mystery Shopping. These are available on the MRS website at www.mrs.org.uk/standards/downloads/mysterycust.doc. This includes the liaison with employees who are the subject of mystery shopping communicating the fact that the technique being used covers the organization from any data protection issue and may be motivating in itself.

Zipping Zapping and Lewd behaviour

Recently the London Business School used cameras filming viewers of TV commercials to try to identify behaviour during advertisement breaks. As media-buying is based on audiences for programmes, LBS tried to categorize behaviour during commercial breaks to see whether companies were truly buying the number of TV rating points they believed.

The cameras were left in place for sometime and whilst in the early stages viewers were clearly aware of the cameras, after a while they clearly had forgotten that they were there and resumed their normal Friday night behaviour.

Source: FT/LBS Feb 2003.

How is observation research used?

Activity 6.3

Reflecting on the various approaches to observation research, think about the potential applications for observation research. Brainstorm as many ideas as you can and then go to the text books to fill in the gaps.

International issues

The use of observation is appropriate in all markets. Indeed, in some international markets it may be the preferred method.

In addition to the usual international caveats of cost, comparability and availability of resources, e.g. CCTV, we have to add the problem of interpretation. The interpretation of body language, signs (semiotics) and non-verbal behaviour is culturally determined.

For example, in certain African countries it is normal for men to hold hands as they are walking together.

In other markets colours may mean something very different from the UK. In China, red means good luck while in others it means danger.

In some other markets green is the colour for danger.

In the UK, white is the colour representing purity and is worn by brides at their weddings. In Japan, white is the colour of mourning and in Brazil, purple is the colour of mourning.

International marketing is fraught with these difficulties but they are certainly not insurmountable.

One way to manage this is to use James Lee's idea of self reference criteria (Lewis, K. and Housden, M., 1999). The researcher should interpret the behaviour in response to his own domestic culture, identify the factors affected by his cultural bias, isolate them and interpret the observation through an understanding of this bias.

Otherwise, it is important to use local agencies who can interpret the behaviour observed from their own cultural perspective. One person's aggressive argument might be a lively discussion between friends in other markets.

Summary

In this unit we looked at observation research. We looked at the types of research.

These are:

1. Natural versus contrived
2. Visible versus hidden
3. Structured versus unstructured
4. Mechanized versus human
5. Participant versus non-participant.

In particular, we looked at the audit process. We looked at the key supplier of audit data in the UK – ACNeilsen and TN Sofres.

We looked in depth at the role of mystery shopping in observation research and at the ethical constraints on its use. We saw that its main function was:

- To act as a diagnostic tool identifying failings and weak points in service delivery
- To encourage and reward staff
- To assess competitors.

We saw that other purposes of observational research were:

- To improve customer service
- To improve store layout
- To improve staffing levels to ensure reduced waiting time at call centres or at service points
- To generate information to inform reward and recognition schemes
- To monitor time spent on any activity, e.g. TV consumption
- To measure the amount of product consumed
- To look at product combinations
- To explore alternative product uses
- To explore product interaction.

International observation research was covered, and the use of self reference criteria in the interpretation of results was advised.

We looked at the mechanical devices used for capturing data both on and off-line.

A range of mechanical observation techniques are used in observation research these include:

- Psychogalvanometers
- Eye cameras
- Tachistoscopes.

Finally, we looked at issues to do with online observation including the use of cookies.

Further study

Question 5

You work as a marketing manager for a major car dealership. The dealership has 150 sites throughout the UK. Your Customer Satisfaction Scores have been falling recently. You have been to an MRS training course on Mystery Shopping and feel that this technique might help identify the causes for the fall in satisfaction.

Write a report to your director outlining why you feel that this might help.

Discuss the role of mystery shopping in delivering service quality.

What are the benefits and limitations of this technique?

Your report should outline what other research techniques might help uncover the cause of the problem.

Bibliography

Lewis, K. and Housden, M. (1999). *International Marketing*, Kogan Page.

MRS (1997). Best practice in mystery customer research.

MRS (2003). www.mrs.org.uk.

Wilson, A. (2003). *Marketing research: an integrated approach*, FT Prentice Hall.

unit 7 qualitative research

Learning objectives

After completing this unit you will be able to:

- Define qualitative data
- Identify and apply methods for collecting qualitative data
- Understand the process of analysing qualitative data
- Understand the techniques of online qualitative research
- Understand how to use qualitative research to inform marketing decision-making
- Complete syllabus elements 4.4, 4.5, 4.6.

Key definitions

Projective techniques A form of disguised questioning that encourages participants to attribute their feelings, beliefs or motivations to another person, object or situation. Examples of projective techniques are word association, sentence completion and thematic apperception tests (ESOMAR, 2003).

Focus groups A number of respondents gathered together to generate ideas through the discussion of, and reaction to, specific stimuli. Under the steerage of a moderator, focus groups are often used in exploratory work or when the subject matter involves social activities, habits and status (MRS, 2003).

Moderator An individual who facilitates but does not influence a group discussion.

One way window A device used to allow researchers to view respondents without themselves being seen.

Depth interviews A variety of data collection techniques, mainly for qualitative research undertaken with individual respondents rather than groups (MRS, 2003).

Topic or discussion guide An outline of the structure, themes and timing of a focus group or depth interview.

Content analysis software Computer software that helps with the textual analysis of qualitative research.

Respondent An individual or organization from whom information is sought, directly or indirectly, which could, in whole or in part, form the results of a research project (MRS, 2003).

Brand personality tests Asks respondents to describe a brand as a person.

Study Guide

This unit should take you around 3 hours to complete. You should set aside another 3 hours to complete the activities outlined throughout the unit.

Introduction

Qualitative research accounts for between 10 and 15 per cent of total research expenditure in the UK. It is growing in importance as marketing professionals recognize its vital role in providing depth of understanding about customers and their behaviour. This unit will introduce you to the methods used in qualitative research and the major applications supported by this methodology.

Qualitative research defined

So how can qualitative research be defined? The MRS defines qualitative research as 'A body of research techniques which seeks insights through loosely structured, mainly verbal data rather than measurements. Analysis is interpretative, subjective, impressionistic and diagnostic' (MRS, 2003).

Crouch and Housden's definition is 'Qualitative research is so called because its emphasis lies in producing data which is rich in insight, understanding, explanation and depth of information, but which cannot be justified statistically' (Crouch, S. and Housden, M., 2003).

Alan Wilson in the course text defines qualitative research as 'Research that is undertaken using an unstructured research approach with a small number of carefully selected individuals to produced non quantifiable insights into behaviour motivations and attitudes' (Wilson, A., 2003).

What are the essential characteristics of qualitative research?

- It is unquantifiable and is not representative of larger populations
- Data collection techniques are unstructured
- It involves small samples of individuals or groups of people
- It seeks to reveal opinions, motivations and attitudes
- It is about insight and depth of understanding
- It is subject to a high degree of interpretation by skilled researchers
- It usually precedes quantitative work
- It can inform the nature of quantitative research.

Data collection techniques in qualitative research

Focus groups or group discussions

Wilson defines group discussions as 'depth interviews with a group of people; they differ in that they involve interaction between respondents' (Wilson, A., 2003).

The MRS defines group discussions or focus groups as 'A number of respondents gathered together to generate ideas through the discussion of, and reaction to, specific stimuli. Under the steerage of a moderator, focus groups are often used in exploratory work or when the subject matter involves social activities, habits and status' (MRS, 2003).

Focus groups are generally made up of around 6–12 respondents. The most common number is 8. A lower number may be used when a particularly specialist topic is being discussed. The higher number would be used for a wide-ranging discussion. This design aspect is determined by the need to reflect the range of views held on a subject by the target market or concerned population.

They are run and managed by an interviewer, usually called a moderator. The moderator maybe the same researcher who produced the research proposal, maybe a specialist consultant or maybe employed from a field work agency. The moderator will control the group keeping the discussion on track and probing for further information when needed. The moderator will introduce other tasks that may occur within the group. The main aim of the group is to ensure that the group members discuss the topic amongst themselves; the moderator's touch should be as light as possible. However, the skilled moderator will use a range of techniques to control the input of particularly vociferous members and to encourage quieter members of the group to make their contribution. Groups will normally last between 45 minutes and 2 hours. Discussions are generally taped, recorded or videoed.

Groups usually occur at the beginning of a research project as they can provide very useful information to explore through other methods. The groups may be observed remotely and agencies offer clients the chance to view groups set up in special rooms, where the client can observe the group through a one-way window. The moderator can be linked by a concealed or a discrete microphone to the observers so that a particularly interesting line of discussion can be probed further.

What makes a moderator?

Sally is an open and friendly woman aged 40. She is a freelance qualitative researcher and has moved into this career after a successful period in advertising planning, where she worked at a senior level on a range of accounts.

She has a degree in Psychology and holds both the CIM and MRS diplomas. She is from London but it is hard to discern any accent. She dresses conservatively.

She is a good listener but can be assertive when required.

Moderators should be:

- highly qualified and experienced in research and, possibly, psychology
- business and marketing aware. They need to be able to translate respondents' feelings into business advantage for their clients
- strong communicators, able to relate to a range of people
- hard to place regionally in terms of socio-economic class
- socially able, relaxed and friendly, but strong enough to control a room of animated, or conversely, disinterested respondents
- flexible and quick thinking, with the ability to respond to the unexpected.

Focus group discussion guide – Bedford

1. Intros – ensure everyone understands nature of the focus group and the objectives, etc., as well as that it is an independent study . . . allow everyone to introduce each other! [5 mins]. As part of this – who do you work for – Franchise or brand owner?
2. What brands would you consider to be successful brands? [5 mins]
3. Why do you think these brands are so successful? [5 mins]
4. What is your perception of our brand [for this you will create some visual ideas]?
   We will base this on the following:
   a. If the brand was a famous personality, who would it be – Popstar or Politician? [10 mins]
   b. If it was a place, where would it be? What would the weather be like? [10 mins]
5. What do you feel our customers see as important? [10 mins]
6. How do you think you can make a difference to what is important? [7.5 mins]
7. If you were the boss, what would you do to change the image/brand, if anything? [7.5 mins]

Close.

Thanks and incentives.

Stimulus material

Stimulus material may include a range of physical objects which respondents can use to reflect upon or use to express their views non-verbally.

These may include:

- Creative samples: Proofs, animated outlines of TV commercials, concept or storyboards, mail copy or print advertisements
- Mocked-up product packs
- Product samples
- Materials for projective work (discussed on pages 105–106).

Recruitment of respondents

The recruitment of respondents is an important part of the process. Participants may be recruited in a number of ways:

- through screening interviews at home or in the street
- through professional recruitment services identified in the research buyer's guide, or the MRS website.

The use of recruiters may save time and money but can have the drawback of recruiting 'professional' group respondents who are not typical of an audience. Screening questions should ensure that respondents fit the overall profile of the population under consideration.

For example,

- male
- over 50
- who has a home computer
- who has bought via the internet in the last month
- who has no connection with the computer or research industry.

Generally, respondents' attendance is incentivized through a cash payment or gift. Refreshments are usually provided. It is advisable to invite more respondents to attend than the minimum required to complete the group, as non attendance can be an issue.

Typically, 4 groups would be carried out but more may be required if looking at sub sectors or regional variations.

Group interviews cost between £1500 and £3000 depending on the type of group (for example, professional groups are more expensive), complexity and the moderator. Group moderation is a highly skilled job, and good moderators are usually highly trained and commercially astute.

The topic or discussion guide

The discussion guide is a route map for the group interview. It outlines a time table of activity and highlights key stages in the process. It is not a list of questions. It covers key themes that should be covered within the group discussion and allows the moderator to mentally or physically cross off areas that have been covered.

Wilson suggests that the guide breaks the group into 3 distinct phases:

1. Introduction
   a. Objectives
   b. Personal introductions
   c. Agenda.
2. Discussive phase
   a. Topic areas
   b. Stimulus material.
3. Summarizing phase
   a. Summarizing discussion
   b. Closing
   c. Administration.

Activity 7.1

Using Wilson's template, write a discussion guide for a car dealership client who has asked you to research new customers' experience of the sales experience. Remember to try to focus on themes rather than questions. Produce an outline timetable for a group lasting one and a half hours.

Focus groups have a number of advantages

- They replicate the dynamic social interactions that occur in the market place
- They provide rich and detailed knowledge of a subject
- They are more efficient in terms of time. One focus group can be done in a day while 14 depth interviews might take at least 2 weeks to complete
- They are cheaper per interviewee than depth interviews
- They allow interaction with physical stimuli, e.g. products
- They can involve multiple techniques within the framework of the focus group.

Depth interviews

The MRS defines depth interviews as a term used to 'describe a variety of data collection techniques, but mainly for qualitative research undertaken with individual respondents rather than groups' (MRS, 2003).

Usually in a study that involves depth interviews, 10–14 interviews will be carried out depending on the nature of the sample. Depth interviews cost between £400 and £700 per interview.

Depth interviews have several advantages:

- They are conducted face to face, and body language can be interpreted
- Proximity may encourage respondents to reveal more than they might in a remote interview
- The respondent is the centre of attention and can be probed at length to explore issues that the researcher feels are important. This is the 'annoying child' syndrome with the researcher asking 'why' (but more subtly) until the issue is explored adequately
- Group dynamics may prevent individuals expressing themselves particularly over areas that are sensitive, like income
- Recruitment tends to be easier
- The logistics are easier, no special rooms are needed
- They reveal depth of understanding
- They are flexible. The line of questioning may evolve within the interview and between interviews
- They can involve a range of techniques.

Generally depth interviews last between 45 minutes and 2 hours. The interviews are tape recorded or videoed to enable the researcher to concentrate on the discussion and its implications rather than writing down notes. As for group discussion, the researcher does not have a list of questions but rather a topic guide as a route map through the interview. The location of the interview may be in the office or in the home. The main thing is that the respondent feels comfortable and relaxed. Interviews generally take place with an individual but interviews may involve more than one respondent if the research question is dealing with a subject in which the respondents may affect each other's decision, for example high involvement purchases like pensions or cars.

Example of topic guide

Questions/discussion guide for in-depth interviews at the strategic level.

Part One

1. Introduction to topic – this research is focused on looking at how relationships can add value. The subject of the research is:

   Does employee behaviour at the retailer level have an impact on brand values?

2. Objectives of the interview – I am looking to understand your thoughts, opinions and feelings at a strategic level to gauge your perception of the brand and the impact of people's behaviour upon its value.

Part Two

1. What factors do you consider important in the creation of a successful brand?
2. What is your current perception of the brand?
3. What is it about the brand that you believe is important to customers?
4. In your opinion, what is your staff's perception of the brand?

5. How do you feel the retailer impacts on brand value?

6. What role do you think the retail staff play in creating a positive brand image?

7. If you had a blank sheet of paper, what would your vision be of the future for the brand?

The interviewer needs to have the same or similar skills as the group moderator. The respondent must feel at ease, and techniques such as positive reinforcement and mirroring of body posture can be used. The interviewer must be skilled in managing depth interviews, and in b2b interviewing the interviewer may need a considerable amount of industry knowledge in order to ask the right questions and know when and how to probe for more information.

What are we like?

Depth interviews are used a great deal to uncover perceptions held by key audiences in a market. This may be used to establish organizational values and mission. It ensures that the current perception of an organization is known. In recent studies, depth interviews were carried out with the following type of people:

- key suppliers
- a range of competitors
- journalists in the national and trade press
- trade association representatives
- key account customers
- trade unions
- employee representative groups

What do they like?

What do they like?

Group interviews were used by a Japanese entrant into the UK food market.

The research objectives were broad and this research was part of an exploratory phase that looked at market potential for their range of instant meals.

Researchers were asked to explore various potential brand names and to taste-test the existing Japanese product range.

The research provided the basis for a successful European launch.

Projective techniques

Projective techniques are designed to allow respondents to 'attribute their feelings, beliefs or motivations to another person, object or situation' (ESOMAR, 2003). They are usually very interesting to administer and reveal some fascinating insight into the research problem. They free respondents from the bonds of language and allow them to express feelings they may find hard to describe in words.

They have several other advantages:

- They are engaging for respondents, are usually fun to do and get respondents motivated
- They provide richer insight than conventional questioning: in the right hands the analysis can be extremely revealing
- They can create excellent ideas for further exploration.

The disadvantage is that they are hard to interpret.

Sentence completion

This technique involves (as the term describes) simply asking respondents to complete sentences or fill in a missing word or words from a sentence. For example:

'I think that McDonald's food is...'

'People who buy Dell computers are...............................'

'CIM workbooks are..'

Story completion

A set of events is related to a respondent who is asked to complete the story or say what he would have done in a similar situation. The respondent may also be asked to explain the behaviour described.

Word association

This technique has been used in psychoanalysis for many years.

It simply asks respondents to state the first word that comes into their head after a cue word is given. Reponses may be spoken or written down.

Researchers may chain responses together to go deeper into the association or probe the reason for the association.

For example, 'Skoda' and 'cheap', reveals something about the Skoda brand but respondents may be thinking about value for money and this would need to be probed further.

Cartoon completion

This involves showing the respondent a cartoon drawing. These may be single images or paired images in which one individual is talking to another. In single images, speech bubbles are left blank, or in paired drawings the second speech bubble is left blank for the respondent to complete.

Mood boards

Mood boards are collages of images that are cut from magazines and assembled together either glued or pinned on a board. This technique can reveal the associations with other products' images and colours that may not come out in conventional research. The same objective lies behind asking respondents to model images relating to a brand in plasticine or clay or to draw them on paper.

Brand personality or brand CVs

Brand personality asks respondents to describe a brand as a person. Another term is the brand CV in which respondents write a mock curriculum vitae for the brand under consideration. This can be very useful in determining the accuracy of positioning in the market.

Activity 7.2

Try the brand CV task with brands of your choice. Try it with friends or colleagues. Are there any differences?. Try it with Volvo.

Association can also be made with objects or known people or celebrities, the reason for the association is the most important thing here. So if a car brand is described as 'Roger Moore' the researcher needs to probe to uncover the meaning of the association. Unfortunately for the brand and Roger Moore, the association in this piece of work was due to the fact that 'he was once glamorous but now past it'.

Brand mapping

Is an extension of the brand personality test that involves multiple brands. Respondents are asked to identify key attributes or dimensions of a product sector and then position brands against those relative to the competition. This can be useful in identifying positioning and segmentation criteria and is very useful in identifying gaps in the market place. The alcopops sector was developed from this type of work. Consumers identify the fact that as children they drink fizzy sweet non-alcoholic drinks and as adults that drink flat, bitter or dry, alcoholic drinks. Alcopops filled the gap for sweet fizzy alcoholic drinks.

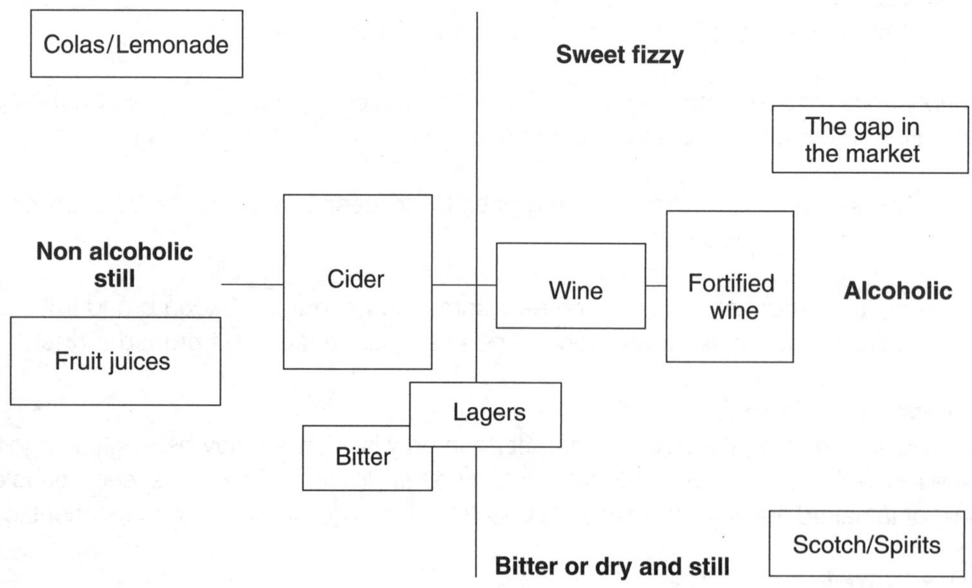

Figure 7.1 Category mapping in the drinks market

These are also known as perceptual maps and in the right hands can be very revealing. Many people, however, simply choose to use standard dimensions to build the maps; most often price and quality.

In the past, this was adequate to differentiate products in markets. Jacobs Creek, for example, entered the UK wine market as a reasonably-priced, reasonably good wine. This was a sustainable position in an undifferentiated market, in which wine choices were often Blue or Black (Blue Nun or Black Tower) and luxury was a bottle of Mateus Rose. Today, wines labelled Tastes Great with Chicken and Tastes Great with Beef are available. New differentiated positions in this market are hard to imagine. Maybe Tastes Great with Chicken Wings!!

In most of today's competitive markets, price and quality are inadequate dimensions to make a difference or to differentiate one product from another. The dimensions can usefully be developed from research or the perceptual maps can be used to assess alternative positions in the market. For example, Lucozade was effectively repositioned as an adult fitness drink through understanding that the brand's values of adding recovery from illness could be translated into a more positive and contemporary positioning: enabling recovery from exercise and today allowing you to exercise longer.

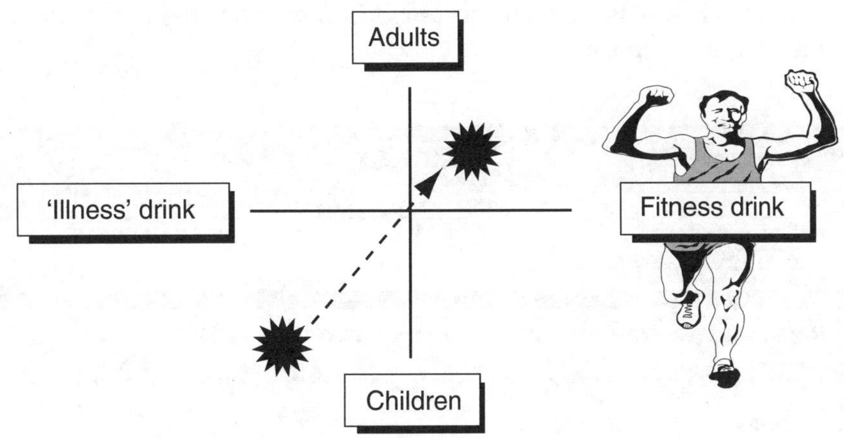

Figure 7.2 Lucozade brand repositioning

Thematic apperception tests or TAT tests

Images are shown to the respondents and they are asked to place the image in a story context. Or respondents are asked to describe what is happening and what will happen next.

Photo sorts

Images of different people are presented and classified as to the brands they would and would not use.

Role play

Respondents are asked to act out a scene. If used in groups, it is important that the group is well motivated and prepared to participate fully.

Role play is a pain

In a well-known example, respondents were asked to play the victim of a headache, the pain and the pain relief. Some described the pain as sharp, aggressive and violent; others described it as dull, nagging and annoying. The pain relief was either aggressive or gentle. This research led to the development of a positioning for over-the-counter pain relief.

Online qualitative research

The web is increasingly being used for a range of research activities and this applies equally to qualitative research. This includes depth interviews and focus groups.

Focus groups use chat room technology to manage the interaction. People interact using their computers to talk to each other. Newsgroup technology is also used. Online bulletin boards are used to post messages and a group of people exchange information about a specific topic.

Respondents are often recruited by e-mail and agree to participate at a certain time, at a certain URL. Each member is able to read the responses of other members and respond to their comments as if in a group situation.

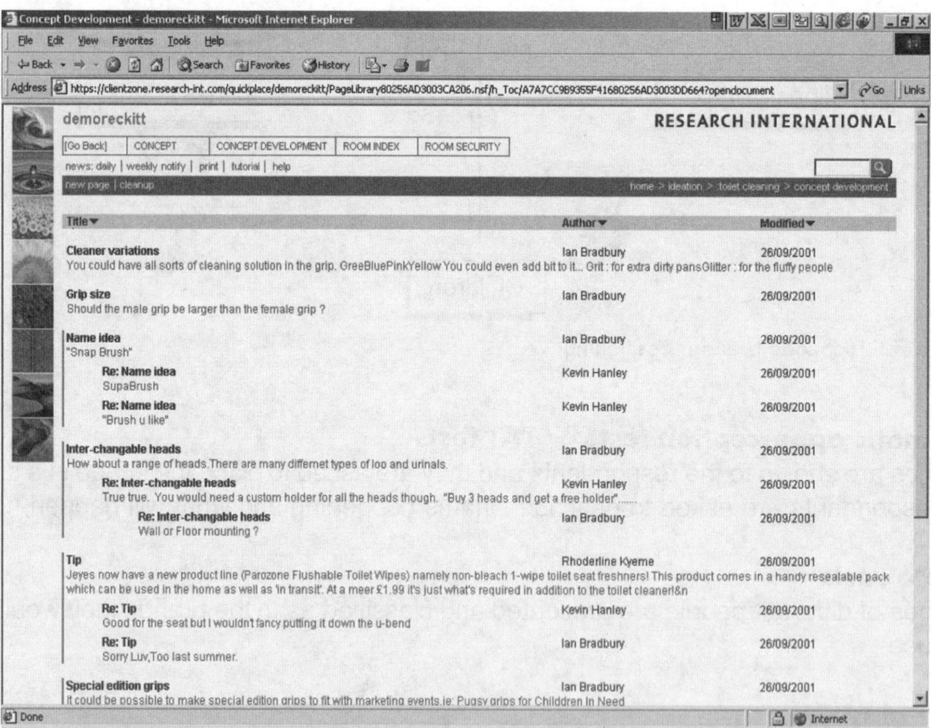

Figure 7.3 Online bulletin board discussions
Source: Research international/Crouch and Housden, 2003

Depth interviewees are recruited in the same way but the communication takes place simply between the respondent and the interviewer.

The web is not the ideal medium to deliver this type of research.

- It is often hard to recruit suitable respondents
- Technical knowledge is required to participate and a common technical platform is required. There are issues over the reliability of the Internet connection, and diverse browsers, etc. Respondents may view screens at different speeds, in different frame sizes and so on
- Interaction is limited and body language cannot be seen although the use of web cams may help this
- It is hard to interpret sarcastic comments other than through the use of emoticons, icons that express emotion, e.g. ☺ or ☹
- It is hard to maintain attention for long periods
- It is a less creative environment for respondents
- It is hard to moderate the contribution of all respondents
- It is hard to establish who exactly is sitting at the terminal.

Advantages include:

- Bringing geographically dispersed samples together
- It may be appropriate for (b2b) markets
- It may be useful for e-commerce businesses.

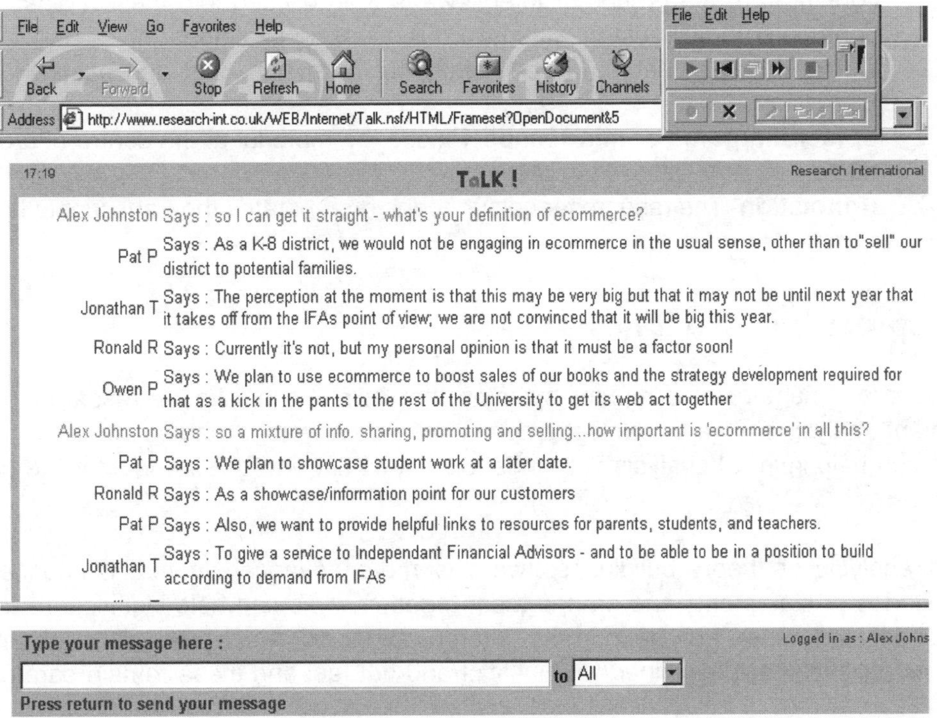

Figure 7.4 Online focus groups
Source: Research international/Crouch and Housden, 2003

Online depth interviews have similar disadvantages but depth interviews online are hard to sustain for more than 10 minutes.

There are some advantages especially in b2b markets where the use of online techniques may fit more easily with the respondents' work practices.

Analysis of qualitative data

The analysis of qualitative data is a skilled job and vital to get maximum value from the research.

It is usual for the moderator or interviewer to carry out the analysis. The starting point is to organize the data, which is contained on tape. These tapes should always be kept. It may be that a written transcript of the tapes has to be made and this can take a significant amount of time, but is nearly always needed to enable effective analysis.

The analysis should enable the broad themes discussed during the research to be explored. We are looking for areas of agreement and disagreement, looking to reflect the range of views held and whether these views were strongly held. We may be trying to report on underlying behaviour and attitudes. Where stimuli have been used, these should be presented in the report and the output analysed.

Organizing the data

Wilson (Wilson, A., 2003) suggests four methods for data organization:

1. **Tabular** In which data is organized according to certain characteristics or themes. The content from the groups or interviews is then divided into these areas. This can be done on spreadsheets or within word processing packages.
2. **Cut and paste** Material is physically cut from transcript and pasted into separate thematic sections.
3. **Spider diagrams or mind maps** Places the material at the centre of a diagram with responses emanating from the centre.
4. **Annotation** The researcher colour codes or annotates the transcript to bring together common themes.

Computer-based analysis

There are a number of computer systems that help the qualitative researcher in his task. Content analysis software counts the number of time a word or phrase appears in a transcript. This can help in initial analysis but tends to be a bit flat and gives a feel for the data but little more.

Text analysis or theory building software is more advanced in that it attaches codes to categories of statements and groups them together. This can help significantly in organizing data but still does not help in its interpretation, in which the skills of analysis and contextualization are combined with instinct and gut feel and these remain paramount.

The leading suppliers of qualitative data analysis software are QSR. They supply 3 packages – Nvivo, N6, the updated version of NUD*IST, and N4 for Mac operators.

Look at their website at www.qsr.com.

Activity 7.3

Write down a list of the applications of qualitative research. Use your text books when you run out of ideas.

Summary

In this unit we looked at the area of qualitative research. We saw that among other definitions, qualitative research can be defined as 'Research that is undertaken using an unstructured research approach with a small number of carefully selected individuals to produce non quantifiable insights into behaviour motivations and attitudes' (Wilson, A., 2003).

We saw that the essential characteristics of qualitative research are:

- It is unquantifiable and it is not representative of larger populations
- Data collection techniques are unstructured
- It involves small samples of individuals or groups of people
- It seeks to reveal opinions, motivations and attitudes.

We looked at the various data collection methods that are used in this area including focus groups, depth interviews and projective techniques. We looked at the advantages and disadvantages of each technique.

We looked in detail at the skills required of the moderator or interviewer.

Moderators should be:

- Highly qualified and experienced in research and, possibly, psychology
- Business and marketing aware. They need to be able to translate respondents' feelings into business advantage for their clients
- Strong communicators, able to relate to a range of people
- Hard to place regionally in terms of socio-economic class
- Socially able, relaxed and friendly, but strong enough to control a room of animated, or conversely, disinterested respondents
- Flexible and quick thinking, with the ability to respond to the unexpected.

We saw that the topic guide is a route map and timetable for both group and depth interviews and that the guide should break the interview into three distinct phases:

1. The introduction phase
2. The discussive phase
3. The summarizing phase.

We looked at the advantages of focus groups:

- They replicate the dynamic social interactions that occur in the market place
- They provide rich and detailed knowledge of a subject
- They are more efficient in terms of time. One focus group can be done in a day. Fourteen depth interviews might take at least two weeks to complete
- They are cheaper per interviewee than depth interviews
- They allow interaction with physical stimuli, e.g. products
- They can involve multiple techniques within the framework of the focus group.

And depth interviews:

- They are conducted face to face, and body language can be interpreted
- Proximity may encourage respondents to reveal more than they might in a remote interview
- The respondent is the centre of attention and can be probed at length to explore issues that the researcher feels are important. This is the annoying child syndrome with the researcher asking 'why?' (but more subtly) until the issue is explored adequately
- Group dynamics may prevent individuals expressing themselves particularly over areas that are sensitive, like income
- Recruitment tends to be easier
- The logistics are easier, no special rooms are needed
- They reveal depth of understanding
- They are flexible. The line of questioning may evolve within the interview and between interviews
- They can involve a range of techniques.

We explored the use of projective techniques and saw that these techniques can be revealing and interesting to administer. Techniques included:

- Sentence completion
- Story completion
- Word association
- Cartoon completion
- Mood boards
- Brand personality or brand CVs
- Brand mapping
- Thematic apperception tests or TAT tests
- Photo sorts
- Role play.

We explored the online applications of qualitative research. We saw that there are problems in carrying out qualitative work online.These included:

- It is often hard to recruit suitable respondents
- Technical knowledge is required to participate, and a common technical platform is required
- Interaction is limited and body language cannot be seen
- It is hard to interpret the meaning of words without the tone of voice and body language
- It is hard to maintain attention for long periods
- It is a less creative environment for respondents
- It is hard to moderate the contribution of all respondents
- It is hard to establish who exactly is sitting at the terminal.

Finally we looked at the techniques for analysing the data, both off-line and using the computer packages that are available. We saw that there are several ways of organizing qualitative data:

- **Tabular** In which data is organized according to certain characteristics or themes
- **Cut and paste** Material is physically cut from transcript and pasted into separate thematic sections

- **Spider diagrams or mind maps** Places the material at the centre of a diagram with responses emanating from the centre
- **Annotation** The researcher colour codes or annotates the transcript to bring together common themes.

Finally, an exercise brought together the various applications discussed in the unit.

Further study

Question 6

As the marketing research executive of a leading confectionery company, you have been asked to commission qualitative research into the positioning of your leading brand in the market place. You have to select a moderator to facilitate the groups.

What is the role of the moderator in managing focus groups?

Describe the key skills required by a moderator of focus groups.

How would you make your final decision?

Bibliography

Crouch, S. and Housden, M. (2003). *Marketing Research for Managers* 3rd edition. Butterworth-Heinemann.

ESOMAR (2003). www.esomar.nl.

MRS (2003). www.mrs.org.uk.

Wilson, A. (2003). *Marketing research: an integrated approach*, FT Prentice Hall.

unit 8 quantitative data

Learning objectives

After completing this unit you will be able to:

- Define quantitative data
- Understand the methods for collecting quantitative data
- Identify online methods for online quantitative data capture
- Define and describe the use of CAPI, CATI and CAWI
- Explore the range of applications enabled by quantitative research
- Complete syllabus elements 4.4, 4.5, 4.6.

Key definitions

Quantitative data Research which seeks to make measurements as distinct from qualitative research (MRS, 2003).

CAPI Computer Aided Personal interviewing.

CAWI Computer Aided Web interviewing.

CATI Computer Aided Telephone interviewing.

Surveys 'The systematic collection, analysis and interpretation of information about some aspect of study. In market research the term is applied particularly to the collection of information by means of sampling and interviews with the selected individuals' (MRS, 2003).

Omnibus surveys 'A survey covering a number of topics, usually for different clients. The samples tend to be nationally representative and composed of types of people for which there is a general demand. Clients are charged by the market research agency on the basis of the questionnaire space or the number of questions required' (MRS, 2003).

Postal survey Self administered surveys are delivered to the respondents who then complete the questionnaire and return it.

Telephone interviewing Interviews carried out using the telephone.

Face-to-face interviews These are interviews that are carried out with respondents in face-to-face contact with the interviewer. Results are recorded on paper or digitally on a Personal Digital Assistant, palmtop or laptop computer.

Study Guide

This unit should take around 3 hours to complete.

Introduction

Quantitative data is the best known currency of marketing research. It is quantitative data that gives us the state of the opinion polls or allows companies to claim that 9 out of 10 customers prefer their product. It is quantifiable because data is collected in a way that allows generalizations to be made about a general population from taking a sample of that population. We will deal with this later. In this unit we are going to look at how data is collected, exploring the principal methods of data collection and their application.

What is quantitative data?

The MRS defines quantitative data as 'Research which seeks to make measurements as distinct from qualitative research' (MRS, 2003).

Wilson (Wilson, A., 2003) defines quantitative research as ' research that is undertaken using a structured research approach with a sample of the population to produce quantifiable insights into behaviour motivations and attitudes'.

Wilson identifies 5 key characteristics of quantitative data:

1. Data gathering is more structured
2. Research involves larger samples than qualitative research
3. The data gathered can provide answers that will quantify the incidence of particular behaviour motivations and attitudes in the population under consideration
4. Studies can be more easily replicated and direct comparisons can be made between studies
5. Analysis is statistical in nature and will usually be done with the help of computer software.

Survey methods

Surveys are defined by the MRS as 'The systematic collection, analysis and interpretation of information about some aspect of study. In market research, the term is applied particularly to the collection of information by means of sampling and interviews with the selected individuals' (MRS, 2003).

In this unit we are looking at the first element of this definition, i.e. the collection of data. There are many ways of gathering research data in a structured way and almost every medium is capable of delivering research questions. These media have a range of capabilities and strengths and weaknesses relating to them. As a CIM delegate, you will need to understand the range of data collection methods used and the relative strengths and weaknesses of these methodologies.

The 2 broadest categories are self-completion and interviewer-administered surveys.

We will start with interviewer-administered surveys.

Face-to-face interviews

These are interviews that are carried out with respondents in face-to-face contact with the interviewer; results are recorded on paper or digitally on a Personal Digital Assistant, palmtop or laptop computer. These can be distinguished from interviewer-administered surveys that are carried out remotely via the telephone or a 'help me' button on a web page.

Marks for Marks

Marks and Spencer use face-to-face interviewing for evaluating consumer reaction to the store experience.

Interviewers can approach respondents as they leave the store when the experience of the store is fresh in their minds.

The advantages of face-to-face contact methods are many:

- There is greater acceptance of the validity of the research if an interviewer can introduce the reasons for the research and show professional membership cards
- The interview process is more efficient as non-eligible respondents can be screened out more effectively
- They improve response rates as the interviewer can answer questions or help with any difficulty in completing the questionnaire
- Personal contact creates a sense of obligation and this can be useful with long surveys. This can reduce the incidence of incomplete or unfinished interviews
- Complexity can be introduced into the survey – for example, the use of show cards or other stimuli material is more easily managed
- Empathy and encouragement can enable deeper consideration of the questions and ensure accuracy of some claims – for example, gender and age.

There are some disadvantages:

- Costs particularly in business-to-business (b2b) research may be high, but this must be offset against a higher response rate
- It can take a considerable amount of time to complete a survey

- Interviewers may be demotivated and may take short cuts to ensure that their quota of completed surveys is made
- Interview bias is a problem. Bias may affect:

  - Who is interviewed – interviewers may select those people who want to be interviewed. An Australian researcher used to do all his interviews on the beach at Bondi
  - The way questions are asked – with a negative inflection or a preceding ad libbed comment 'I know this sounds stupid but . . .'
  - The way an interviewer responds verbally and visually to an answer – a raised eyebrow or expression of shock is not required!
  - The way an answer is recorded, the interpretation of a response may be biased.

- Safety of interviewing staff may be an issue in some areas
- The training and control of field staff is important and adds to costs
- A dispersed sample geographically, for example regional store mangers, is clearly difficult to administer in this way and other data collection methods might need to be considered.

The Interviewer Quality Control Scheme

The Market Research Society operates a scheme to ensure the quality of fieldwork. The Interviewer Quality Control Scheme aims to institute and maintain quality fieldwork. In 2002, 84 companies were members of the scheme.

The scheme covers:

1. Consumer, social and qualitative research

2. Consumer and retail panels, and audits

3. Hall tests

4. Telephone research.

The scheme lays down minimum standards for recruitment, office procedures, supervision, training, quality control (IQCS standards are in line with BS 5750) and survey administration.

Each member company is visited annually by an independent inspector, and required to produce documentation and other evidence that it conforms to or exceeds the minimum standards.

Inspection can be made with a minimum of 24 hours' notice. If accepted as a member of the scheme, this is shown in the Market Research Society listing of organizations and providing market research services, in the Research Buyer's Guide. Members of the IQCS are also listed in its own annual handbook,

'IQCS Minimum Service Standards for Market Research Data Collection'.

That booklet and full details of the IQCS standards will be sent, on request by IQCS. e-mail: gwareing@lineone.net.

In home or doorstep interviews

These are interviews carried out at the home of the respondent. These may be important if the sample is determined by post code or type of dwelling. They have the advantage of putting the respondent at their ease but are generally hard to manage and with the number of women in paid employment outside the home, their value in terms of ensuring access is reduced.

Street interviews

These are perhaps the most visible form of marketing research. Respondents describe their mixed feelings on seeing the smiling face of the interviewer approaching them. However, street interviewing has a number of advantages:

- They are less expensive than home interviews
- They allow respondents who conform to quota specifications to be identified and approached – for example women with children or older men.

Disadvantages include:

- Some shopping centres charge a fee or do not allow researchers to interview customers
- Respondents are unlikely to stop in the open air if it is raining
- Interviews need to be as short as possible
- There are many distractions to the respondent – for example, children or friends who are impatient.

Executive interviewing

This involves interviewing business people at their place of work. It is expensive and time consuming. As for depth interviews, researchers must be knowledgeable and access may be difficult over a dispersed sample. Generally for b2b interviews alternative data collection methods are more appropriate.

Others

Other types of face-to-face interviewing do exist. These may take place in other public places, for example, in galleries or on buses and trains.

What makes a good interviewer?

From the above, it is clear that the weak point in the collection of survey data is often the interviewer.

Activity 8.1

What do you think makes a good market research interviewer? Write your list and compare it with the list in the debrief.

Face-to-face interviews may be carried out:

- In the home
- In the street
- In the office (executive interviews)
- In other public places.

We looked at the personal qualities of good interviewers and at the IQCS as a means for ensuring quality of field work.

We went on to look at CAPI and its advantages:

- Data entry is much simpler
- There is no print production, so it is cheaper
- The computer can check for inconsistent replies – for example, a respondent has said that he is a non-smoker and later tells an interviewer he smokes on average three cigarettes a week.

Telephone is one of the fastest growing media to collect data. We looked at the reasons for this:

- Changing environment
- Telephone research mirrors many business processes and distribution networks
- Mobile phones and mobile Internet means that research can use a range of methods to reach and stimulate respondents
- Technology enables very efficient calling procedures.

We looked at the advantages and disadvantages of using the telephone.

Advantages:

- The cost
- Control
- It is very good for international or other geographically dispersed samples
- It is fast
- It is convenient
- Third generation mobile phones, mobile Internet and SMS text messaging have extended the capability of the phone as a medium for data capture.

Disadvantages:

- Lower response rates
    - Respondents find it easier to say 'no' on the telephone
    - They may screen their calls
    - They may be ex-directory
    - They may not engage fully with the interview process and fail to complete the questionnaire
- Research design is restricted
- Some social classes have a greater preponderance of ex-directory numbers
- Access to mobile telephone numbers may be difficult to obtain
- It is intrusive and may be irritating
- In certain cases international access might be a concern
- Attitudes to the use of telephone in market research may be less positive than in the UK.

We examined CATI and its advantages. These were:

- CATI can facilitate the design administration and analysis of telephone interviewing
- Questionnaires can be customized and verbal comments can be recorded
- Inconsistencies can be highlighted and the researcher can probe to correct the inconsistency
- Automated dialling allows for efficient management of the interviewer
- Completely automated telephone interviews are more possible and may be used to capture simple research data, e.g. satisfaction data.

We saw that web-based interviews could be interviewer-aided and that the use of CAWI is helping this process.

Self-administered surveys or surveys that are delivered to the respondents who then complete the questionnaire and return them, covered postal hand delivered, fax and e-mail or web questionnaires.

We looked at each in turn discussing the advantages of each.

Postal surveys were seen to have several advantages:

- Cheap
- It is useful for geographically dispersed and larger samples
- It reduces interview bias

- Questionnaires can be piloted and revisions made
- It is very convenient
- Longer questionnaires can be delivered and completed effectively
- They allow respondents to confer and this may be desirable when researching high involvement purchases.

The disadvantages:

- Response rate may be low
- Research design is limited
- They may take time to complete and this can lead to low response
- The availability of lists to form sample frames
- There is limited control over the respondent
- A high incidence of incomplete questionnaires or inconsistent answers may be expected
- There is potential for bias in responders as those who respond may be those who feel strongly about an issue.

We looked briefly at fax and hand delivered surveys, and in more depth at online surveys:

Online methods were seen to have a number of advantages:

- They are cheap to administer, design, deliver and analyse
- They are flexible in content
- They are fast to administer and to report on
- They have immediate and low cost global reach
- They can replicate customer behaviour in both consumer and business markets
- They can be used automatically
- They are easy to control
- They can be completed at the respondents' convenience.

There are several disadvantages:

- Technology may not be supported by all computers
- The amount of unsolicited e-mails or spam may affect perception of the questionnaire
- Samples might be difficult to construct
- It may be hard to validate who has responded
- People remain suspicious of the Internet and confidentiality needs to be ensured
- There may be a cost to the respondent especially if the questionnaire takes time to download
- The ease of use in some organizations has led to very poor 'research' being carried out on an ad hoc basis.

Finally, we looked at Omnibus surveys, hall tests and reviewed the use of panel data.

Omnibus surveys were seen to have the following advantages:

- Cheap
- Fast
- Representative
- Flexible.

Disadvantages:

- The sample cannot be changed
- Questions must be phrased simply
- Not suitable for opinions or attitudes
- Question order may affect responses.

Finally we looked at hall tests, simulated test markets, placement and panel data.

Further study

Question 7

As an executive of a leading research agency, you are pitching to persuade a client to extend the qualitative work they have carried out on their brands to include quantitative work, using face-to-face interviews.

Write a report to the client outlining the advantages and disadvantages of quantitative research.

What are the advantages and disadvantages of face-to-face interviewing?

How can the disadvantages be countered?

Bibliography

Crouch, S. and Housden, M. (2003). *Marketing research for managers* 3rd edition, Butterworth-Heinemann.

MRS (2003). www.mrs.org.uk.

Wilson, A. (2003). *Marketing research: an integrated approach*, FT Prentice Hall.

unit 9 questionnaire design

Learning objectives

After completing this unit you will be able to:

- Define the questionnaire
- Understand and outline the questionnaire design process
- Understand questionnaire formats
- Understand how to word a questionnaire
- Understand the issues in question sequencing
- Outline the role of piloting in the delivery of the questionnaire
- Outline the use of software packages to enable design
- Complete syllabus elements 4.4, 4.5.

Key definitions

Questionnaire A structured data collection mechanism involving a range of question formats and completed orally or in print. Questionnaires may be administered by interviewers or self completed by the respondent.

Coding Turning responses into a form that enables analysis usually by allocating a unique number to each response.

Semantic differential A scaling question that asks respondents to indicate the strength of their views on normally a 5 or 7 point scale between bipolar adjectives or statements.

Open questions Questions that ask for the respondent's own response.

Dichotomous questions Questions for which there are two possible replies.

Multiple choice questions Questions with a number of predetermined answers.

Closed questions Questions to which there are a limited number of predetermined responses.

Forced scale A scaling question that does not allow for a neutral reponse.

Likert scales A scaling approach that asks respondents to indicate their strength of agreement or disagreement with a range of statements on a 5 point scale.

Scaling questions Questions assigning numerical values to subjective concepts.

Skip questions Questions that take respondents to other questions determined by the answer.

Biased question A question that is phrased so that it influences the respondent's answer.

Pilot study A small scale test of a completed questionnaire.

Study Guide

This unit should take about 3 hours to complete.

Introduction

A questionnaire is a structured data collection mechanism involving a range of question formats and completed orally or in print. As we have seen, questionnaires may be administered by interviewers or self completed by the respondent. The design of the questionnaire is a key task in the research and proves good design can make the difference between a successful project and a failure.

The questionnaire has four main purposes:

- It is designed to collect relevant data
- To remove bias
- To make data comparable
- To motivate the respondent.

This unit will outline the process of developing a good questionnaire.

The questionnaire design process

Wilson (Wilson, A., 2003) identifies a process for questionnaire development:

1. Develop question topics
2. Select question and response formats

3. Determine sequence
4. Design layout and appearance
5. Pilot test
6. Undertake the survey.

Developing question topics

This process will draw on the results of any exploratory, desk or qualitative research carried out already. The research objectives laid down in the research brief and proposal will also be drawn on to inform the process. The idea is to make the questionnaire as efficient as possible. The questionnaire should produce the maximum amount of required information at minimum time.

The characteristics of the respondents should also be considered:

- Do they have the information we are asking for?
- Will they be able to remember the information?
- Are they likely to want to tell us the information we are asking for? Is it particularly sensitive data, e.g. income, sexual practices, etc.
- How literate and numerate are they? Will they be able to articulate the information?
- Will they understand the questions?
- Will they be interested in the survey?

Question and response formats

What does a questionnaire contain?

There are 3 parts to any questionnaire:

1. Identification data
2. Classification data
3. Subject data.

Identification data Is usually completed by the interviewer. It contains identification of the respondent, maybe name, address and a contact number. It also includes the time, data and place of the interview and the name of the interviewer. This data is required to allow check backs to be made. It is important to note that the MRS code of conduct aims to ensure the anonymity of the respondent. These questions may be kept to the end of the questionnaire to allow sufficient rapport to be built-up between the interviewer and the respondent.

Classification data Is the data that is required to classify respondents. It may include:

- Age
- Gender
- Income
- Job title
- Marital status.

This allows the information to be analysed effectively and also to help the interviewer ensure that the respondent has the characteristics of the sample that is required to be interviewed.

Subject data Refers to the nature of the information that is being gathered to meet the survey objectives. This may be laid down in a flow diagram which allows us to begin to plan the question sequence.

This flow chart is a route map through the questionnaire to be created in outline and allows the designer to introduce what are known as 'skip' or 'filter' questions to take the respondent through the questionnaire.

For example:

Do you drink wine?

If YES go to Q.2

If NO go to Q.9

Care needs to be taken in the use of skip questions, too many can be confusing to a respondent who is self completing or to an inexperienced interviewer. The use of CATI and CAPI systems can help here as the computer will go to the appropriate question automatically, given the response to the skip question.

What type of questions can be asked?

There are 4 main question types. These are:

1. Closed questions
    a. Dichotomous
    b. Multiple choice
2. Open ended
3. Rating scales.

Closed questions – dichotomous

Simply these are questions to which there are only two possible answers, e.g. yes and no. This sounds simple but the question asked must fit into this answer structure. A question that asks:

'Do you intend to go on holiday in the next 12 months?' may be answered

'It depends'

For completeness a 'don't know' option is usually offered. For example:

Do you bank online?

	Code
Yes	1
No	2
Don't know	3

Each of these is given a code number for analysis.

Closed questions – multiple choice

These appear straightforward but are quite difficult to construct as the designer needs to know all possible answers. This is known as being 'collectively exhaustive'. This can be achieved by piloting the questionnaire to ensure that all possible answers are offered.

To avoid this, the 'other' response is often used and this usually leaves a space to allow the response to be written onto the questionnaire. Other answers are coded later to produce a full list of codes for analysis (a coding frame).

'How do you usually travel to work?'

	Code
Car	1
Train	2
Bus	3
Bicycle	4
Walk	5
Motorbike or scooter	6
Other	

It is important that when multiple choice questions are being designed the answers are mutually exclusive. This means that there is no overlap between responses. This is important in dealing with details of age or quantities and is easy to miss.

A major petrol retailer produced a questionnaire with the following question

On average what mileage do you get each year?

0–5,000

5,000–10,000

10,000–15,000

15,000–20,000

More than 20,000

Spot the problem?

Yes, there is overlap. The responses are not mutually exclusive.

Red faces all round.

Other issues with multiple choice responses include the number of potential responses. This may mean that the respondent cannot remember the first answers. In face-to-face interviews the responses may be put on a show card. This is not always possible in other media.

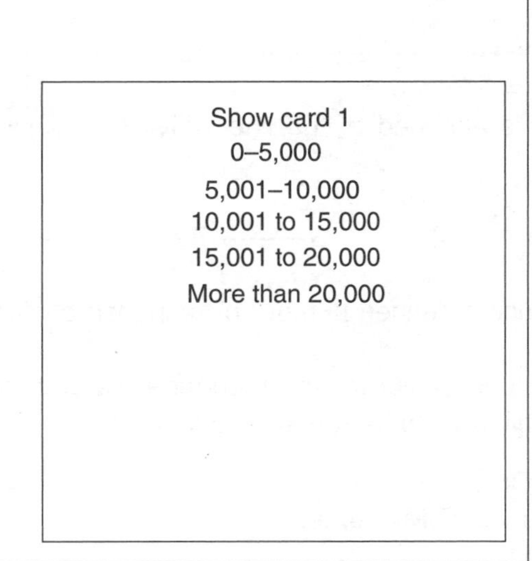

Figure 9.1 Show cards

Open-ended questions

Open-ended questions are questions in which an answer is not suggested. The respondent is free to respond in any way. Because of this, they are sometimes known as unstructured questions. It may be that a one-word answer is required or it may be that a longer response is needed. For example:

- Why did you choose to study with the CIM?
- What do you enjoy most about your course?
- What would you like to change about the course?

The problem with open questions is analysis. If there are very many categories of answers, then it may be hard to code the responses and it may reduce the effectiveness of the analysis.

Much depends on the skill of the researcher in these cases.

One way around this is to pilot the survey and produce a pre-coded list of potential responses which allows the interviewer to interpret the response and code it.

Open-ended questions can be very useful and the difficulties in managing them within a questionnaire are not huge. Their value can certainly outweigh these difficulties.

Scaling questions

There are many types of scaling questions. They are very useful in quantifying complex and multi-dimensional concepts such as opinions, attitudes and motivation. A scale question will ask a respondent to indicate the strength of feeling about that concept. This may be done on a multi-dimensional basis. For example, exploring the range of different aspects of a brand or company or it may be done on a single dimension – for example the satisfaction with that brand or company.

The quantification allows comparison to be made.

Graphic versus itemized scales

Scales can be itemized or graphic.

Graphical scales ask respondents to indicate the level they associate with the issue under consideration on a line:

Dissatisfied --X -- Satisfied

Occasionally, a value is attached to the line whilst still allowing respondents to select any position:

Dissatisfied --------- 1----------2 --------- 3----------4----------5 --------- X----------6 --------- Satisfied

Itemized scales introduce a defined number of response choices.

Itemized scales tend to be easier for the respondent and they are easier to analyse as the graphical responses still have to be turned into value.

Indicate your opinion about CIM courses

CIM courses are
Poor value for money 1 2 3 4 5 Good value for money

Figure 9.2 Itemized scale questions

Comparative versus non comparative assessments

Wilson (Wilson, A., 2003) defines comparative rating scales as scales that ask respondents to compare the organization or issues in relation to a common frame of reference. Non-comparative allows the respondents to select their own frame of reference.

The comparative approach can be used to allow companies to rate their performance relative to other companies, or in evaluating the features that a consumer values in a product.

An example from industry can be seen in train companies asking customers to rank speed of journey, the price of the journey, on-board facilities and station facilities.

Forced versus non forced scales

Forced scales do not allow a neutral position

For example:

A forced scale:

Do you think that CIM courses are

Very inexpensive	Inexpensive	Expensive	Very expensive

An unforced scale:

Do you think that CIM courses are

Very inexpensive	Inexpensive	Neither inexpensive nor expensive	Expensive	Very expensive

Forced scales can be used when it is believed that there will be few neutral respondents. These are used also to force those who are in the neutral position to decide and can lead to spurious data being obtained.

Balanced versus unbalanced scales

Balanced scales have a balanced number of positive and negative responses. Unbalanced may be used when piloting suggests that there will be fewer of any particular response and to explore the more common position with more sensitivity.

Number of scale positions

There are no hard and fast rules as to the number of positions on a scale. The most common number is 5. Some researchers use 7 or 9. The idea is that there is greater sensitivity in using a higher number. The key consideration is that respondents are able to make a clear distinction between the various options.

Labelling and pictorial representation of positions

Scales generally require at least two 'anchor' labels at each end of the scale. As we have seen earlier, it is also possible to label each position.

It is also possible to use emoticons; smiley faces or thumbs up or down can be useful in certain markets and may be useful in international markets but you need to be careful with thumbs up which has very rude meaning in some markets.

Commonly used scales

Respondents divide certain points or other units (possibly currency) between a number of attributes.

This gives a rank order of attributes and an indication of the scale of difference between these attributes.

Train companies have used this type of research, allocating consumers a number of pounds and giving them a range of investment opportunities on which to spend them.

Likert scales

A commonly used scale, the Likert scale asks respondents to indicate their level of agreement with a range of statements. Responses are scored from 1 to 5 and the result is an average score for each statement indicating the level of agreement with the statement.

Strongly agree	Agree	Neither agree nor disagree	Disagree	Strongly disagree	CIM courses are good value	CIM courses are relevant to my needs, etc

Figure 9.3 Likert scales

The strength of the Likert Scale depends on the way that the statements are selected. This involves filtering and pretesting a range of statements before the final statements are selected. The initial list may be generated as a result of qualitative or exploratory research.

Activity 9.1

Create a list of 20 statements for a Likert Scale about a product of your choice.

Test this list on a friend or colleague. How effective was your list? What have you learned from the test?

Semantic differentials

Semantic differentials use words or statements and their opposites and measure the strength of opinion between them.

The words are generated from exploratory or qualitative research.

Expensive	1	2	3	4	5	Inexpensive
Effective	1	2	3	4	5	Ineffective
For career women	1	2	3	4	5	For the housewife
Modern	1	2	3	4	5	Old fashioned

This can be used to rate a single brand or to compare brands.

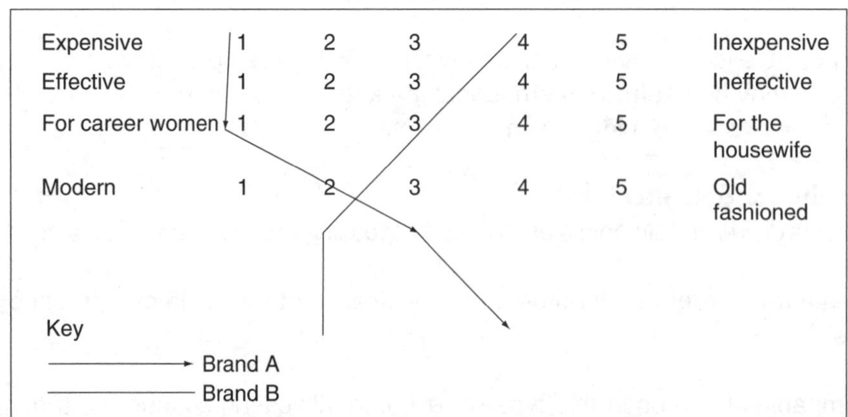

Figure 9.4 Semantic differentials

Stapel scales

Uses a single descriptor rather than a pair and ranks opinion of this descriptor. It is rarely used in market research due to its complexity. It asks the respondents to score statements depending on how accurate they believe the statement to be, the more accurate, higher the mark, the more inaccurate, lower the score.

+5	+5	+5	+5
+4	+4	+4	+4
+3	+3	+3	+3
+2	+2	+2	+2
+1	+1	+1	+1
Expensive	Effective	For career women	Modern
−1	−1	−1	−1
−2	−2	−2	−2
−3	−3	−3	−3
−4	−4	−4	−4
−5	−5	−5	−5

Purchase intent scales

These scales are used to measure the respondents' intention to buy a product or a potential product.

They look like the following example:

If this car was priced at £5,999, would you

Definitely buy	1
Probably buy	2
Probably not buy	3
Definitely not buy	4

Select wording and phrasing

The next stage of the questionnaire is to word the questions. At each stage of the process, the researcher should stop and ask 'Is the question really necessary?' Each question should be carefully evaluated on its own, in relation to other questions on the questionnaire and the overall objectives of the study. If the question does not contribute to the overall purpose of the research, it should not be included in the questionnaire.

There are many rules on questionnaire wording:

- Ensure meaning is understood
  For example, is dinner a meal consumed at night or at 'lunch' time. In international markets this is more important. Translation of questionnaires can cause major problems. The secret is to translate and then back translate into the original language. A question that was asked to young people 'What was the prime motivator behind your impulse purchase of confectionery countlines?' is clearly inappropriate for the audience. The language of the audience is important and this is one of the functions of qualitative research to allow the questionnaire to be constructed using appropriate terms.

Sexual health and the researcher

The AIDS virus has meant that an understanding of the sexual behaviour of the population is important for health budgeting and provision. Market research has been used to find out this very sensitive and important information.

A questionnaire was designed to present a range of behaviours in language that all respondents could understand.

Qualitative research via focus groups informed the language of the questionnaire.

Whilst the terms cannot be repeated here, it meant that the quantitative phase of the study was far more successful.

Use clear and simple language. Use words of one or two syllables. Use simple English:

- Instead of 'observe', use 'look'
- Instead of 'construct', use 'build'
- Instead of 'regarding', use 'about'
- Instead of 'at this moment in time', use 'now'.

Use what is known as demotic language or the language of the people. It is very easy to produce stiff and inaccessible written words. Remember, very often the questionnaire will be read out loud. It is good practice to speak the question.

- Avoid ambiguity:

  'Do you buy a newspaper regularly?'
  What does regular mean? Every day? Once a month? Once a year?

- Avoid two questions in one:

  'What do you think of our prices and product quality?'
  This is impossible to be answered accurately

- Avoid leading or loaded questions:

  'Should the council spend money regenerating the poor environment in Brookmill ward?'
  It is hard for anyone to disagree with this question
  'Most people think that our membership of the EU is a good thing, Do you?' Is a classic leading question
  The aim has to be to reduce the potential to lead respondents

- Avoid assumptions:

  'When driving, do you listen to your CD player?'
  This makes a number of assumptions about the respondent. That he drives, that his car has a CD player, even that he is not hearing impaired!!

- Avoid generalization:

  'How much do you usually spend on beer in a week?' There are much better observational or panel methodologies to ensure accuracy here. If the respondent is spending more than a few pounds, the chances are that he won't remember in any case!

- Avoid negative questions:

  'You don't think that drink driving should be more strictly regulated, do you?' is confusing and leads to problems

- Avoid hypothetical questions:

  'If West Ham were relegated, would you still buy a season ticket?'
  Speculation and guesswork is an outcome of this type of question.

A poor questionnaire. But why?

- Are you single?
  (A sensitive question, ask the respondent to state what their marital status is.)

- What is your average weekly disposable income?
  (A sensitive question and hard for respondents to work out.)

- How regularly do you come here?
  (Ambiguous. Once a year or once a week.)

- Do you buy green vegetables?
  (Cabbage, fair trade or organics?)

- Do you by are frozen and canned foods?
  (Spelling is poor, and two questions in one.)

- What about our chilled and ambient ready meals?
  (Two questions in one, and what are ambient ready meals? Will the respondent understand the question?)

- How much did you spend on food last year?
  (Can *you* remember this?)

- Most people say our new store layout is really good. What do you think?
  (A leading and loaded question.)

- Does your husband come with you?
  (Assumption about marital status, an unnecessary question given the opening question)

- When do you leave the car?
  (Assumption and 'when' does the researcher mean? – Overnight? When we go on holiday?)

- Are you against drug abuse?
  (A leading question, this would not produce a varied response.)

- You don't think council tax is too high, do you?
  (Use of negative and a leading question.)

- If we moved to the high street would you come more often?
  (A hypothetical question.)

- How old are your children?
  - 0–3
  - 3–5
  - 5–10
  - 10–15
  - 15+

  (Overlapping categories and what about parents of grown-up children?)

A better approach.

This is an extract from a questionnaire evaluating a new newsagent.

- What is your postcode? ....
- How did you get from home to this store?

  Car ○
  Motorcycle ○
  Bus ○
  Train ○
  Foot ○
  Cycle ○
  Other
  Please state: ....
- Did you buy any of the following today (SHOW CARD):

  Newspapers and Magazines ○
  Sandwiches ○
  Other snacks ○
  Drinks ○
  Confectionery ○
  Other
  Please state ....
- On a scale of 1–5, how would you rate the following aspects of this store, where 1 is very poor and 5 is very good.

	1	2	3	4	5
Cleanliness of the store	○	○	○	○	○
Product selection	○	○	○	○	○
Helpfulness of staff	○	○	○	○	○
Speed through the checkout	○	○	○	○	○

Thank you for your help.

Sequencing

Wilson suggests that the questionnaires should be funnel sequenced, i.e. going from the broad to the narrow. The interviewer asks the most general questions about the subject and moves to narrower and more focused questions.

For example:

- How do you rate the quality of management education in the UK?
- How do you rate the quality of business education in the marketing research sector?
- How do you rate the MRS diploma?

It is useful to start the questionnaire with some fairly straightforward questions to get the interview going. Questions about identity, occupation, family and marital status, and educational level might be included here.

Classification questions may have to be asked early to ensure the respondent fits the intended responder profile.

This questionnaire about marketing includes classification questions as the first section:

Section 1: We need to know a few things about you:

1. Title: Mr/Mrs/Ms/Miss/Dr/Professor/Other (please state): ____________________
2. First name: ____________________
3. Last name: ____________________
4. Job title: ____________________
5. Company: ____________________
6. Number of employees working in your company: ____________________
7. Number of employees working in marketing: ____________________
8. What are your key areas of responsibility (please tick all those that apply)?

- ❑ Public relations
- ❑ Advertising
- ❑ Exhibitions
- ❑ Sales force management
- ❑ Database management
- ❑ Product management
- ❑ Campaign management
- ❑ Media buying
- ❑ Other (please state): ____________________
- ❑ Planning
- ❑ Internet
- ❑ Research
- ❑ Brand management
- ❑ E-commerce
- ❑ Data analysis
- ❑ Call centre management
- ❑ Sales promotion
- ❑ Intranet
- ❑ Events

9. Which of the following marketing publications do you read?

	Every week	From time to time
Marketing	❑	❑
Marketing week	❑	❑
Admap	❑	❑
Campaign	❑	❑
Creative review	❑	❑
Precision marketing	❑	❑
Direct marketing week	❑	❑
Revolution	❑	❑
New media age	❑	❑
DM business	❑	❑
Media week	❑	❑
Customer relationship Management	❑	❑
Marketing direct	❑	❑
Direct response	❑	❑
Other	❑	❑

Please give title(s): ______________________________

Other sensitive questions, for example, on age or income might be better left to the end of the questionnaire to ensure that a rapport has been established.

Design, layout and appearance

The physical appearance of the questionnaire will determine levels of response even if the questionnaire is interview-administered. It needs to be:

- Spaced effectively, not squashed onto one page – it may save money but will reduce response
- Set in a serif type face. The serifs are the feet on the letters of a serif type face that keep the eye on the line, they are known to increase comprehension
- If it is to be used outside, a book format might protect the questionnaire better
- In at least 10 point font so that people can read the questionnaire
- Produced to a high quality with no literals and printed on high quality paper
- It should look interesting. Colour can help
- A range of question types can help make the questionnaire more engaging
- Coding and interviewer instructions must be clearly distinguished from the questions
- Use skip and filter questions and routing instructions to help the interviewer or respondent work through the questionnaire.

A self-completion questionnaire

College Leavers' Survey – 2003

Please take some time to complete this questionnaire as the results will help us improve the experience of students at the college.

When you have completed all the questions, please return the questionnaire to the reception.

1. Please indicate if you are:

   ❑ Male ❑ Female

2. How old were you on 1 September 1998? ....

3. During your course, have you been able to learn in ways that suit you?

   ❑ Always ❑ Mostly ❑ Sometimes ❑ Never

4. Has your course stretched you in your studies?

   ❑ Very much ❑ Quite ❑ Not very much ❑ Not at all

5. Are you satisfied in your own efforts to attend regularly and get to classes on time?

   ❑ Very much ❑ Quite ❑ Not very much ❑ Not at all

6. Are you satisfied in your efforts to complete your work within agreed deadlines?

   ❑ Very much ❑ Quite ❑ Not very much ❑ Not at all

7. How would you rate your overall progress on the course?

   ❑ Much better than you expected ❑ Better than you expected

   ❑ Worse than you expected ❑ Much worse than you expected

8. Have you been encouraged to update your Record of Achievement?

   ❑ Yes ❑ No

9. Have you had the opportunity to produce a current CV?

   ❑ Yes ❑ No

10. How many times during your course have you individually reviewed your overall progress with a tutor?

    ❑ More than once a term ❑ Once a term

    ❑ Once a year ❑ Never

11. If you have been given advice about your career, has this been helpful?

❑ Extremely helpful ❑ Helpful

❑ Very helpful ❑ Not helpful

❑ I have not been given any advice

12. If you have used the library, have you found this useful?

❑ Extremely useful ❑ Very useful

❑ Useful ❑ Not useful

❑ I have not used the library

13. If you have used the information in the Careers section of the library, have you found this useful?

❑ Extremely useful ❑ Very useful

❑ Useful ❑ Not useful

❑ I have not used careers information

14. If you have used the Open Access IT facility in the library, have you found this useful?

❑ Extremely useful ❑ Very useful

❑ Useful ❑ Not useful

❑ I have not used Open Access IT

15. If you have used the Learning Support Workshop in the library, have you found this useful?

❑ Extremely useful ❑ Very useful

❑ Useful ❑ Not useful

❑ I have not used the Learning Support Workshop

16. Please add any comments you wish to make on the Library, Open Access IT, Careers Advice and Learning Support facilities:

____

____

____

____

17. If you have had any personal or financial difficulties during your course, what have you done?
(Please tick as many boxes as appropriate)

- ❑ Discussed it with friends
- ❑ Discussed it with your personal tutor
- ❑ Discussed it with another lecturer
- ❑ Discussed it with the Student Adviser
- ❑ Kept it to yourself
- ❑ Discussed it with someone else in college
- ❑ Discussed it with parents
- ❑ I have not had any personal difficulties
- ❑ Other (please state) ______________________________

____

____

18. If you discussed a personal/financial difficulty with the Student Adviser, was this helpful?

- ❑ Extremely helpful
- ❑ Helpful
- ❑ Very helpful
- ❑ Not helpful
- ❑ I have not been given any advice

19. If you discussed a personal/financial difficulty with your personal tutor or lecturer, was this helpful?

- ❑ Extremely helpful
- ❑ Helpful
- ❑ Very helpful
- ❑ Not helpful
- ❑ I have not had any such discussions

20. How often have you met INDIVIDUALLY with your personal tutor?

- ❑ Weekly
- ❑ Monthly
- ❑ Termly
- ❑ Never, if never go to Q. 22

21. Have you found your INDIVIDUAL meetings with your personal tutor helpful?

- ❑ Extremely helpful
- ❑ Helpful
- ❑ Very helpful
- ❑ Not helpful

22. How often have you met as a GROUP with your personal tutor?

- ❑ Weekly
- ❑ Monthly
- ❑ Termly
- ❑ Never, if never go to Q. 24

23. Have you found your GROUP meetings with your personal tutor helpful?

❑ Extremely helpful ❑ Helpful

❑ Very helpful ❑ Not helpful

24. Please add any comments you wish to make about your personal tutorial sessions:

____

____

____

____

25. How long, in total, have you spent on work experience during your course?

❑ 1–10 days ❑ 11–20 days ❑ 21–30 days

❑ More than 30 days ❑ I have not had any work experience

If you have not had work any experience, please go to Q. 29; if you have had work experience please answer the following questions:

26. How many work experience placements have you had during your course?

❑ 1 ❑ 2 or 3 ❑ More than 3

27. Was your work experience helpful?

❑ Extremely helpful ❑ Helpful

❑ Very helpful ❑ Not helpful

28. Please add any comments you have on work experience:

____

____

____

____

29. What have you particularly liked about your course?

____

____

____

30. What have you disliked about your course?

____

____

31. Would you recommend your course to other people?

❑ Yes ❑ No

32. What have you particularly liked about the College?

____

____

____

____

____

____

33. What have you disliked about the College?

____

____

____

____

____

34. Would you recommend the College to other people?

❑ Yes ❑ No

Thank you for you help, please return this questionnaire to the reception.

Pilot

Piloting or testing the questionnaire is crucial.

- It allows problems to be corrected
- Helps with the coding process
- Improves question sequencing
- Improves wording of questions.

Piloting can be done with a small sample but it must be done. If many changes are made, the revised questionnaire should also be piloted. Piloting should be carried out by the staff who will administer the questionnaire, in a comparable environment and with respondents who share the characteristics of the sample.

The debriefing method means the respondents should be asked after completing the questionnaire what their thought processes were as they completed the questionnaires. The protocol method allows the respondent to talk through the process of completing the questionnaire.

Questionnaire checklist

- Are the objectives right?
- Will the data specified meet the objectives?
- Will the questions listed collect all the data required?
- Is every question essential?
- Will the right type of data be collected for:

    fact?
    opinion?
    motive?
- Will all the identification data required be collected?
- Will all the classification data required be collected?
- Is the question sequence logical?
- Are the types of question being used appropriate:

    dichotomous?
    multiple-choice?
    open-ended?
    rating scales?

- Is the question wording:

  simple to understand?
  unambiguous?
  clear?

- Have cushion statements been used when necessary?
- Is it reasonable to expect the respondent to answer every question?
- Will the answers be easy to record?
- Will the answers be easy to process?
- Does the questionnaire look good?
- Will it, and any show material, be easy for the interviewers to use?
- Has the questionnaire been piloted?
- Is the right type of questionnaire being used:

  personal?
  postal?
  telephone?
  online?

Source: Crouch and Housden, 2003.

Summary

In this unit we looked at the process of designing a questionnaire.

The questionnaire has four main purposes:

- It is designed to collect relevant data
- To remove bias
- To make data comparable
- To motivate the respondent.

We looked at a process for questionnaire development:

1. Develop question topics
2. Select question and response formats
3. Determine sequence
4. Design layout and appearance
5. Pilot test
6. Undertake the survey.

We looked at the process of developing question topics.

We explored in depth the types of questions that can be asked which included closed dichotomous questions, closed multiple choice questions, open questions and scale questions. We looked in detail at each of these:

- Likert scales
- Stapel scales
- Semantic differential
- Intention to buy scales
- Forced and unforced scales.

We explored the wording of questions and their sequencing. We saw that there were a number of rules of right wording and phrasing of questionnaires.

- Use clear and simple language
- Avoid ambiguity
- Avoid two questions in one
- Avoid leading or loaded questions
- Avoid assumptions
- Avoid generalization
- Avoid negative questions
- Avoid hypothetical questions.

We looked at the design and appearance of the completed questionnaire and the various ways of improving this aspect of questionnaire design. We saw that it should be:

- Laid out effectively in a clear font
- In a practical format
- Produced to a high quality with no literals and printed on high quality paper.
- It should look interesting with a range of question types
- Coding and interviewer instructions must be clearly distinguished from the questions.

Finally we looked at the importance of the pilot test, a small scale test of the completed questionnaire and a checklist was provided to help judge the quality of the questionnaire.

Further study

Question 8

a. Why is questionnaire design so important in the research process?
b. What is the role of piloting in the questionnaire design process?

Hints and Tips

Go to the MRS website and download the document Questionnaire Design Guidelines. Read this and add it to your study resource pack.

Bibliography

Wilson, A. (2003). *Marketing research: an integrated approach*, FT Prentice Hall.

unit 10 sampling

Learning objectives

After completing this unit you will be able to:

- Define sampling
- Understand how to construct a sample for a survey
- Understand and identify the sampling process
- Understand and apply the statistical basis of sampling
- Understand and evaluate different sampling methods
- Understand the concepts of population, census and sample
- Understand how the sampling frame is constructed
- Complete syllabus elements 4.6, 5.1.

Key definitions

Sample A part or subset of a population taken to be representative of the population as a whole.

Sampling frame A list of the population of interest that is used to draw the sample in a survey.

Population A population is the total number of people in any defined group of interest.

Census A survey of the entire population.

Sample element An individual member of the sample frame.

Confidence level The probability that the true population value will fall within a known range.

Probability sampling A sampling method that uses objective sample selection so that every member of a population has a known probability of being selected.

Cluster sampling A procedure in which clusters of population units are selected at random and then all or some of the units in the chosen clusters are studied.

Non-probability sampling Non-probability sampling involves a subjective selection of respondents. Therefore, the probability of selecting respondents is unknown. This means that because the sample is not chosen objectively it is not possible to state results with any degree of statistical certainty.

Quota sampling A sampling method that selects a sub sample based on known proportions in the population.

Convenience sampling Based on the convenience of the researcher. It may be that the section is made in the street, in the office or from a database. As long as the sample fits with the population as a whole, it is legitimate.

Judgement or purposive sampling The researcher consciously selects a sample considered appropriate for the study.

Sample error The error in a survey caused by using a sample to estimate the value of a parameter in the population.

Simple random sampling A probability sampling method in which respondents are selected using random numbers.

Systematic sampling A probability sampling method in which respondents are selected using a 1 in 'n' approach.

Stratified random sampling A probability sampling method in which the sample is forced to contain respondents from each of the key segments of a population.

Standard deviation A measurement of dispersion that calculates the average distance of the values in a data set from the mean value.

Snowball sampling A type of non-probability sampling where initial respondents are selected at random and subsequent respondents are then selected by referrals or information from the earlier respondents.

Study Guide

This unit of the coursebook will take you 3 hours to complete. You should add time to complete the exercises.

Introduction

This unit is concerned with the process of deciding which individuals will be asked to provide information. It is very unusual for an entire population to be surveyed. A population refers to the total number of people in a group of interest. One of the few examples of this is the 10-year census in the UK. Rather like a chef tastes his food in order to determine the taste of the entire dish, so the market researcher seeks the views of a sample of the population under consideration. However, the market researcher must also ensure that all the ingredients have been used and that the ingredients have been correctly mixed.

Key to the accuracy of this is the determination of the characteristics of the sample. Wilson (Wilson, A., 2003) highlights 5 key questions that inform the sampling process:

1. We need to understand the nature of the people we wish to survey
2. We need to know where they are
3. We need to know how we select them
4. We need to know the number of people we wish to survey
5. We need to understand how representative this sample is of the population as a whole.

This unit outlines the sampling process.

What is a sample?

Crouch and Housden define a sample as 'A sample is a small number taken from a large group for testing and analysis, on the assumption that the sample is representative of the population as a whole' (Crouch, S. and Housden, M., 2003).

The MRS defines a sample as 'A part or subset of a population taken to be representative of the population as a whole for the investigative purposes of research' (MRS, 2003).

Sampling is used to make an estimate of the characteristics of the population as a whole. Sampling overcomes the impossibility in almost every market of asking all members of a population their opinion:

- It is efficient
- It is easier to manage
- It is cheap
- It is subject to statistical verification
- It allows for a high degree of precision.

The sampling process

Wilson (Wilson, A., 2003) outlines a six-stage sampling process

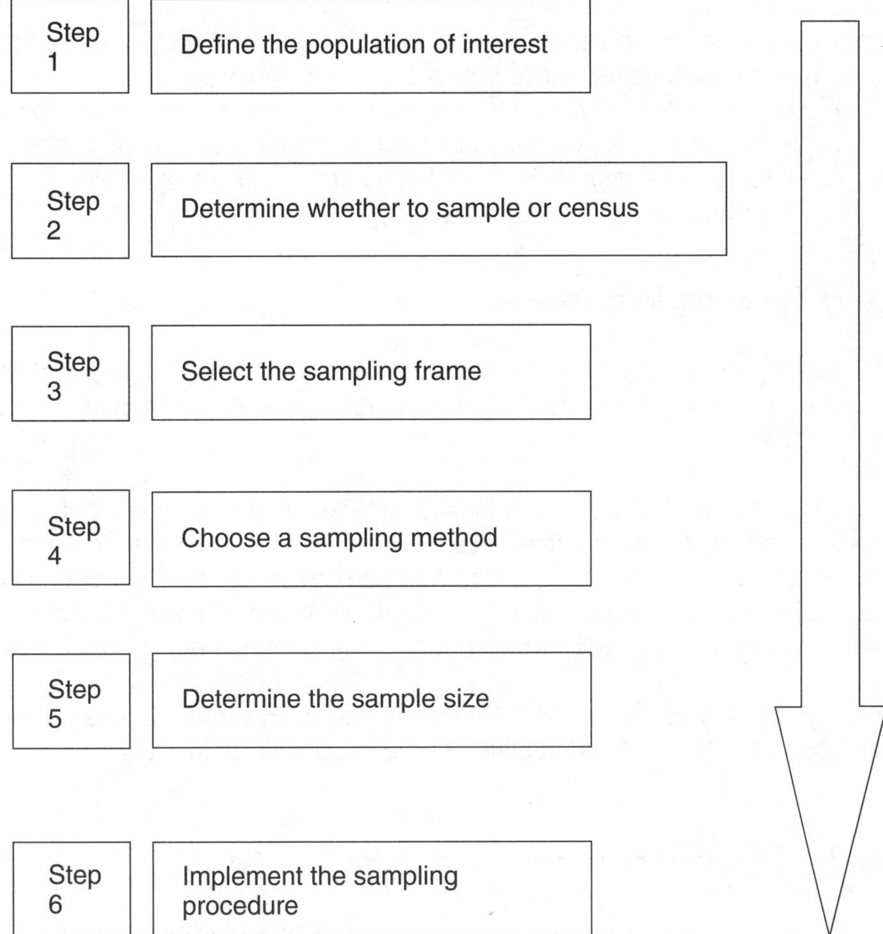

Figure 10.1 The sampling process

Define the population of interest

Samples are selected from populations. The population is the total number of individuals in the group in which we are interested. This may be established at any level. We may be interested in all car dealers, we may be interested in Renault dealers, or we may be interested in Renault dealers in London and the south-east.

The definition of the population of interest is of vital importance. It is possible that the definition will produce a very low number of people in the sample. This has implications that we will explore below.

The key thing is that the definition of the population informs the whole research process. It will determine the methodology, the nature of questions asked and the interview process. The interviewer will be given screening criteria on which to select and deselect potential respondents.

For example, 'Women living in Essex who are working, and who have applied for child tax relief in the last three months'.

Some people in the defined population will be deselected by virtue of other characteristics. They work in market research and are employed by the benefits agency or Inland Revenue.

Sample or census?

Remember the difference? A census covers the entire population; a sample is a part of that population. It is unusual for a census to take place unless the population is small. This may take place in certain business-to-business (b2b) markets – for example regional distributors of industrial machinery. Here the population is small and a census is appropriate. However, it is more usual that the population may include thousands or millions of individuals – for example, supermarket shoppers, voters, or council tax payers.

Selecting the sample frame

ESOMAR defines the sampling frame as 'A list of the population of interest that is used to draw the sample in a survey, e.g. a telephone directory or a list of members of a profession' (ESOMAR, 2003).

Sample frames are used to select the individual who will be interviewed. It is important that the sample frame reflects the characteristics of the population and a number of lists may need to be combined to ensure this. Wilson (Wilson A., 2003) points out that a telephone directory may not include all elements of a population, for example those who are ex-directory, those who use a mobile phone or those with no telephone. This is known as sample frame error.

If there is no suitable list, a list of the general population may be used and classification questions used to select respondents who fit the population of interest.

Activity 10.1

You have been commissioned to conduct research into marketing directors of companies involved in food and drinks production in the UK. What lists may be available to help you develop a sample frame?

Choosing a sampling method

There are two broad sampling methods

Probability sampling

The key characteristic is that every member of the population of interest has a known chance of being selected, independent of any subjective selection by the researcher. For example, each member of a sample frame is given a number, and respondents are randomly selected until the required sample is selected.

Advantages are that the results can be projected onto the population as a whole subject to a known sampling error. This means that we can identify the limits of error for any particular result. For example, a research report might state that results are correct at the 95 per cent confidence level +/–3%.

What does this mean?

First that the sample has a 1 in 20 chance of being wrong and secondly, that a result of say 45 per cent actually will fall between 48 and 42 per cent, i.e. 45 +3 or 45 –3.

It should be clear that when a small sample is used to reflect the views of a population this calculation can only be approximate. The larger the sample, the greater confidence we can have that the sample will reflect accurately the population as a whole and the closer the views of the sample will be to the population as a whole. We will look at this in detail later.

Of course the way that respondents are selected adds to the cost of the survey.

Non-probability sampling

Non-probability sampling involves a subjective selection of respondents. Therefore, the probability of selecting respondents is unknown. This means that because the sample is not chosen objectively it is not possible to state results with any degree of statistical certainty.

Non-probability sampling has advantages and disadvantages.

Advantages:

- Lower cost
- Faster
- Smaller sample sizes
- Important respondents can be targeted

Disadvantages:

- Results are purely indicative
- Sampling error cannot be computed
- The degree of representativeness of the sample to the population is not known
- Assumptions need to be made about the groupings with the population of interest.

Probability sampling

There are 4 commonly used methods of probability sampling:

1. Simple random sampling
2. Systematic sampling
3. Stratified random sampling
4. Cluster sampling.

Simple random sampling

Each member of the population has an equal chance of being selected for the survey. Members are randomly selected by a computerized random number generator or tables until the required sample size is filled.

Probability of selection is worked out as population size/sample size.

Activity 10.2

What is the probability of selection for a sample of 500 from a population of 20,000?

Systematic sampling
This is easier than random sampling as it does not use random number generation. In the previous activity, we looked at a sample size of 500 from a population of 20,000. In systematic random sampling, the figure of 40 would be used as what is known as a skip interval and every 40th name would be selected from the list.

Stratified random sampling
This method divides the population into two or more mutually exclusive groups.

For example, men or women, users or non users of a product and takes random samples from within them using either of the methods above.

This can be done ***proportionately*** where potential respondents or units are selected in proportion to the total number in each subset or ***disproportionately*** which takes more units from the subset with fewer respondents, i.e. where there is greater variation.

Whilst the disproportionate method is efficient and reliable, the proportionate method is more commonly used as the researcher may not know in advance the level of diversity within each subset.

Cluster sampling

Cluster sampling is described by Wilson (Wilson, A., 2003) as 'A procedure in which clusters of population units are selected at random and then all or some of the units in the chosen clusters are studied'.

The technique works by identifying clusters within a population and selecting randomly from these clusters. The technique works when a population can easily be divided into representative clusters, for example in membership directories.

Disadvantages include the difficulty of forming a mini version of the population which maintains the characteristics of the population as a whole. Rather like Dr Evil and Mini Me, the characteristics may change and may be hard to control!!

Wilson (Wilson, A., 2003) identifies three approaches to cluster sampling:

1. **One stage** Clusters are selected randomly and data is gathered from all people in the clusters
2. **Two stage** Clusters are selected randomly and data is gathered for a random sample of people in the selected clusters
3. **Area sampling** Geographical clusters are created and a random sample of individuals is selected.

Multi-stage sampling
This is a method which has several advantages. The chief is to concentrate a dispersed sample into convenient locations.

For example in surveying UK households, a random selection of constituencies might be made, this would be followed by a random selection of wards, then polling districts and finally a selection of streets and then individuals can be made.

Advantages include the fact that the creation of the sample frame is easier and the final interviews end up being geographically clustered reducing cost of face-to-face interviews.

Limitations of random sampling

- It is expensive
- Respondents selected must be interviewed to ensure the integrity of the process. This means that up to 3 call backs to individuals may be made before classifying a non response
- The cost of pulling together a large sample frame may be prohibitive
- The random selection of a sample means that all members of a national population would have the same chance of being selected. This means that interviewers may have to cover Lands End to John O' Groats.

Non-probability sampling

There are 4 types of non-probability sampling these are:

Convenience sampling

Is based on the convenience for the researcher. It may be that the section is made in the street, in the office or from a database. As long as the sample fits with the population as a whole, it is legitimate.

Judgement or purposive sampling

The researcher consciously selects a sample considered appropriate for the study. This may be based on certain companies representing a sector. For example a researcher in the cutlery market might include all major department stores in the sample as well as a random selection of other outlets. This is designed to reflect the relative importance of department stores in the retail market.

Quota sampling

Is defined by ESOMAR as 'A type of non-probability sample where the required number of units with particular characteristics are specified' (ESOMAR, 2003). This is based on the idea that if known characteristics of the population are reproduced in the same proportion in the sample, it is representative of that population; for example, age, sex and social class can be used to select quotas.

A researcher may be required to interview equal split of men and women and a certain number of men of a certain age. The researcher selects respondents that comply with the quota laid down.

	Required	Achieved	Total
Male	100		
Age			
16–34	40		
35–54	40		
55+ ages	20		
Class			
ABC1	40		
C2	35		
DE	25		

Figure 10.2 Quota sheets

Advantages include:

- Speed and cost
- Allows sampling to take place where a sample frame may not be available but key characteristics of the population are known – for example, in overseas b2b research
- Interviewers do not have to interview named individuals, they are screened in or out via a small number of classification questions
- The data, when compared to random methods which are perhaps double the cost, has been proved to be acceptable provided that the research is managed effectively
- Cost savings may be used to improve the quality of research through increasing sample sizes or using a different method in support of the survey
- Its popularity shows that it works!

Disadvantages include:

- Whilst known characteristics may be distributed in correct proportions, unknown characteristics that may be relevant to the survey may not be. Hidden bias may exist that is not discovered
- Researchers may be biased as to the type of respondents they choose to interview or the location where they choose to carry out the interviews. A quota for young people may be filled at one youth club but will not be truly representative of the population as a whole.

Snowball sampling

Is defined by ESOMAR as 'A type of non-probability sampling where initial respondents are selected at random and subsequent respondents are then selected by referrals or information from the earlier respondents' (ESOMAR, 2003).

This is very useful in markets where there is low incidence of the population – in b2b markets, where buyers of competitive intelligence or where unusual behaviour is under consideration.

Online issues

The same methods can be used in online research but the problem is that sample frames are less available. A range of panels have been set up to counter this; for example Nielsen net ratings.

Determining the sample size

There is no necessary relationship between the size of the population and the sample. Whilst the larger the sample size the more accurate the results, this has to be traded off against the cost of producing this effect and the complexity, and therefore cost of managing the collection of and processing large amounts of data.

The cost of producing more response is normally proportional, i.e. the percentage increase in the cost of producing a percentage increase in sample size will be the same. However, the increase in accuracy is not proportional. As Wilson (Wilson, A., 2003) points out, sampling error tends to decrease at a rate equal to the square root of the relative increase in sample size. A sample increased by 100 per cent will improve accuracy by 10 per cent.

Sample size is often determined by past experience. Previous studies will indicate:

- The degree of variability in the population – the more the variability, the larger the sample size will need to be
- The likely response rates – if these are believed to be low, the sample will need to be larger
- The incident rate of the characteristic being researched – if this is common, the sample may be smaller
- The number of subgroups within the data – the smaller groups will have larger sampling errors and a larger sample might be needed to ensure that subgroups can be effectively analysed.

Statistical techniques

For probability samples, statistical methods are used to establish sample sizes.

We need 3 pieces of information to work this out

1. The degree of variability of the population known as standard deviation
2. The required limit of accuracy or sampling error
3. The required level of confidence that the results will fall within a certain range.

There are 2 different ways of working out sample sizes for random samples, and these depend on whether we are measuring averages or proportions.

For studies involving averages or means

The formula to work out sample size is $N = \frac{Z^2\sigma^2}{E^2}$

Where, Z is the confidence level

σ is the population standard deviation

E is the acceptable level of precision.

Specify the level of precision

The level of precision is worked out by clients and researchers and reflects the budget available and the acceptable margin of error or degree of risk attached to the outcome of the research. If there is a need for accurate data, the sample size may be larger and the level of precision would be tighter.

Determine the acceptable confidence interval

The concept of normal distribution says that any number of observations will fall symmetrically and in a bell shape around the average of the observations.

There is no need in the CIM syllabus to understand this in detail.

The rules state that 68.27 per cent of the observations fall within standard deviation of the mean.

95.45 per cent fall within +/–2 standard deviations.

99.73 per cent fall within +/–3 standard deviations.

For our purpose, marketers generally use 95 per cent or 99 per cent confidence limits. These relate to 1.96 and 2.57 standard deviations and these are the Z values that are used.

These mean that at the 95 per cent confidence interval there is a one in twenty chance of the sample being wrong and at the 99 per cent confidence level, there is a one in a hundred chance of the sample being wrong.

Estimate the standard deviation

It is impossible to know this before carrying out the survey, so an estimate is required. This can be based upon:

- Previous studies
- Secondary research
- The result of pilot surveys
- Judgement.

Once the study is completed, the sample mean and standard deviation can be calculated, and the exact confidence level and limits of error can be worked out.

Activity 10.3

Wilson presents an example in which the Z value is 1.96. Standard deviation is 40.8 and the limit of error is 5. What happens if we wish to increase the confidence limit to 99 per cent?

Studies involving proportions

For studies measuring the proportion of a population having a certain characteristic, a different formula is needed.

$$N = \frac{Z^2[P(1-P)]}{E^2}$$

Z is, let's say, 1.96 or the 95 per cent confidence level

E is the limit of error let's say +/–3 per cent, written as a decimal 0.03

P is the estimated percentage of the population who have the characteristic. In this case we will look at the number of people who may respond to a mailing and we estimate that 15 per cent may respond. This is written as 0.15.

So, let's work this through:

$$N = \frac{1.96 \times 1.96\,[0.15(1 - 0.15)]}{0.03^2}$$

$$N = \frac{3.84 \times (0.15 \times 0.85)}{0.0009}$$

$$N = \frac{0.72}{0.0009}$$

$$N = 544$$

Adjustment for larger samples

We have said, there is no direct relationship between population and sample size to estimate a characteristic with a level of error and confidence.

The assumption is that that sample elements are drawn independent of one another. This cannot be assumed when the sample is higher than 10 per cent of the population. If this is the case, an adjustment is made called the finite population correction factor.

The calculation reduces the required sample:

$$N1 = \frac{nN}{N + n - 1}$$

N1 is the revised sample size

n is the original sample size

N is the population size

For example, if the population has 2000 elements and the original sample size is 400, then,

$$N1 = \frac{400 \times 2000}{2000 + 400 - 1}$$

$$N1 = 333$$

Other rules of thumb factors to consider in setting sample sizes:

- Trade of cost against reliability and accuracy
- Minimum subgroup sizes should be more than 100 respondents. It is difficult to be confident in figures lower than this.
- The average sample size in national surveys in the UK is around 1500–2000 respondents. Minimum sample sizes in the FMCG markets are 300–500 respondents.

Implementing a sampling procedure

Once the sample size is worked out, the researcher can start to gather data. We have already discussed the fact that a sample will always vary in some way from the population. There are a number of reasons for this:

Sampling error

Sampling error is the error in a survey caused by using a sample to estimate the value of a parameter in the population (ESOMAR, 2003).

'Sampling error is the difference between the sample value and the true value of a phenomenon for the population being surveyed' (Wilson, A., 2003).

Sampling error is inherent in the process of sampling and is reflected in the accuracy of estimates about the total population that can be made from the data.

Sampling errors can be estimated using statistics but other errors can occur. These are called non sampling errors.

Non sampling error

Sampling frame error – This is the error that occurs due to the fact that the sampling frame is different from the entire population. This can be reduced by combining lists to reinforce the frame.

Non response error – This may be due to refusal or the non availability of respondents. Refusals can be reduced by incentivizing the process and through using trained, experienced interviewers and well-designed questionnaires.

Data error – This may be through respondent error, responders give the wrong information deliberately or unintentionally. This can be reduced through careful analysis of inconsistency in the responses, through the use of well-designed questionnaires and the use of skilled interviewers.

Interviewer errors – These occur as a result of the interviewer making mistakes in asking questions or recording answers. These can be reduced through careful training and back checking to ensure that the interview was carried out, that the respondent matched the required profile, that all questions were asked and that the code of conduct of the MRS was adhered to. The IQCS ensure minimum standards for back checking.

Data analysis error – These can be caused by key stroke or software problems. They can be reduced by checking for consistency and manually profiling hard data against that held in the computer.

Weightings

Weightings are used to correct problems due to sampling error. Responses from subgroups are given a statistical weight reflecting the importance of the subgroup in the population of interest.

The weighting is most often used to bring the sample into line with known proportions in the population, for example age or gender.

Summary

In this unit, we explored the process of sampling and looked in detail at the stages involved in the process.

They cover:

- The definition of the population
- The decision to sample or census
- The creation of the sampling frame
- The sampling method.

We looked in detail at probability and non-probability sampling and the various approaches under each. Probability sampling includes random sampling, systematic sampling, stratified random sampling, cluster sampling and area sampling.

Non-probability techniques include convenience sampling, judgement sampling, quota sampling and snowball sampling. We looked at the constraints on the choice of sampling method.

The sample size was then discussed. Sample size is determined by financial, managerial and statistical considerations. We looked in detail at the statistical basis of establishing sample size.

Finally, we looked at the error involved in sampling and suggested ways of managing error and the process of weighting.

Further study

Question 9

You have been appointed as marketing manager to an online retailer of intimate apparel (underwear). They have succeeded in difficult times to grow their business but have appointed you to look at the marketing research function within the business. Your first piece of research is based on a quota sample. The MD of the business is sceptical.

Produce a report for the MD outlining what quota sampling is.

What benefits does it have? What are its disadvantages and how can these be overcome?

What other sampling techniques may have been considered and why would they have been rejected?

Hints and Tips

Go to the MRS website and look at the guidelines for qualitative research. Add this to your study pack.

Bibliography

Crouch, S. and Housden, M. (2003). *Marketing research for managers,* Butterworth-Heinemann.

ESOMAR (2003). www.esomar.nl.

MRS (2003). www.mrs.org.uk.

Wilson, A. (2003). *Marketing research: an integrated approach*, FT Prentice Hall.

unit 11 quantitative data analysis

Learning objectives

After completing this unit you will be able to:

- Understand the process of data management, entry, editing, coding and cleaning
- Understand concepts of tabulation and statistical analysis
- Understand the main techniques of statistical analysis including descriptive statistics, statistical significance and hypotheses testing, the measurement of relationships and multivariate analysis
- Understand the use of computer packages that can help with the process
- Cover syllabus elements 4.6, 5.1.

Key definitions

Coding The process that allocates a number to each answer and it is this that allows analysis to take place.

Editing The process of computer or manual checking of the data to look for respondent or interview errors.

Frequency distributions Counts of the numbers of respondents who gave each possible answer to a particular question.

Nominal data Numbers assigned to objects or phenomena as labels or identification numbers that name or classify but that have no true numeric meaning (Wilson, A., 2003).

Ordinal data Numbers with the labelling characteristics of nominal data but which also have the ability to communicate the rank order of the data. They do not indicate absolute quantities and do not imply that the intervals between the numbers are equal (Wilson, A., 2003).

Interval data Similar to ordinal data but with the added dimension that intervals between the values on a scale are equal (Wilson, A., 2003).

Ratio data Actual or real numbers that have a meaningful or absolute zero (Wilson, A., 2003).

Descriptive statistics Statistical devices that help to summarize data, these include measures of central tendency, mode, mean, median, and measures of dispersion range, interquartile range and standard deviation.

Factor analysis Studies the relationships between variables to simplify data into a smaller set of composite variables or factors.

Correlation Examines the strength of the relationship between variables using an index.

Cross tabulations Table setting out responses to one question relative to others.

Coefficient of determination Measure of the strength of linear relationship between a dependent and an independent variable.

Conjoint analysis Analysis that asks respondents to make decisions between various attributes measuring their relative importance.

Chi square A test measuring the goodness of fit between the observed sample values and the expected distribution of those values.

Z test A hypothesis test about a single mean where the sample is greater than 30.

T Test A hypothesis test about a single mean where the sample is less than 30.

Spearman's rank-order correlation Correlation for ordinal data.

Pearson's product moment correlation A correlation technique for interval and ratio data.

Null hypothesis The hypothesis that is tested.

Alternative hypothesis A hypothesis competing with the null hypothesis.

Least squares A regression method that produces a line of best fit for a data set involving a dependent and independent variable.

Independent variable A variable that has influence on the value of the dependent variable.

Dependent variable The response measure studied.

Regression Examines the relationship between 2 variables.

Study Guide

The unit should take around 3 hours to complete. You will need another 3 hours to ensure that you complete and understand the exercises. You will need to refer to other course texts throughout this unit and should have access to Alan Wilson's text.

Introduction

The analysis of data is a key skill of the marketing manager. Very often people find the introduction of statistics a little daunting. However, an ability to understand basic methods of data analysis is very important. This unit will take you through the process of preparing data and analysing that data to inform marketing decisions. For the less numerate, it will try to show you what the various techniques do to data, and how and why they are used. Many people find that describing what the techniques do in words makes the whole task more manageable and accessible.

Data analysis can be done easily now using computer packages such as Excel and SPSS. However, the lack of understanding of the techniques remains.

Editing and coding

Before data is processed, it is assessed for completeness and coherence. The editing process involves computer or manual checking of the data to look for respondent or interview errors or inconsistencies. If errors are identified, the respondent may be called back and if the questionnaire cannot be rescued then it may be rejected.

Coding is the process that allocates a number to each answer and it is this that allows analysis to take place. As discussed earlier, the coding process may take place as the questionnaire is administered either manually by the interviewer ringing a number on the questionnaire or it may be managed through computer assisted methods.

After this process is completed the data will look like this:

	Question 1	Question 2	Question 3	Question 4	Etc.
Record 1	1	3	1	10	
Record 2	1	4	5	15	
Record 3	2	2	3	12	
Etc. . . . 4					

The questionnaire might have looked like this:

Question 1	**Code**
Sex M	1
F	2
Question 2	
What is your age?	**Code**
18–25	1
26–35	2
36–45	3
46–55	4
55+	5

And so on.

Coding open questions involves using a sample of the completed questionnaires and developing a coding frame or a list of codes for all possible responses to an open question. This process may categorize and group certain diverse responses into a manageable number. This process must be handled carefully to reduce the processing error that might occur.

Data entry

Data entry may be carried out automatically through CAPI, CAWI and CATI systems or scanned into the computer using optical character recognitions software or they may be entered by hand. After this process, the data will be once again checked or cleaned for key stroke or character recognition problems.

Once this is complete, the data can be analysed.

Tabulation and statistical analysis

There are 4 types of data that can be analysed.

These are:

Nominal data

These refer to values that are given to objects that in themselves have no intrinsic numerical value. For example, we assigned a value to gender – 1 for men and 2 for women.

We can count them and create percentages.

Statistics based on frequency counts can be used with this type of data. These include mode and chi-square tests.

The mode is the most frequently occurring figure in a set of data (see page 179). For example, this may be used to say that brand x was the most frequently mentioned brand.

Chi-square tests measure the significance between cross tabulated data. For example, we may have data that shows that men buy more beer than women. Whilst we might assume that this is the case, we will have a range of values in each cell. The problem is to determine if the difference in the values is real or a result of using a sample of the population.

Ordinal data

These data represent rank order data. They do not imply that there is an equal gap between items ranked and there is no other meaning than the rank order.

Examples include asking consumers to rank a number of products 1–5 around a certain attribute.

For example:

Rank the following online banks 1–5 in order of their reputation for service where 1 is the bank which offers the best service and 5 is the bank that offers the worst service.

- Smile
- Cahoot
- First direct
- Egg
- Intelligent finance.

We can use mode and median analysis with this data.

The median is the middle value when responses are arranged in order (see page 179).

Interval data

Is rank order in which the intervals between the data are equal. These are also known as interval scales. Interval scales rank elements relative to each other and there is no fixed point. This means that ratio analysis between values is not possible.

Rank the following online banks 1–5 in order of their reputation for service where 1 is the bank which offers the best service and 5 is the bank that offers worst service.

o Smile	1	2	3	4	5
o Cahoot	1	2	3	4	5
o First direct	1	2	3	4	5
o Egg	1	2	3	4	5
o Intelligent finance	1	2	3	4	5

This data allows means and standard deviations to take place and a range of other statistical tests can be carried out.

The mean is the average of the results (see page 179).

Standard deviation is a measure that looks at the distribution of results around the average value of the results.

Ratio data

Ratio data has an absolute zero or observable origin. For example, shoe size, products bought or age.

This means all analyses are possible.

Tabulations

Tables give researchers a feel for data. Frequency distributions are simply counts of the numbers of respondents who gave each possible answer to a particular question.

Hole counts and frequency

Frequency distributions or hole counts are simply counts of the numbers of respondents who gave each possible answer to a particular question. They are used to help the researcher form the next stage of analysis.

Cross-tabulations (cross-tabs)

These tables 'cross' the answers to one question with the answers to another, for example age and products purchased.

Q. 15 When do you plan to buy a new car?

Base: All those who intend to replace their car

		Age	
	Total	**21–44**	**44+**
Base	127 (100%)	63 (100%)	64 (100%)
Within a month	12 (9%)	2 (3%)	10 (15%)
Within six months	45 (35%)	25 (40%)	20 (31%)
Within the year	55 (43%)	30 (48%)	25 (39%)
Longer	15 (12%)	10 (16%)	5 (8%)

These tables can be presented graphically

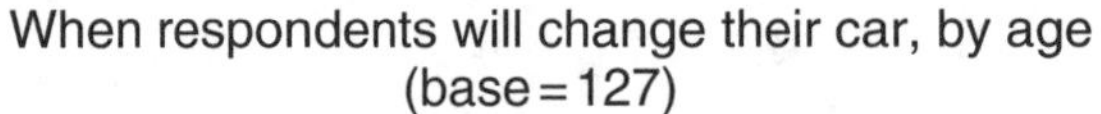

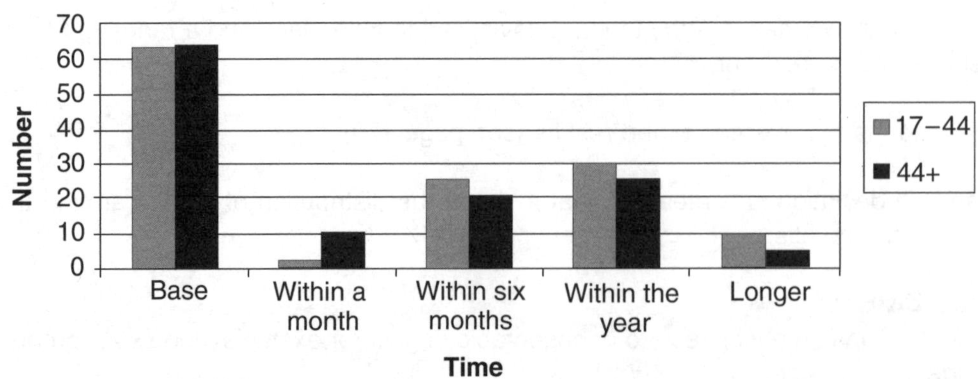

Figure 11.1 Cross tabulations

It is easy to generate cross tabs using computers. The skill is to decide which are relevant and significant.

Descriptive statistics

These data are used to give the researcher a view of the location of the data and its spread. These are known as measures of central tendency and measures of dispersion or variability.

Measures of central tendency indicate typical values for data sets. These are the mean, median and mode.

The mean is the arithmetic average. To calculate the mean, divide the total values by the number of cases.

The median is the value of the middle case in a series of numbers put in ascending or descending order.

The mode is the value in a set of data that appears most frequently. A data set may have more than one mode – a number of categories may be equal and share the highest frequency.

For example, shoe sizes bought in one hour:

5	6	6	7	8
9	8	8	8	8
9	9	9	8	8
11	10	10	9	9
11	12	12	13	5
Mode = 8	Median = 9	Mean = 8.72		

Measures of dispersion

These indicate how spread out or dipersed a data set is. They include the range, variance and standard deviation.

The range is the interval from the highest to the lowest value in a data set. In the example above, the range is 13 – 5 = 8.

The shoe example is straightforward. However, if the size 13 man had bought 5 pairs of shoes, then the sample would be skewed towards the higher range. This is managed by using what is called the interquartile range, this removes any values that fall outside the 75th and 25th percentile and then calculates the range.

Variance is a measure of how spread out a data set is. We work it out by looking at the average squared deviation of each number from its mean. There are different formulae for working out variance but the one most commonly used in market research takes into account the potential bias in a sample.

The formula is

$$s^2 = \sum_{i=1}^{n} \frac{(X_i - \overline{X})^2}{n - 1}$$

X is the individual value in an array of data

$\overline{X}$ is the mean of the array

n is the number of values in an array

For example, for the numbers 1, 2, 3, 4 and 5, the number of values is 5, and the variance is 2.

$1-3=-2 \times -2=4$

$2-3=-1 \times -1=1$

$3-3=0 \times 0=0$

$4-3=1 \times 1=1$

$5-3=2 \times 2=4$

Sum of the squared differences $4+1+0+1+4=10$

10 divided by $5-1=10/4$

Variance $= 2.5$

Standard deviation is used to compare the spread of data sets. The more spread a set of values the look at data sets.

Standard deviation is the square root of the variance.

$$SD = \sqrt{\frac{\sum (x_i - \bar{x})^2}{n-1}}$$

where

x_i = the value of each data point

$\bar{x}$ = the average of all the data points

$\sum$ = the greek letter sigma, meaning 'sum of'

n = the total number of data points

Statistical significance

There are advantages to using samples rather than collecting data from the whole population under review. However, the data from a sample will always be subject to error. We cannot be sure that the difference between two results is a real change in those values or simply a result of the sampling error.

Clearly, there may be a mathematical difference between two values but if the difference is large enough not to have occurred through chance or error, then the difference is defined as statistically significant.

Hypothesis testing

A hypothesis is defined by Wilson as an assumption about a characteristic in the population. Research will allow the researcher to conclude something about the population.

For example, advertising recall tests show a decrease in spontaneous recall from 59 per cent to 54 per cent. Is this difference significant and must we change our advertising strategy?

The testing of hypothesis follows a simple structure.

First, establish the hypothesis.

There are 2 forms of hypotheses:

1. The Null hypothesis or H_0 is the one that will be tested, i.e. the existing situation where no difference is expected
2. The Alternative hypothesis or H_1 is the one in which a difference is expected.

For example, our recall problem could be expressed as:

The Null hypothesis or H_0 Mean recall rates are stable at 59 per cent.

The Alternative hypothesis or H_1 Mean recall rates have fallen to 54 per cent.

The hypotheses will either be accepted or rejected depending on the outcome of the results.

There are a range of significance tests available and the most frequently used are:

- Chi-square test
- Z test
- T test.

Significance tests measure whether the difference between two percentages is significant or not, or whether the difference between two means from different samples is significant. In order to carry out these tests three concepts must be considered.

Degrees of freedom

Degrees of freedom are defined as the number of observations minus 1. A sample n has $n-1$ degrees of freedom. Degrees of freedom are used to reflect potential bias in a example.

Independent versus related samples

Selection of the appropriate test technique may involve considering whether samples are independent or related. In related samples, the measurement of the variable of interest in one sample might affect the measurement of the variable of interest in another.

Errors in hypothesis testing

Two types of error are known – type one and type two. A concept called the alpha level defines the probability of committing such an error and is commonly set at 0.05 or a 5 per cent chance of the error occurring.

Type one errors happen when the null hypothesis is rejected when it is true. Type two errors mean accepting the null hypothesis when it is false.

Reducing the alpha level increases the chance of a type one error occurring.

The Chi-square test

Measures whether the differences in cross tabulated data sets are significant, this is also known as 'goodness of fit' between observed distribution and expected distribution or the variable. It compares one or more sets of data to indicate if there is a real difference.

Activity 11.1

A test mailing plan produced the following responses:

Pack A 5909
Pack B 5810
Pack C 6350

Using the Chi-square formula, work out if there is a variation between the packs.

$\sum$ = sum of
f_o = observed
f_e = expected (mean)

$$\chi^2 = \sum \frac{(f_o - f_e)^2}{f_e}$$

Before proceeding look at the debrief to this activity.

Chi square test of two or more variables can be used to test, for example, the difference between male and female respondents to the mailing.

Hypotheses about means

Where sample data produces a mean or a proportion, researchers can use a Z or a T test to test hypotheses relating to them.

Z tests are used if the researcher is aware of the population's mean and variance. This may be the real mean or variance, or assumed figures. The sample must be higher than 30. T tests are used if the mean and variance are unknown or if a sample is less than 30. T tests are more frequently used by researchers. They allow the researcher to work out if the difference between the 2 averages is real or significant, or simply due to the fact that the figures are derived from a sample. For example, if a customer satisfaction survey ranks your brand higher than average, is this a real difference or due to sampling error?

In a sample of 1500 people on a scale of 1–5 your customer satisfaction was 4.5, the average of your competitors was 3.8. The sample standard deviation was 1.6.

The formula for a Z test is as follows:

$$Z = \frac{\text{sample mean} - \text{population}}{\text{estimated standard error}}$$

Standard error = standard deviation/the square root of the sample size

$$\text{Standard error} = \frac{1.6}{\sqrt{1500}} = 0.04$$

$$Z = 4.5 - 3.8/0.04 = 17.5$$

This is larger than the Z value of 1.64 at 0.05 level of significance and we can say that at 95 per cent confidence the results are correct.

Try changing some of these figures, the standard deviation for example, you will see that if the results were more dispersed, Z score would reduce.

T tests are generally used to determine the results from smaller surveys with a sample size of under 30.

The formula for T tests involving a mean and one sample is:

$$T = \frac{\text{sample mean} - \text{mean under null hypothesis}}{\text{estimated standard error of the mean}}$$

For comparing the mean in two samples the following formula is used:

$$T = \frac{\text{mean from sample 1} - \text{mean from sample 2}}{\sqrt{[(\text{standard error for sample 1})^2 - (\text{standard error for sample 2})^2]}}$$

Measuring relationships

Correlation and regression

These techniques measure the degree of association between two variables such as income and number of foreign holidays or customer satisfaction and product repurchase, or advertising spend and sales.

Bivariate techniques measure the relationship between two variables. This does not prove that one variable causes the other but rather indicates the degree of relationship between the variables. Often a cause and effect link is assumed but this is not a proven relationship. It is important to apply common sense in the interpretation of the results.

Variables are labelled dependent and independent. Independent variables are those assumed to influence the dependent variable.

There are two types of correlation analysis.

Pearson's product movement correlation is used with interval and ratio data. It produces a correlation coefficient which can have a maximum value of +1 and a minimum value of –1.

Perfect positive correlation between two sets of variables is indicated by +1. This means that if there is a movement of 5 per cent on one variable, it is accompanied by a movement in the same direction of 5 per cent on another variable. For example, when satisfaction increases by 5 per cent, sales rise by 5 per cent. Perfect negative correlation means the two variables have a perfect negative relationship. If for every 10 per cent increase in price the sales volume decreased by 10 per cent then the correlation coefficient would be –1.

When changes in one variable are not associated with changes in the other variable the correlation coefficient will be calculated as zero.

Generally, correlation coefficients above +0.7 or below –0.7 are believed to show an increasing degree of association. This might require further research to explore the association in more detail from larger samples.

When ordinal data is being considered, Spearman's rank order correlation is used. This might be used to compare ranking of companies' promotional expenditure with a ranking of their sales turnover.

It is important to note that low coefficients do not mean that there is no association. It only implies absence of a linear association. It may be that a non-linear association exists. Again think about your market and apply common sense to your work.

Activity 11.2

Work through the examples of Pearson's product movement coefficient of correlation in your texts. What other examples of the application can you think of?

$$R = \frac{n\sum xy-(\sum x)(\sum y)}{\sqrt{[n\sum x^2-(\sum x)^2][n\sum y^2-(\sum y)^2]}}$$

This example looks at the relationship between restaurant capacity and sales. Work out R for this example.

Restaurant	Capacity	Turnover (£100,000)
1	210	£1.10
2	80	£0.74
3	80	£0.99
4	160	£1.14
5	100	£1.01
6	70	£0.92
7	160	£1.08
8	60	£0.80
9	300	£1.10
10	200	£1.16
11	150	£1.09
12	50	£0.68
13	80	£0.78
14	150	£1.08
15	100	£1.12
16	100	£0.90
17	90	£0.94
18	170	£0.91
19	80	£0.85
20	110	£1.05

Simple regression analysis

Regression analysis is concerned with dependence. For example, sales volume may be predicted based on other variables.

In the insurance industry, this is used to measure the chance of a customer not renewing a policy and explores the number of inbound calls and customer complaints.

The allocation of dependent and independent variable is more important in regression analysis.

Remember, movement in the dependent variables depends upon movement in the independent variables.

Often, correlation analysis and regression analysis are both carried out on the same data sets. If correlation analysis indicates which variables have a relevant association with, say sales volume, regression analysis can be used to predict sales volume, given a set of decisions about marketing variables and assumptions about probable movements in external variables. Sales forecasters use regression analysis. However, it is clear that the movement in a market is caused by a number of factors and this is dealt with through multivariate techniques which we will look at later.

Least squares is the most common approach to regression. Least squares identifies a line of best fit between observations and this allows us to produce an estimated regression function that indicates the relationship. To do this we need to look at the slope of the line and the line of intercept. Simple regression analysis may be enhanced through the coefficient of determination. This measures the strength of the relationship between variables.

Activity 11.3

Using the formula, calculate the relationship between turnover and capacity.

$$\hat{b} = \frac{\sum x_i y_i - n\bar{x}\bar{y}}{\sum x_i^2 - n(\bar{x})^2}$$

$$\hat{a} = \bar{y} - \hat{b}\bar{x}$$

Restaurant	Capacity	Turnover (£100,000)
1	210	£1.10
2	80	£0.74
3	80	£0.99
4	160	£1.14
5	100	£1.01
6	70	£0.92
7	160	£1.08
8	60	£0.80
9	300	£1.10
10	200	£1.16
11	150	£1.09
12	50	£0.68
13	80	£0.78
14	150	£1.08
15	100	£1.12
16	100	£0.90
17	90	£0.94
18	170	£0.91
19	80	£0.85
20	110	£1.05

This can be plotted as follows:

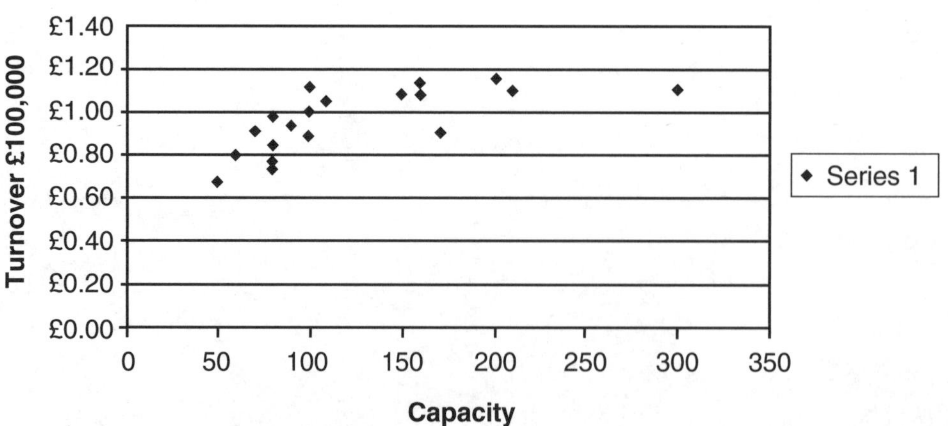

Figure 11.2 Turnover and capacity

What is the impact of increasing capacity on turnover?

Multivariate analysis techniques

These techniques analyse two or more variables simultaneously and present a more realistic approach to marketing decision-making.

There are six key techniques:

Multiple regression analysis

These allow the researcher to understand the relationship between 3 or more variables and the impact on the value of a dependent value, based on the values of 2 or more independent values. For example, response to mailings and the impact of re-mailing or telephone follow-up.

Wilson points out that there are three common uses.

- The impact of marketing mix variables on sales
- The importance of components or aspects of satisfaction on overall satisfaction
- Determining the impact of different consumer characteristics on sales.

Multiple discriminant analysis

This technique is used to classify individuals based on 2 or more independent variables. For example, readiness to buy a car based on age of car, length of time spent on the website and in bound calls.

The major discriminating factor between shoppers and non-shoppers in a particular department store was found, through discriminant analysis, to be the perceived price level within the store. Subsequent advertising of lower-priced lines resulted in an increase in the number of shoppers.

Factor analysis

Factor analysis reduces a large number of variables to a more manageable smaller set of factors based on the interrelationships between them.

It provides insight for the groupings that emerge and allows for more efficient analysis of complex data.

It is often used for rating scales or attitude statement.

Factor analysis is a subjective process as any set of factors can be rejected and new sets created. One way of managing this is to split the sample into 2 groups and if the same factors are created from each group, more confidence can be placed in them.

Cluster analysis

This technique groups objects or respondents into mutually exclusive and exhaustive groups. The technique is often used in data base marketing to create segments based on behaviour across a range of variables.

Multidimensional scaling or perceptual mapping

Consumers rate objects, often brands, by the relative strength of an attribute compared to other objects or brands. This creates a perception of a 'position' in the market and is very useful for determining brand perception and repositioning.

Conjoint analysis

Conjoint analysis is a way of looking at customers' decisions as a trade off between multiple attributes in products or services.

In conjoint analysis, consumers are asked to make decisions about various attributes, trading lower price for comfort, for example, in car purchases.

There are two approaches to this process:

1. The full profile approach describes the full product or service – respondents may rank all possible combinations of, for example, product quality, price and after sales service.
2. The pairwise approach presents attributes in pairs and respondents put each in rank order. This approach is generally easier for respondents to manage and care must be taken that the list of attributes is not too long.

Software packages

Do not despair if this unit has left you slightly boggle eyed!. There are many software packages on the market that will do most of this for you. The key thing is to understand what these packages will do to your valuable data and to produce efficient analysis which allows a focus on the research problem.

Excel is perfectly adequate for most of the key formulae outlined above but there are specialists, perhaps the best known software packages include:

SPSS www.spss.com

SNAP www.mercator.co.uk

Activity 11.4

Visit www.spss.com and www.mercator.co.uk, make a list of the services that are available and add these to your favourites.

Summary

In this unit, we looked at the process of data analysis. We saw that data needs to be entered, coded, edited and cleaned before data analysis can be carried out.

We saw that there are four types of data. These are:

1. Nominal
2. Ordinal
3. Interval
4. Ratio.

The type of analysis that can be carried out is dependent on the type of data that is being analysed.

We looked at the process of tabulation. In order to obtain a first look at data, we saw examples of frequency distributions or hole counts and cross tabulation.

We went on to look at the types of analysis that can be carried out looking in detail at the following:

- Descriptive statistics
- Statistical significance and hypotheses testing
- The measurement of relationships
- Multivariate analysis.

We looked in detail at methods under each of these categories.

Further study

Question 10
What tasks have to be done before data can be analysed and after surveys have been completed?

Describe the tasks and outline their role in producing effective analysis.

Hints and Tips

There are many online tutorials that cover the area of statistical analysis. A web search on the key terms above generates some great examples and exercises.

Bibliography

Wilson, A. (2003). *Marketing research: an integrated approach*, FT Prentice Hall.

unit 12 presenting marketing research

Learning objectives

After completing this unit you will be able to:

- Identify the structure for the presentation of a research report
- Outline the key features of an oral presentation
- Know how to make the most of a presentation
- Understand the use of graphics in presentation of data
- Complete syllabus elements 5.2, 5.3, 5.4.

Key definitions

Oral presentation A verbal presentation of research findings using a range of supporting material.

Executive summary A précis of the report.

Study Guide

This unit should take you around 1.5 hours to complete.

Introduction

The final report to the client is perhaps the most important part of the research planning process. For the external agency, it is the moment of truth when the proposed methodology is presented to the client. For the client, it is the chance to consider the course of action based on the results. For individuals, it is the chance to impress senior colleagues and enhance their reputation. No wonder people get a little fractious and nervous as the deadline looms!

The ability to present data in the most appropriate and accessible way, whilst ensuring that the research problem is effectively dealt with, is a highly-developed skill. The results are generally presented in written format and this may or may not be supported by an oral presentation supported by slides.

The written report

The structure of a written report is standard and this helps considerably with the process of producing the document. Before producing the report, it helps to consider the objectives of the study again and the nature of the audience who will read and use the report. What are the key points that the audience is interested in? What are the key constraints on marketing decisions recommended in the report? What is the business position and are the resource implications of decisions adequately considered?

- Title page
- Contents
- Executive summary
- Introduction
- Situation analysis and problem definition
- Research methodology and limitations
- Findings and analysis
- Conclusions and recommendations
- Appendices

Figure 12.1 Research report format

Title page

This should contain the title of the report. The name and contact details of the agency and the researcher, client details and the date of presentation.

Contents page

This should contain full details of sections and subsections and page numbers. It should include lists of tables and figures. It should make the report navigable. If presenting on the web, the use of hyperlinks which take the browser to the relevant section can be considered.

The executive summary

This should be a short summary of the report and its recommendations. Many say that it should be a one or two page summary, or a maximum of two pages. There are no hard and fast rules. The summary needs to do a job, i.e. summarizing a report, and also needs to be accessible.

Production of the executive summary is a tough job. As Churchill said 'Sorry, for such a long letter I didn't have time to write a short one'. It is hard to condense the report into a one or two page summary. It is also the section of the report that will be read by senior managers and so it is worth putting time and effort into its production.

The executive summary should be written after the rest of the report has been written. The executive summary should start the report. Some people feel that it should follow the contents page and some feel that it should precede it. Some companies produce a separate summary of the work and this can be useful for wider and more efficient distribution of the key findings of the report.

Introduction

The introduction should outline the key objectives of the research, the reasons why the research has been carried out and the constraints that the researchers are working to. It may include profiles and key responsibilities of the researchers.

Situation analysis and problem definition

This section outlines the background to the problem and reviews business and marketing objectives. It drills down into the problem's definition and the detailed objectives for the research programme, and reprises the sections of the brief and proposal.

Research methodology and limitations

This section outlines the detailed methodology for the study. It should cover the research method, the data capture mechanism, the topic or discussion guide or questionnaire, the definition of the population of interest, the sampling approach and the method of data analysis. This section should not be too long. Details should be put into the appendices. It should cover sources of error, including sample size.

Findings and analysis

The main body of the report should cover the findings relevant to the objectives. It should be constructed to present a solution to the problem, not on a question by question basis. The research data should present data to support a line of argument and the focus should be on analysis and insight. Key ideas can be supported by tables or quotes from respondents. It may include tables and graphics, and should be linked by a narrative.

Conclusions and recommendations

This section brings the report to a close. It should present a summary of key findings and recommendations for marketing decisions and future research.

Appendices

Should include all supporting data. It contains material that is relevant to the research but that would be too detailed for the main report. It may include all tables, questionnaires, discussion guides and secondary data. It may be that the appendices are longer than the main report.

Example of a report contents (amended to protect client confidentiality)

1 Abstract

2 Executive summary

3 Acknowledgements

4 Introduction

4.1 Industry background – The UK Market

4.1.1 The 'Brand Renaissance'

4.1.2 A radically changing distribution network

4.1.3 Changing consumer values

4.1.4 The franchised dealer

4.2 Background to organization

4.2.1 UK success story?

4.2.2 Brand deficit

4.2.3 The future

5 Research objectives

6 Research methodology

6.1 Sampling procedure and size

6.2 Research methods

6.2.1 In-depth interviews

6.2.2 Staff focus groups

6.2.3 Customer focus groups

7 Data analysis and evaluation

8 Research findings

- 8.1 Primary research overview
- 8.2 Strategic direction of the brand
- 8.3 Staff perception of the brand
- 8.4 Staff and customer value
- 8.5 Loyalty and interaction of staff
- 8.6 Effective communication
- 8.7 Measurement as a behavioural driver
- 8.8 Customer value of experience
- 8.9 Brand decision-making

9 Appendices

- 9.1 Appendix A: In-depth interview guide
- 9.2 Appendix B: Staff focus group discussion guide
- 9.3 Appendix C: Customer focus group discussion guide
- 9.4 Appendix D: Participant invitation letter
- 9.5 Appendix G: CD Rom recording of in-depth interviews
- 9.6 Appendix H: Video footage of focus groups

10 Terms of reference

The oral presentation

The process of delivering an oral presentation may be daunting, but preparation means that it does not have to be too nerve-wracking.

The oral presentation may involve a number of people and a range of audio and visual equipment. The technology is always a problem and it is reassuring to have a back-up.

The key thing in preparing a presentation is that it is not simply a regurgitation of the report. The presentation, of course, draws on the same data and makes the same conclusions but the findings can be presented in a much livelier and, maybe, accessible and memorable way.

Wilson (Wilson, A., 2003) presents a useful structure for research presentations:

Introduction
Thank you.

Introduce the team.

Outline the agenda of the presentation.

Set rules for questions. Will you take them at the end or through the presentation?

Research background and objectives
An outline of the business and marketing background and the objectives of the study.

Research methodology
Describe the methodology and data collection device along with limitations.

Key findings
Supported by graphs and tables. Keep it simple, only present pertinent tables and graphs. Make sure that the tables and graphs are readable and clear.

Conclusions and recommendations
Repeat key findings. Lay down your recommendations.

Questions
A full discussion of the issues. Think about the following points at rehearsal:

1. What questions will come up? Try to pre-empt and prepare
2. Will all presenters handle questions or will the team leader take questions and pass them on to the team's expert?
3. What will you do if you can't answer a question?
4. Tell your audience how you want to deal with questions.

Presentation tips

- Meet your objectives.
- Know your audience; what do they want to hear? How many will be present? Who are they? What positions do they hold?
- Keep it brief and to the point, do not use too many tables or graphs. Use a balanced mixture of words and images.
- Be prepared for interruptions and stop presenting if your audience are distracted. Don't plough on.
- Turn off mobile phones.
- If using PowerPoint technology, make sure that it is compatible with the projection system. Make sure that your slides do not contain too much information and that tables and graphics can be read.
- During the presentation, maintain eye contact with your audience. Try to avoid having a physical barrier between you and your audience.
- Be aware of your body language, relax your shoulders, smile and try to project enthusiasm.
- Relax and use natural movements. Engage with your audience but don't invade their personal space.
- Make eye contact with all people in the room early in the presentation – get them on your side.

- Face your audience rather than the screen.
- Never turn you back to the audience.
- Don't hide behind lecterns and A4 notes.
- Use cue cards if necessary, do not try to ad lib unless you are well rehearsed.
- Provide handouts for your audience of the slides and tables and graphs that may be hard to read.
- If working with a team of presenters, make sure that you support them. When you are not presenting, maintain a positive attitude and listen to the rest of the team. If a team member falters or technology is causing problems act to sort out the situation.
- Keep to time and take responsibility for your own timings.
- Use pictures, video, audio clips to enliven and add variety to the presentation.

  - Research has shown that people forget 30 per cent of what you tell them after just 3 hours and 90 per cent is forgotten after only 3 days. Visual aids can help and variety is the key. The combination of verbal and visual material has been shown to deliver 85 per cent recollection after 3 hours and up to 65 per cent after 3 days. Almost all presentations are made using PowerPoint and the lack of pacing and variety often creates a very flat atmosphere and passive audience. This is often the case as projection equipment may mean that the lights have to be dimmed and the audience sink into a soporific state. Popcorn might be a more appropriate snack than the executive biscuit selection. Liven it up by using a variety of support and dynamic pacing through the presentation.
  - Flipchart.
  - Overhead projector slides.
  - PowerPoint.
  - Story boards.
  - Video and sound clips.

- Practise, practise, practise, remember 'fail to prepare, prepare to fail'.

  - Make sure you carry out a 'dress' rehearsal. Practise speaking out loud.
  - Practise all aspects of the presentation including the transition between speakers and the use of supporting technology or audio visual aids.
  - It may help to record your rehearsal and pick up your verbal tics, the 'you knows' the 'hums' and the 'yeses'. Knowing that you have these verbal tics can help control them. Practise volume and pace and the use of silence.

- Tell them what you will tell them, tell them and tell them what you have told them. Structure the presentation and use staging posts and summarizing slides to close sections and introduce new sections.
- Always finish on a high note.

Use of graphics

Tables and graphs will enliven reports and presentations, but with the range of technology available, overkill is possible.

Tables

Tables should be presented with the title and a number. The tables should be labelled with base numbers, i.e. the figures for the sample and sub samples should be shown, especially when percentages are being used. 75 per cent is impressive. 75 per cent of 10 respondents is less so. If quantities are indicated in the table, you must specify if they are in volumes or value. If numbers are used, specify the units. If currency is used, make sure that it is included in the table decription.

Tables should be structured so that data is ordered from large to small items. The layout should enable data to be read easily. If data is imported, it should always be referenced or sourced.

Beer consumption % Volume 1998–2002 (Base = 550)

	1998	1999	2000	2001	2002
Bitter	27	26	25	24	23
Stout	15	15	15	16	16
Lager	30	31	32	33	34
Other	28	28	28	27	27

Source: RK Associates 2003

Marketing spend by medium 1998–2004 (Euros '000)

Medium\Year	1998	1999	2000	2001	2002	2003f	2004f
Mail	24	28	45	56	43	45	50
Nat press	334	556	667	776	545	680	789
TV	1500	1500	3456	3450	4000	4000	5700
Radio	200	230	340	570	567	789	790
Trade press	35	50	60	76	78	88	98
Telephone	0	0	15	19	40	70	90
Total	**4091**	**4363**	**6583**	**6948**	**7275**	**5672**	**7517**
F = forecast							

Source: Internal marketing data

Figure 12.2 A typical table

Other graphics

Other graphical devices that can be used include

- Pie charts

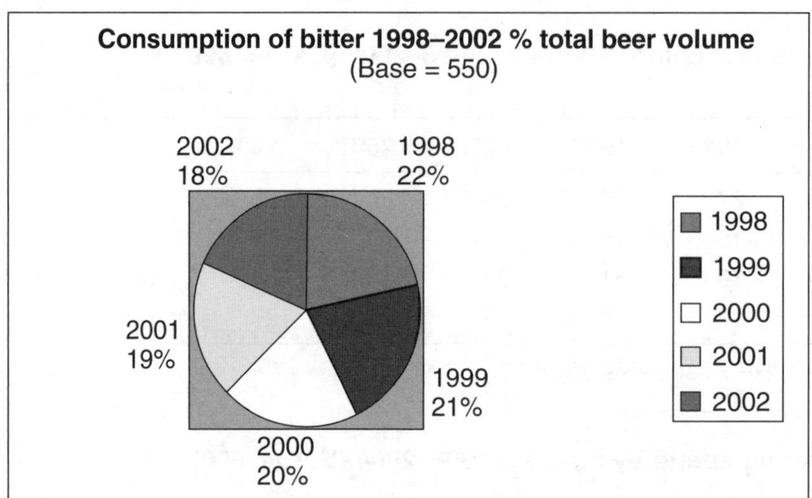

Figure 12.3

- Donuts

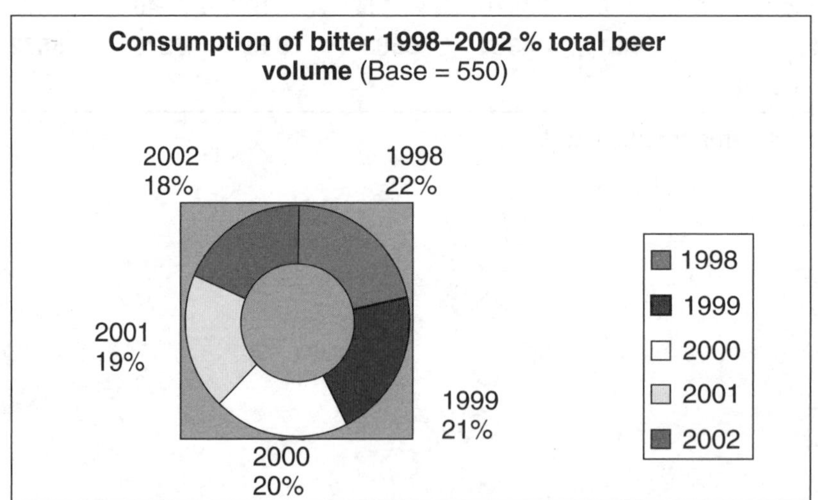

Figure 12.4

- Bar charts

These must present information in an accessible way, not like this

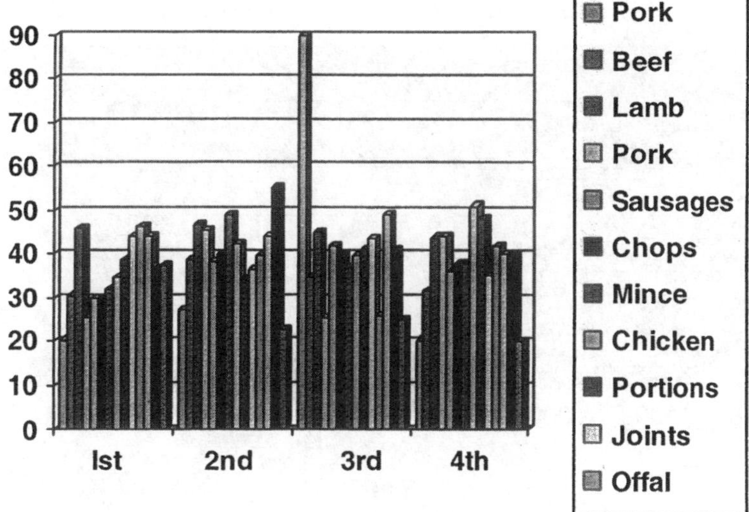

Figure 12.5

This is better:

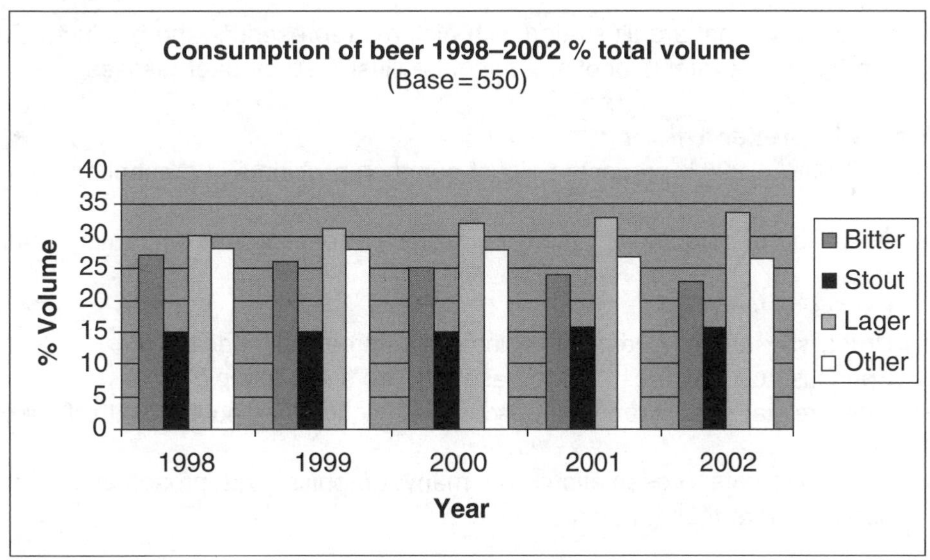

Figure 12.6

- Line graphs

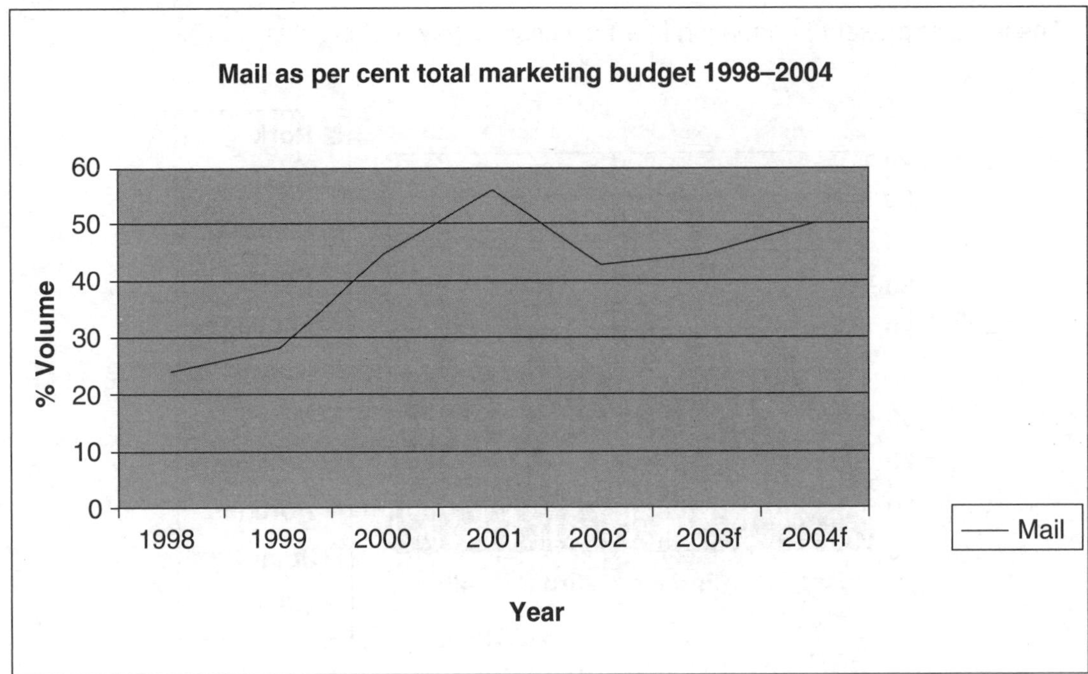

Figure 12.7

- Pictograms

These are graphics that are illustrated with pictures representing the product or object of the graphic. In the beer example above, it might be illustrated by beer glasses.

Problems in presentations

Wilson (Wilson, A., 2003) presents a list of common problems in presenting reports:

- Assuming understanding: there is insufficient background and interpretation given to results
- Excessive length
- Unrealistic recommendations which are commercially naive
- Spurious accuracy: results are based on too small sample sizes
- Obscure statistics: a range of obscure techniques may not be useful if the client cannot use them
- Over elaborate presentation: too many graphics and presentational devices may obscure more than it reveals.

Summary

This unit looked at the process of delivering results from research.

It looked at the structure of a written research report and covered each of these in depth:

- Title page
- Contents
- Executive summary
- Introduction
- Situation analysis and problem definition
- Research methodology and limitations
- Findings and analysis
- Conclusions and recommendations
- Appendices.

We went on to cover the oral presentation of the results and gave tips for presentation success:

- Introduction
- Research background and objectives
- Research methodology
- Key findings
- Conclusions and recommendations
- Questions.

We then looked at the graphical presentation of the results including:

- Tables
- Bar graphs
- Pie charts and donuts
- Line graphs
- Pictograms.

Finally, we looked at common failings in presenting results.

Further study

Question 11

List the sections of a research report and briefly outline what goes into each section.

Hints and Tips

The MRS code of conduct presents the duties of an agency to its clients in the research. Go to www.mrs.org.uk and review this.

Bibliography

Wilson, A. (2003). *Marketing research: an integrated approach*, FT Prentice Hall.

appendix 1 guidance on examination preparation

Preparing for your examination

You are now nearing the final phase of your studies and it is time to start the hard work of exam preparation.

During your period of study you will have become used to absorbing large amounts of information. You will have tried to understand and apply aspects of knowledge that may have been very new to you, while some of the information provided may have been more familiar. You may even have undertaken many of the activities that are positioned frequently throughout your Coursebook, which will have enabled you to apply your learning in practical situations. But whatever the state of your knowledge and understanding, do not allow yourself to fall into the trap of thinking that you know enough, you understand enough, or even worse, that you can just take it as it comes on the day.

Never underestimate the pressure of the CIM examination.

The whole point of preparing this text for you is to ensure that you never take the examination for granted, and that you do not go into the exam unprepared for what might come your way for three hours at a time.

One thing's for sure: there is no quick fix, no easy route, no waving a magic wand and finding you know it all.

Whether you have studied alone, in a CIM study centre, or through distance learning, you now need to ensure that this final phase of your learning process is tightly managed, highly structured and objective.

As a candidate in the examination, your role will be to convince the Senior Examiner that you have credibility for this subject. You need to demonstrate to the examiner that you can be trusted to undertake a range of challenges in the context of marketing, that you are able to capitalize on opportunities and manage your way through threats.

You should prove to the Senior Examiner that you are able to apply knowledge, make decisions, respond to situations and solve problems.

Very shortly we are going to look at a range of revision and exam preparation techniques, and at time management issues, and encourage you towards developing and implementing your own revision plan, but before that, let's look at the role of the Senior Examiner.

A bit about the Senior Examiners!

You might be quite shocked to read this, but while it might appear that the examiners are 'relentless question masters' they actually want you to be able to answer the questions and pass the exams! In fact, they would derive no satisfaction or benefits from failing candidates; quite the contrary, they develop the syllabus and exam papers in order that you can learn and then apply that learning effectively so as to pass your examinations. Many of the examiners have said in the past that it is indeed psychologically more difficult to fail students than pass them.

Many of the hints and tips you find within this Appendix have been suggested by the Senior Examiners and authors of the Coursebook series. Therefore you should consider them carefully and resolve to undertake as many of the elements suggested as possible.

The Chartered Institute of Marketing has a range of processes and systems in place within the Examinations Division to ensure that fairness and consistency prevail across the team of examiners, and that the academic and vocational standards that are set and defined are indeed maintained. In doing this, CIM ensures that those who gain the CIM Certificate (Stage 1), Advanced Certificate (Stage 2) and Postgraduate Diploma (Stage 3), are worthy of the qualification and perceived as such in the view of employers, actual and potential.

Part of what you will need to do within the examination is be 'examiner friendly' – that means you have to make sure they get what they ask for. This will make life easier for you and for them.

Hints and tips for 'examiner friendly' actions are as follows:

- Show them that you understand the basis of the question, by answering *precisely* the question asked, and not including just about everything you can remember about the subject area
- Read their needs – how many points is the question asking you to address?
- Respond to the question appropriately. Is the question asking you to take on a role? If so, take on the role and answer the question in respect of the role. For example, you could be positioned as follows:

  'You are working as a Marketing Assistant at Nike UK' or 'You are a Marketing Manager for an Engineering Company' or 'As Marketing Manager write a report to the Managing Partner'.

These examples of role-playing requirements are taken from questions in past papers.

- Deliver the answer in the format requested. If the examiner asks for a memo, then provide a memo; likewise, if the examiner asks for a report, then write a report. If you do not do this, in some instances you will fail to gain the necessary marks required to pass.
- Take a business-like approach to your answers. This enhances your credibility. Badly ordered work, untidy work, lack of structure, headings and subheadings can be

off-putting. This would be unacceptable in the work situation, likewise it will be unacceptable in the eyes of the Senior Examiners and their marking teams.

- Ensure the examiner has something to mark: give them substance, relevance, definitions, illustrations and demonstration of your knowledge and understanding of the subject area.
- See the examiner as your potential employer, or ultimate consumer/customer. The whole purpose and culture of marketing is about meeting customers' needs. Try this approach – it works wonders.
- Provide a strong sense of enthusiasm and professionalism in your answers; support it with relevant up-to-date examples and apply them where appropriate.
- Try to do something that will make your exam paper a little bit different – make it stand out in the crowd.

All of these points might seem quite logical to you, but often in the panic of the examination they 'go out of the window'. Therefore it is beneficial to remind ourselves of the importance of the examiner. He/she is the 'ultimate customer' – and we all know customers hate to be disappointed.

As we move on, some of these points will be revisited and developed further.

About the examination

In all examinations, with the exception of Marketing Management in Practice at Advanced Certificate (Stage 2) level, the paper is divided into two parts.

- Part A – Mini-case study = 50 per cent of marks
- Part B – Option choice questions (choice of two questions from four) = 50 per cent of the marks (each question attracting 25 per cent).

For the Marketing Management in Practice paper, the same approach is taken. However, all of the questions are directly related to the case study and in this instance the case material is more extensive.

Let's look at the basis of each element.

The mini-case study

This is based on a mini-case or scenario with one question, possibly subdivided into between two and four points, but totalling 50 per cent of overall marks.

In essence, you, the candidate, are placed in a problem-solving role through the medium of a short scenario. On occasions, the scenario may consist of an article from a journal in relation to a well-known organization.

Alternatively, it will be based upon a fictional company, and the examiner will have prepared it in order that the right balance of knowledge, understanding, application and skills is used.

Approaches to the mini-case study

When undertaking the mini-case study there are a number of key areas you should consider.

Structure/content

The mini-case that you will be presented with will vary slightly from paper to paper, and of course from one examination to the next. Normally the scenario presented will be 400–500 words long and will centre on a particular organization and its problems or may even relate to a specific industry. However, please note, for Marketing Management in Practice, the case study is more significant as all the questions are based upon the case materials.

The length of the mini-case study means that usually only a brief outline is provided of the situation, the organization and its marketing problems, and you must therefore learn to cope with analysing information and preparing your answer on the basis of a very limited amount of detail.

Time management

There are many differing views on time management and the approaches you can take to managing your time within the examination. You must find an approach to suit your way of working, but always remember, whatever you do, you must ensure that you allow enough time to complete the examination. Unfinished exams mean lost marks.

A typical example of managing time is as follows:

Your paper is designed to assess you over a three hour period. With 50 per cent of the marks being allocated to the mini-case, it means that you should dedicate somewhere around 100 minutes of your time to both read and write up the answer on this mini-case, leaving a further 80 minutes for the remaining questions. Some students, however, will prefer to allocate nearly half of their time (90 minutes) on the mini-case, so that they can read and fully absorb the case and answer the questions in the context of it. This is also acceptable as long as you ensure that you work extremely 'SMART' for the remaining time in order to finish the examination.

Do not forget that while there is only one question within the mini-case, it can have a number of components. You must answer all the components in that question, which is where the balance of time comes into play.

Knowledge/skills tested

Throughout all the CIM papers, your knowledge, skills and ability to apply those skills will be tested. However, the mini-cases are used particularly to test application, i.e. your ability to take your knowledge and apply it in a structured way to a given scenario. The examiners will be looking at your decision-making ability, your analytical and communication skills and, depending on the level, your ability as a manager to solve particular marketing problems.

When the examiner is marking your paper, he/she will be looking to see how you differentiate yourself, looking at your own individual 'unique selling points'. The examiner will also want to see if you can personally apply the knowledge or whether you are only able to repeat the textbook materials.

Format of answers

On many occasions, and within all examinations, you will most likely be given a particular communication method to use. If this is the case, you must ensure that you adhere to the requirements of the examiner. This is all part of meeting customer needs.

The likely communication tools you will be expected to use are as follows:

- Memorandum
- Memorandum/report
- Report
- Briefing notes
- Presentation
- Press release
- Advertisement
- Plan.

Make sure that you familiarize yourself with these particular communication tools and practise using them to ensure that, on the day, you will be able to respond confidently to the communication requests of the examiner. Look back at the Customer Communications text at Certificate level to familiarize yourself with the potential requirements of these methods.

By the same token, while communication methods are important, so is meeting the specific requirements of the question. This means you must understand what is meant by the precise instruction given. **Note the following terms carefully:**

- **Identify** Select key issues, point out key learning points, establish clearly what the examiner expects you to identify.
- **Illustrate** The examiner expects you to provide examples, scenarios and key concepts that illustrate your learning.
- **Compare and contrast** Look at the range of similarities between the two situations, contexts or even organizations. Then compare them, i.e. ascertain and list how activities, features, etc. agree or disagree. Contrasting means highlighting the differences between the two.
- **Discuss** Questions that have 'discuss' in them offer a tremendous opportunity for you to debate, argue, justify your approach or understanding of the subject area – *caution* it is not an opportunity to waffle.
- **Briefly explain** This means being succinct, structured and concise in your explanation, within the answer. Make your points clear, transparent and relevant.
- **State** Present in a clear, brief format.
- **Interpret** Expound the meaning of, make clear and explicit what it is you see and understand within the data provided.
- **Outline** Provide the examiner with the main concepts and features being asked for and avoid minor technical details. Structure will be critical here, or else you could find it difficult to contain your answer.
- **Relate** Show how different aspects of the syllabus connect together.
- **Evaluate** Review and reflect upon an area of the syllabus, a particular practice, an article, etc., and consider its overall worth in respect of its use as a tool or a model and its overall effectiveness in the role it plays.

Source: Worsam, M., *How to Pass Marketing*, Croner, 1989.

Your approach to mini-cases

There is no one right way to approach and tackle a mini-case study, indeed it will be down to each individual to use their own creativity in tackling the tasks presented. You will have to use your initiative and discretion about how best to approach the mini-case. Having said this, however, there are some basic steps you can take.

- Ensure that you read through the case study at least twice before making any judgements, starting to analyse the information provided, or indeed writing the answers.
- On the third occasion read through the mini-case and, using a highlighter, start marking the essential and relevant information critical to the content and context. Then turn your attention to the question again, this time reading slowly and carefully to assess what it is you are expected to do. Note any instructions that the examiner gives you, and then start to plan how you might answer the question. Whatever the question, ensure the answer has a structure: a beginning, a structured central part and, finally, always a conclusion.
- Keep the context of the question continually in mind: that is, the specifics of the case and the role which you might be performing.
- Because there is limited material available, you will sometimes need to make assumptions. Don't be afraid to do this, it will show initiative on your part. Assumptions are an important part of dealing with case studies and can help you to be quite creative with your answer. However, do explain the basis of your assumptions within your answer so that the examiner understands the nature of them, and why you have arrived at your particular outcome. **Always ensure that your assumptions are realistic.**
- Only now are you approaching the stage where it is time to start writing your answer to the question, tackling the problems, making decisions and recommendations on the case scenario set before you. As mentioned previously, your points will often be best set out in a report or memo type format, particularly if the examiner does not specify a communication method.
- Ensure that your writing is succinct, avoids waffle and responds directly to the questions asked.

Part B

Each Part B is comprised of four traditional questions, each worth 25 per cent. You will be expected to choose two of those questions, to make up the remaining 50 per cent of available marks. (Again please note that the structure is the same for Marketing Management in Practice, but that all questions are applied to the case study.)

Realistically, the same principles apply for these questions as in the case study. Communication formats, reading through the questions, structure, role-play, context, etc. – everything is the same.

Part B will cover a number of broader issues from within the syllabus and will be taken from any element of it. The examiner makes the choice, and no prior direction is given to students or tutors on what that might be.

As regards time management in this area, if you used about 100 minutes for the mini-case you should have around 80 minutes left. This provides you with around 40 minutes to plan and write a question, to write, review and revise your answers. Keep practising – use a cooker timer, alarm clock or mobile phone alarm as your timer and work hard at answering questions within the time-frame given.

Specimen examination papers and answers

To help you prepare and understand the nature of the paper, go to www.cimeduhub.com to access Specimen Answers and Senior Examiner's advice for these exam questions. During your study, the author of your Coursebook may have, on occasions, asked you to refer to these papers and answer the questions. You should undertake these exercises and utilize every opportunity to practise meeting examination requirements.

Each of the Advanced Certificate (Stage 2) coursebooks have, at the end of them, some examination questions and guidance provided by the authors and senior examiners, where appropriate, to provide you with some insight into the types of questions asked.

The specimen answers are vital learning tools. They are not always perfect, as they are answers written by students and annotated by the Senior Examiners, but they will give you a good indication of the approaches you could take, and the examiners' annotations suggest how these answers might be improved. Please use them.

Other sources of information to support your learning through the Virtual Institute are 'Hot Topics'. These give you scope to undertake a range of associated activities related to the syllabus and study areas, and will also be very useful to you when you are revising.

Key elements of preparation

One Senior Examiner suggests the three elements involved in preparing for your examination can be summarized thus:

- Learning
- Memory
- Revision.

Let's look at each point in turn.

Learning

Quite often students find it difficult to learn properly. You can passively read books, look at some of the materials, perhaps revise a little, and regurgitate it all in the examination. In the main, however, this is rather an unsatisfactory method of learning. It is meaningless, shallow and ultimately of little use in practice.

For learning to be truly effective it must be active and applied. You must involve yourself in the learning process by thinking about what you have read, testing it against your experience by reflecting on how you use particular aspects of marketing, and how you could perhaps improve your own performance by implementing particular aspects of your learning into your everyday life. You should adopt the old adage of 'learning by doing'. If you do, you will find that passive learning has no place in your study life.

Below are some suggestions that have been prepared to assist you with the learning pathway throughout your revision.

- Always make your own notes, in words you understand, and ensure that you combine all the sources of information and activities within them
- Always try to relate your learning back to your own organization
- Make sure you define key terms concisely, wherever possible

- Do not try to memorize your ideas, but work on the basis of understanding and, most important, applying them
- Think about the relevant and topical questions that might be set – use the questions and answers in your Coursebooks to identify typical questions that might be asked in the future
- Attempt all of the questions within each of your Coursebooks since these are vital tests of your active learning and understanding.

Memory

If you are prepared to undertake an active learning programme then your knowledge will be considerably enhanced, as understanding and application of knowledge does tend to stay in your 'long-term' memory. It is likely that passive learning will only stay in your 'short-term' memory.

Do not try to memorize in parrot fashion; it is not helpful and, even more important, examiners are experienced in identifying various memorizing techniques and therefore will spot them as such.

Having said this, it is quite useful to memorize various acronyms such as SWOT, PEST, PESTEL, STEEPLE, or indeed various models such as Ansoff, GE Matrix, Shell Directional Policy Matrix, etc., as in some of the questions you may be required to use illustrations of these to assist your answer.

Revision

The third and final stage to consider is 'revision', which is what we will concentrate on in detail below. Here just a few key tips are offered.

Revision should be an ongoing process rather than a panic measure that you decide to undertake just before the examination. You should be preparing notes *throughout* your course, with the view to using them as part of your revision process. Therefore ensure that your notes are sufficiently comprehensive that you can reuse them successfully.

For each concept you learn about, you should identify, through your reading and your own personal experience, at least two or three examples that you could use; this then gives you some scope to broaden your perspective during the examination. It will, of course, help you gain some points for initiative with the examiners.

Knowledge is not something you will gain overnight – as we saw earlier, it is not a quick fix; it involves a process of learning that enables you to lay solid foundations upon which to build your long-term understanding and application. This will benefit you significantly in the future, not just in the examination.

In essence, you should ensure that you do the following in the period before the real intensive revision process begins:

- Keep your study file well organized, updated and full of newspaper and journal cuttings that may help you formulate examples in your mind for use during the examination
- Practise defining key terms and acronyms from memory
- Prepare topic outlines and essay answer plans
- When you start your intensive revision, ensure it is planned and structured in the way described below. And then finally, read your concentrated notes the night before the examination.

Revision planning

You are now on a critical path – although hopefully not too critical at this time – with somewhere in the region of between four and six weeks to go to the examination. The following hints and tips will help you plan out your revision study:

- You will, as already explained, need to be very organized. Therefore, before doing anything else, put your files, examples, reading material, etc. in good order, so that you are able to work with them in the future and, of course, make sense of them.
- Ensure that you have a quiet area within which to work. It is very easy to get distracted when preparing for an examination.
- Take out your file along with your syllabus, and make a list of key topic areas that you have studied and which you now need to revise. You could use the basis of this book to do that, by taking each unit a step at a time.
- Plan the use of your time carefully. Ideally you should start your revision at least six weeks prior to the exam, so therefore work out how many spare hours you could give to the revision process and then start to allocate time in your diary, and do not double-book with anything else.
- Give up your social life for a short period of time. As the saying goes 'no pain – no gain'.
- Looking at each of the subject areas in turn, identify which are your strengths and which are your weaknesses. Which areas have you grasped and understood, and which are the areas that you have really struggled with? Split your page into two and make a list on each side. For example:

Planning and control

Strengths	Weaknesses
Audit – PEST, SWOT, Models	Ratio analysis
Portfolio analysis	Market sensing
	Productivity analysis
	Trend extrapolation
	Forecasting

- Break down your list again and divide the points of weakness, giving priority in the first instance to your weakest areas and even prioritizing them by giving each of them a number. This will enable you to master the more difficult areas. Up to 60 per cent of your remaining revision time should be given over to that, as you may find you have to undertake a range of additional reading and also perhaps seeking tutor support, if you are studying at a CIM Accredited Study Centre.
- The rest of the time should be spent reinforcing your knowledge and understanding of the stronger areas, spending time testing yourself on how much you really know.
- Should you be taking two examinations or more at any one time, then the breakdown and managing of your time will be critical.
- Taking a subject at a time, work through your notes and start breaking them down into subsections of learning, and ultimately into key learning points, items that you can refer to time and time again, that are meaningful and that your mind will absorb. You yourself will know how you best remember key points. Some people try to develop acronyms, or flowcharts or matrices, mind maps, fishbone diagrams, etc., or various connection diagrams that help them recall certain aspects of models. You could also develop processes that enable you to remember approaches to various options. (But do remember what we said earlier about regurgitating stuff, parrot fashion.)

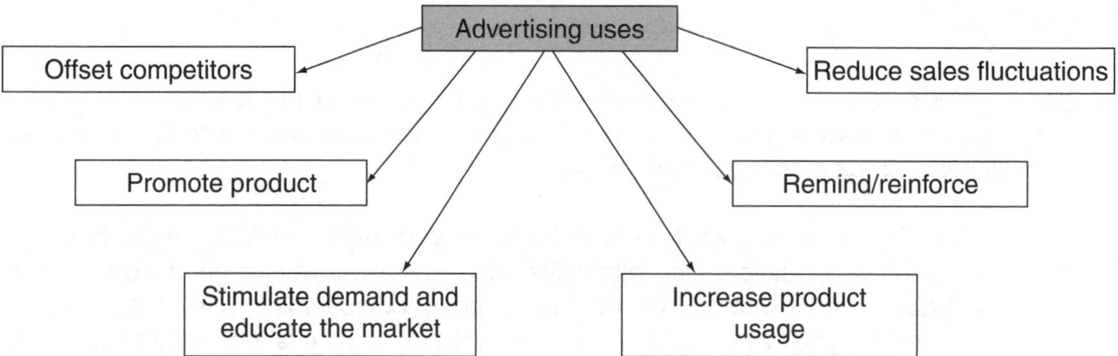

Figure A1.1 Use of a diagram to summarize key components of a concept
Source: Adapted from Dibb, Simkin, Pride and Ferrell, *Marketing Concepts and Strategies,* 4th edition, Houghton Mifflin, 2001.

Figure A1.1 is just a brief example of how you could use a 'bomb-burst' diagram (which, in this case, highlights the uses of advertising) as a very helpful approach to memorizing key elements of learning.

- Eventually you should reduce your key learning to bullet points. For example: imagine you were looking at the concept of Time Management – you could eventually reduce your key learning to a bullet list containing the following points in relation to 'Effective Prioritization'.
  - Organize
  - Take time
  - Delegate
  - Review.

Each of these headings would then remind you of the elements you need to discuss associated with the subject area.

- Avoid getting involved in reading too many textbooks at this stage, as you may start to find that you are getting confused overall.
- Look at examination questions on previous papers, and start to observe closely the various roles and tasks they expect you to undertake, and importantly, the context in which they are set.
- **Use the specimen exam papers and specimen answers** to support your learning and see how you could actually improve upon them.
- Without exception, find an associated examination question for the areas that you have studied and revised, and undertake it (more than once if necessary).
- Without referring to notes or books, try to draft an answer plan with the key concepts, knowledge, models and information that are needed to successfully complete the answer. Then refer to the specimen answer to see how close you are to the actual outline presented. Planning your answer, and ensuring that key components are included and that the question has a meaningful structure, is one of the most beneficial activities that you can undertake.
- Now write the answer out in full, time-constrained and written by hand, not with the use of IT. (At this stage, you are still expected to be the scribe for the examination and present handwritten work. Many of us find this increasingly difficult as we spend more and more time using our computers to present information. Do your best to be neat. Spidery handwriting is often off putting to the examiner.)

- When writing answers as part of your revision process, also be sure to practise the following essential examinations techniques:

  - Identify and use the communication method requested by the examiner
  - Always have three key parts to the answer – an introduction, a middle section that develops your answer in full, and a conclusion. Where appropriate, ensure that you have an introduction, main section, summary/conclusion and, if requested or helpful, recommendations
  - Always answer the question in the context or role set
  - Always comply with the nature and terms of the question
  - Leave white space. Do not overcrowd your page; leave space between paragraphs, and make sure your sentences do not merge into one blur. (Don't worry – there is always plenty of paper available to use in the examination)
  - Count how many actions the question asks you to undertake and double-check at the end that you have met the full range of demands of the question
  - Use examples – to demonstrate your knowledge and understanding of the particular syllabus area. These can be from journals, the Internet, the press, or your own experience
  - Display your vigour and enthusiasm for marketing. Remember to think of the Senior Examiner as your Customer, or future employer, and do your best to deliver what is wanted to satisfy their needs. Impress them and show them how you are a 'cut above the rest'
  - Review all your practice answers critically, with the above points in mind.

Practical actions

The critical path is becoming even more critical now as the examination looms. The following are vital points:

- Have you registered with CIM?
- Do you know where you are taking your examination? CIM should let you know approximately one month in advance
- Do you know where your examination centre is? If not find out, take a drive, time it – whatever you do don't be late!
- Make sure you have all the tools of the examination ready. A dictionary, calculator, pens, pencils, ruler, etc. Try not to use multiple shades of pens, but at the same time make your work look professional. *Avoid using red and green as these are the colours that will be used for marking.*

Summary

Above all, you must remember that you personally have invested a tremendous amount of time, effort and money in studying for this programme and it is therefore imperative that you consider the suggestions given here as they will help to maximize your return on your investment.

Many of the hints and tips offered here are generic and will work across most of the CIM courses. We have tried to select those that will help you most in taking a sensible, planned approach to your study and revision.

The key to your success is being prepared to put in the time and effort required, planning your revision, and equally important is planning and answering your questions in a way that will ensure that you pass your examination on the day.

The advice offered here aims to guide you from a practical perspective. Guidance on syllabus content and developments associated with your learning will become clear to you as you work through this Coursebook. The authors of each Coursebook have given subject-specific guidance on the approach to the examination and on how to ensure that you meet the content requirements of the kind of question you will face. These considerations are in addition to the structuring issues we have been discussing throughout this Appendix.

Each of the authors and Senior Examiners will guide you on their preferred approach to questions and answers as they go. Therefore where you are presented with an opportunity to be involved in some activity or undertake an examination question either during or at the end of your study units, do take it. It not only prepares you for the examination, but also helps you learn in the applied way we discussed above.

Here, then, is a last reminder:

- Ensure you make the most of your learning process throughout
- Keep structured and orderly notes from which to revise
- Plan your revision – don't let it just happen
- Provide examples to enhance your answers
- Practise your writing skills in order that you present your work well and your writing is readable
- Take as many opportunities as possible to test your knowledge and measure your progress
- Plan and structure your answers
- Always do as the question asks you, especially with regard to context and communication method
- **Do not leave it until the last minute!**

The writers would like to take this opportunity to wish you every success in your endeavours to study, to revise and to pass your examinations.

Karen Beamish
Academic Development Advisor

appendix 2 undertaking CIM assignments and the integrative project

Introduction – the basis to the assignments and the integrative project

Within the CIM qualifications at both Stage One and Stage Two there are several assessment options available. These are detailed in the outline of modules below. The purpose of an assignment is to provide another format to complete each module for students who want to apply the syllabus concepts from a module to their own or a selected organization. For either qualification, there are three modules providing assessment via an assignment and one module assessed via an integrative work-based project. The module assessed via the integrative project is the summative module for each qualification.

	Entry modules	Research & analysis	Planning	Implementation	Management of Marketing
STAGE 3	Entry module–Stage 3	New syllabus to be launched in September 2004			
		Currently all modules assessed via examination route only			
STAGE 2	Entry module–Stage 2	**Marketing Research & Information**	**Marketing Planning**	**Marketing Communications**	**Marketing Management in Practice**
		All assessed via examination or assignment			***Exam/Integrative Project***
STAGE 1		**Marketing Environment**	**Marketing Fundamentals**	**Customer Communications**	**Marketing in Practice**
		All assessed via examination or assignment			***Exam/Integrative Project***
Introductory Certificate		Supporting marketing processes (research & analysis, planning & implementation)			

Adapted from the outline of CIM 'standard' syllabus, October 2002

The use of assignments does not mean that this route is easier than an examination. Both formats are carefully evaluated to ensure that a grade B in the assessment/integrative project route is the same as a grade B in an examination. However, the use of assignments does allow a student to complete the assessment for a module over a longer period of time than a three-hour examination. This will inevitably mean work being undertaken over the time-span of a module. For those used to cramming for exams, writing an assignment over several weeks which comprises a total of four separate questions will be a very different approach.

Each module within the qualification contains a different assignment written specifically for the module. These are designed to test understanding and provide the opportunity for you to demonstrate your abilities through the application of theory to practice. The format and structure of each module's assignment is identical, although the questions asked will differ and the exact type of assignment varies. The questions within an assignment will relate directly to the syllabus for that particular module, thereby giving the opportunity to demonstrate understanding and application.

The assignment structure

The assignment for each module is broken down into a range of questions. These consist of a core question, a selection of optional questions plus a reflective statement. The core question will always relate to the main aspects of each module's syllabus. Coupled with this are a range of four optional questions which will each draw from a different part of the syllabus. Students are requested to select two optional questions from the four available. In addition, a reflective statement requires a student to evaluate their learning from the module. When put together, these form the assessment for the entire module. The overall pass mark for the module is the same as through an examination route, which is set at 50 per cent. In addition, the grade band structure is also identical to that of an examination.

Core question

This is the longest and therefore the most important section of your assignment. Covering the major components of the syllabus, the core question is designed to provide a challenging assignment which both tests the theoretical element and also permits application to a selected organization or situation. The question itself will require a written answer of approximately 2,500 words (Stage One) or 3,000 words (Stage Two) in addition to any further information you may wish to provide. This additional information should be in the form of appendices. However, the appendices should be kept to a minimum. Advice here is that they should be no longer than five pages of additional pertinent information.

Optional questions

There are a total of four questions provided for Stage One and Stage Two of the syllabus from which a student is asked to select two. Each answer is expected to provide a challenge, although the actual task required varies. The word counts are also lower than the core question at 1,000 words (Stage One) and 1,500 words (Stage Two).

These are designed to test areas of the syllabus not covered by the core question. As such it is possible to base all of your questions on the same organization although there is significant benefit in using more than one organization as a basis for your assignment. Some of the questions specifically require a different organization to be selected from the one used for the core question. This only occurs where the questions are requiring similar areas to be investigated and will be specified clearly on the question itself.

Within the assignment, there are several types of questions that may be asked, including:

- ***A report*** The question requires a formal report to be completed, detailing an answer to the specific question set. This will often be reporting on a specific issue to an individual.
- ***A briefing paper or notes*** Preparing a briefing paper or a series of notes which may be used for a presentation.
- ***A presentation*** You may be required to either prepare the presentation only or deliver the presentation in addition to its preparation. The audience for the presentation should be considered carefully and ICT used where possible.
- ***A discussion paper*** The question requires an academic discussion paper to be prepared. You should show a range of sources and concepts within the paper. You may also be required to present the discussion paper as part of a question.
- ***A project plan or action plan*** Some questions ask for planning techniques to be demonstrated. As such, the plan must be for the timescale given and costs shown where applicable. The use of ICT is recommended here in order to create the plan diagrammatically.
- ***Planning a research project*** Whilst market research may be required, questions have often asked for simply a research plan in a given situation. This would normally include timescales, the type(s) of research to be gathered, sampling, planned data collection and analysis.
- ***Conducting research*** Following on from a research plan, a question can require student(s) to undertake a research gathering exercise. A research question can be either an individual or a group activity depending upon the question. This will usually result in a report of the findings of the exercise plus any recommendations arising from your findings.
- ***Gathering of information and reporting*** Within many questions, information will need gathering. The request for information can form part or all of a question. This may be a background to the organization, the activities contained in the question or external market and environmental information. It is advisable to detail the types of information utilized, their sources and report on any findings. Such a question will often ask for recommendations for the organization – these should be drawn from the data and not simply personal opinion.
- ***An advisory document*** A question here will require students to evaluate a situation and present advice and recommendations drawn from findings and theory. Again, any advice should be backed up with evidence and not a personal perspective only.
- ***An exercise, either planning and/or delivering the exercise*** At both Stage One and Stage Two, exercises are offered as optional questions. These provide students with the opportunity to devise an exercise and may also require the delivery of this exercise. Such an activity should be evidenced where possible.
- ***A role-play with associated documentation*** Several questions have asked students to undertake role plays in exercises such as team-building. These are usually videoed, and documentation demonstrating the objectives of the exercise provided.

Each of these questions related directly towards specific issues to be investigated, evaluated and answered. In addition, some of the questions asked present situations to be considered. These provide opportunities for specific answers relating directly to the question asked.

In order to aid students completing the assignment, each question is provided with an outline of marking guidance. This relates to the different categories by which each question is marked. The marker of your assignment will be provided with a detailed marking scheme constructed around the same marking guidance provided to students.

For both the core and optional questions, it is important to use referencing where sources have been utilized. This has been a weakness in the past and continues to be an issue. There have been cases of plagiarism identified during marking and moderation, together with a distinct lack of references and bibliography. This becomes more important at Stage Two where the nature of the syllabus lends itself to a more academic approach. It is highly recommended that a bibliography be included with each question and sources are cited within the text itself. The type of referencing method used is not important, only that sources are referred to.

The reflective statement

This is the final aspect to each module assignment. The purpose of the reflective statement is for each student to consider how the module has influenced him/her as an individual and reflected upon his/her practice. A shorter piece of work than for other aspects at 500 words (Stage One) or 750 words (Stage Two), it is also more personal in that your answer will often depend upon how you as an individual have applied the learning from the module to your work and other aspects.

A good reflective statement will comprise a number of aspects, including:

- Details of the theoretical aspects that you found beneficial within the module, and their reasons. If you have found particular resources beneficial, state this and the reason why
- How these concepts have affected you as a practitioner with examples of application of concepts from the module to your work and/or other activities
- How you intend to progress your learning further after completing the module assessment.

When looking at the reflective statement, your tutor or an assessor will try to award marks for your demonstration of understanding through the module together with how you have applied the theoretical concepts to practice. They are looking for evidence of learning and application over time, rather than a student simply completing the question because they have a deadline looming. The result of this marking tends to be that students who begin to apply the module concepts early, often achieve higher marks overall.

Integrative project structure

The integrative project is designed to provide an in-company approach to assessment rather than having specified assignments. Utilized within the summative module element of each level's syllabus, this offers a student the chance to produce a piece of work which tackles a specific issue. The integrative project can only be completed after undertaking other modules as it will rely on information in each of these as guidance. The integrative project is approximately 5,000 words in length and was introduced from September 2002 at the Stage One level. It will be introduced from September 2003 at Stage Two with the commencement of the new syllabus. The integrative project is marked by CIM assessors and not your own tutors.

Stage Two assignments – Marketing Research and Information

This module covers five different elements all relating to the subject area of marketing information. This covers the use of ICT and databases, together with the entire marketing research process. The result is a range of opportunities for questions relating to the module and its element to be asked. Questions can cover the role of ICT in an organization, together with planning market research or the use of market research data.

Element 1– Information and research for decision-making

This element forms the foundation for all other aspects within the module by setting the role and purpose of marketing information into context. The purpose of information is covered within the element together with issues of marketing information requirements and support systems. This leads towards questions which centre on the need for information and how it may be used:

Your manager has asked you to prepare a presentation on the use and value of marketing information. This will form part of an all-day set of workshops and presentations used within the in-company programme 'Run-around'. This aims to give employees throughout the organization an insight into other job roles and activities. The presentation is to last approximately 30 minutes together with associated handout(s).

The first aspect of this question is the setting. The organization's employees could come from any area or job role. As such, the presentation will need to assume no knowledge whatsoever, aiming to build-up an understanding and appreciation of the subject. Elements contained within an answer to this question include:

- Setting the scene; the organization itself together with a picture of the typical roles and activities of the employees. This can be part of the introductory setting within the presentation or a separate component of the answer.
- An introduction to marketing information and its purpose, together with the setting of marketing information within marketing and market research. This is required due to the audience comprising employees from every part of the organization.
- The need for information and knowledge management will require explaining as part of the presentation.
- The application of information to different issues needs to be covered. Incorporating examples from a range of organizational areas would be beneficial here.
- Finally, within the presentation the use of support systems is required.
- The presentation should be supplied on disk together with a paper copy. In addition, there needs to be a handout containing the presentation plus notes at a level appropriate to the non-marketer. A good handout will cover more than simply the presentation – it will often come in a typed format, with suitable examples to illustrate the points made in the presentation.

Element 2 – Customer databases

The second element of the module addresses aspects of the role of databases together with database management. This draws into consideration aspects of the role of databases, customer profiling and the use of databases within market research. Questions drawn from this element will use databases as their foundation, building in other aspects of the syllabus in order to cover the element.

Taking an organization of your choice, investigate the current customer database in operation and its use for Customer Relationship Management. Make appropriate recommendations for the potential use of the database together with a consideration of how this data can be used for improved marketing performance.

Element two covers the use of databases in detail. Therefore an answer to a question will require an in-depth analysis of issues deriving from the element. With this element comprising only 15 per cent of the module syllabus, it is unlikely that an entire core question would be drawn from this element. An answer needs to include the following:

- A background to the organization selected for the question, their use of information and current approach to Customer Relationship Management.
- The second component of an answer would cover the use of information within the organization. This includes how customer records are kept and accessed.
- An answer would examine how information is utilized and the process of gathering market research from customer data. Where this is not undertaken, later recommendations would cover the process of establishing a data collection and analysis mechanism.
- Recommendations made would centre around improved use of data and customer information. They should incorporate both a theoretical and practical perspective, relating theory to practice.
- The format of a response to the question should be laid out as a report, directly relating to the organization type selected in the answer.

Element 3 – Marketing research in context

This element forms the foundation of study regarding market research. It identifies the role market research has to play, together with the market research process, issues regarding research and a market research proposal. This will provide several opportunities to ask questions regarding the basis for market research and the process itself.

Your class has been approached to develop the proposal for a market research activity investigating issues of stakeholder perceptions of the CIM centre/an organization of your choice. The supplier's brief for the proposal includes the following elements:

- A research brief
- A specification of the research proposed
- Types of secondary/primary data to be used
- Sampling
- Any social/ethical issues arising from the proposed research.

Individually, develop a research proposal and presentation covering all the aspects.

The brief provides little information regarding the type of research required. Therefore, there exists considerable scope to provide an answer aimed at a situation selected by the student. The answer would need to cover the components of element 3. In addition, part of element 4 is drawn into the question as an answer requires a consideration of both primary and secondary data plus the sampling approach. An answer would consist of:

- A description of the situation given. This needs to cover the issue selected and a description of the stakeholders involved. For example, a college would have a range of stakeholders including the students, employees, local and national government, suppliers, businesses together with the local and wider population.
- The market research process needs explaining, plus the components of a marketing plan. This draws the theoretical perspective and combines theory with a practical situation.
- The types of information required by the client can be defined next within an answer plus a decision as to whether primary or secondary data is appropriate in each circumstance.

- It would be beneficial to propose a sampling methodology as part of the research plan and incorporate this into the proposal report given to the client.
- The final stage would be to prepare a presentation for the client outlining the research approach. The question does not ask for the presentation to be made, only that this is prepared. A presentation needs to be provided on disk in addition to paper format.

Element 4 – Research methodologies

The fourth component of the module is aimed at the specifics of data gathering methodologies. These cover both quantitative and qualitative mechanisms, including primary and secondary data. In addition, the element includes sampling and the roles of each data type. Questions which arise from this module include:

Your line manager wishes to gather data to answer a specific research problem. Evaluate the types of data available, both primary and secondary. Compare and contrast each type of research mechanisms to meet data gathering requirements, together with a discussion of the value and methods of sampling.

An answer to this question could cover a wide range of aspects. As this element is the most likely to form a core question, an answer will be quite detailed. The information needed here will range from an organizational setting to the evaluation of appropriate research methods to solve an identified problem.

- The setting of an answer is the first component here. This will require both an organization plus a specific research problem.
- The second element is to consider the available research, in order to identify potential sources of primary and/or secondary data.
- Each of the sources should be identified, drawing on the components of element 4. This needs to include an evaluation of the benefits and limitations of both primary and secondary data, together with the respective types of research. In addition, the use of qualitative and quantitative data should also be evaluated.
- An answer needs to incorporate issues of sampling and types of sampling, in order for the research to be appropriate and valid.
- Finally, the format of an answer to the question is not given. An appropriate choice would be a report, identifying the research problem and organization, leading into a discussion of the available sources of data. The answer would then lead onto an evaluation of potential data sources and recommendations made.

Element 5 – Presenting and evaluating information to develop business advantage

The final element in the Market Research and Information module covers the use of data that has already been gathered. Building on all other aspects of the module, the element covers issues such as data analysis, presentation of data and the development of recommendations built on findings. As such, this element leads to two types of questions. The first type of question draws in element 4 (Research methodologies) and would require a research project to be conducted, analysed and presented with recommendations made. The second type of question takes already gathered data and presents findings. Two example questions are shown below:

A regional charity has a declining base of donors, and little use of customer information. As their advisor, you have been asked to give a presentation on their chances for success in gaining funding. However, the data available shows that there is little opportunity for sources of funding from current donors. Therefore, you should incorporate a discussion on potential research and sources of information that will highlight both donor data and other data sources.

or

As part of the management of your CIM course, the college is intending to identify a range of perceptions regarding the quality of the college and your course in particular with the aim of using customer data for improved CRM. Identify a range of potential sources of information which would enable accurate and detailed data to be gathered. Evaluate these sources, preparing a research proposal which details the planned research methodology. Conduct the research and analyse the data. Prepare a presentation and report demonstrating your findings with suitable recommendations drawn from the data.

Both of these relate to the presentation of data, which is element 5. They draw in components from other elements, with the charity question considering customer (donor) data and the CIM centre question drawing in sections of elements 3 and 4. The second question would also act as a stand-alone core question due to the volume of research and analysis required. Covering the presentation aspect, a typical answer would include:

- A background to the situation and the available research. This would set the scene for either question.
- The data should be shown visually in both PowerPoint and word-processed format. Where possible, statistics need to be given to back up any points made.
- Recommendations should be drawn from the data. A recommendation is best related directly back to the data, emphasizing the point(s) made.
- A presentation would normally include a handout containing the notes, with the answer being submitted in both paper format and electronically on disk or CD-ROM.

Assignment regulations

There have been a number of changes to the assignment structure compared with previous years, timed with the introduction of the new syllabus. These have been designed to provide consistency in approach for a student whether they are completing the assessment for a module by examination, assignment or integrative project. The more significant changes include:

- For the current academic year, tutors at CIM centres will mark assignments. These are then moderated by CIM assessors. An integrative project is marked by CIM assessors only.
- No resubmission of assignments, as per an examination. In previous years a range of assignments were being submitted. Where a student does not achieve the 50 per cent pass mark, they are requested to re-take the assessment for the module through examination or assignment/integrative project.
- Whichever assessment route is selected, it is fixed rather than having the option to change at the last minute. Past history has shown that students sometimes begin on an assignment route, change to an examination at the last minute due to not meeting a deadline and then score badly in the examination. The paths to an assignment and to an examination are different and therefore it is unadvisable to switch, which is the reason for the change of rule.
- In the 2002–3 academic year word limits for questions and assignments were introduced. This was introduced due to assignments being submitted which were of a wide variety of lengths. These ranged from under 2,000 words to over 25,000 words.

Where a student is completing four modules by assignment this would equal over 100,000 words – the equivalent of a medium-sized textbook or novel. As such it became impossible for two assignments to be considered together. Therefore the word-limit guidance was introduced in order to provide equality for all students undertaking assessment by assignment.

- Two sets of assignments per year as with the examination route. With this change students are required to complete the assignment aimed at the nearest examination session. Previously students had between 3 months and 9 months to complete an assignment depending upon whether it was given out in September for a June deadline or March for the June deadline. Therefore a decision was made to follow the examination route with the intention of giving all students equal time to complete an assignment.

These summarize the key changes which have occurred due to the introduction of new syllabuses with the assignment/integrative project route in order that there is parity of assessment at all levels and using all formats. Some of these changes have been significant, others minor. However, all the changes have been considered thoughtfully and with the best intentions for the student in mind.

Use of case studies

For anyone who is not working or has difficulty in access to information on their or another organization, there are a number of case studies available which allow the completion of a module using a case-based approach rather than basing it upon an organization identified by the student. These case studies are provided on a request-only basis through your accredited CIM centre and should only be used as a last resort. Using a case study as the basis for your assignment will not mean an easier approach to the assignment. However, they do provide an opportunity to undertake assignments when no other alternative exists. Each case study comes with a certain amount of information which can be used specifically for the completion of a question. Additional information may need to be assumed or researched in order to create a comprehensive assignment.

Submission of assignments/integrative project

The following information will aid both yourself and your tutor who marks your work and also the CIM assessor who will be moderating your work and the integrative project. In addition, the flow diagram represents the process of an assignment/integrative project from start to final mark.

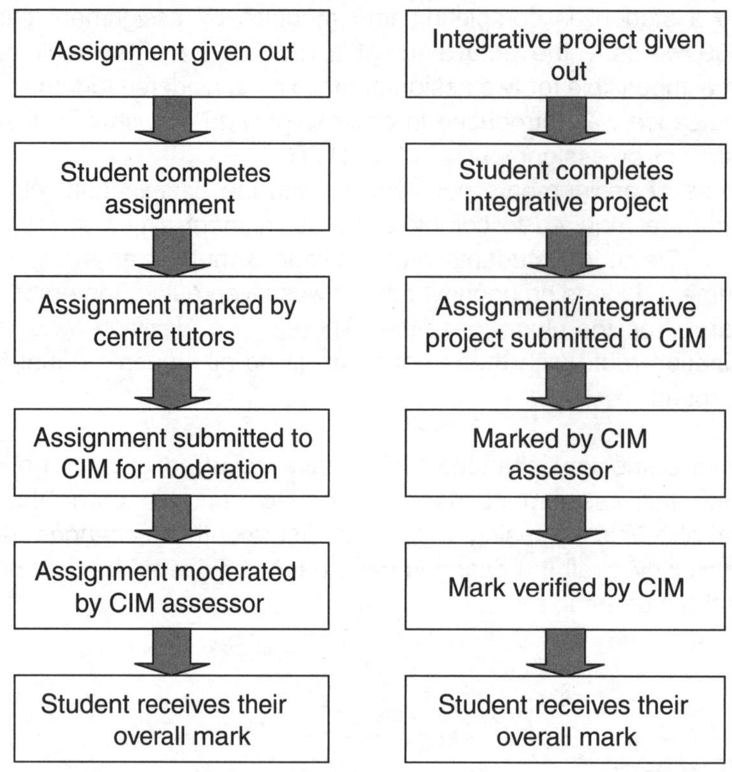

When completing and submitting assignments or the integrative project, refer to the following for guidance:

- Read through each question before starting out. Particularly with the core question, there will be a considerable amount work to undertake. Choose your optional questions wisely.
- Answer the question set and use the mark guidance given regarding the marking scheme.
- Reference each question within the assignment and use a bibliography.
- Complete all documentation thoroughly. This is designed to aid both the CIM and yourself.
- Ensure that the assignment is bound as per instructions given. Currently, assignments are requested not to be submitted in plastic wallets or folders as work can become detached or lost. Following the submission instructions provided aids both the CIM administrators and the CIM assessor who will be marking (integrative project) or moderating (assignments) your work.
- Complete the candidate declaration sheet showing that you have undertaken this work yourself. **Please note that if you wish the information contained in your assignment to remain confidential you must state this on the front of the assignment.** Whilst CIM assessors will not use any information pertaining to your or another organization, CIM may wish to use the answer to a question as an example.

An assignment will be marked by a tutor at your CIM centre followed by moderation by a CIM assessor. The integrative project will be marked by a CIM assessor as per an examination with moderation by the CIM. To ensure objectivity by CIM assessors, there exists a mark-in meeting prior to any marking in order that standardization can occur. The senior assessor for each subject also undertakes further verification of both examinations and assessments to ensure parity between each type of assessment.

David C. Lane
Senior Moderator (Advanced Certificate)
February 2003

appendix 3 exam questions

Learning objectives

After completing this unit you will be familiar with the type of questions that may be asked in the exam.

You will be able to identify the structure to answer these questions.

Question 1

You are the marketing manger for a major supplier of computer hardware, mainly to the consumer market. The company has a database of 350,000 active customers. The company wishes to enter the small office/home office sector. You have been given the job of researching and contributing to the development of the marketing plan for this new venture. The board feels that their investment on the database should be adequate to inform the development process.

Write a report to the board outlining the following:

- How the database and marketing research will work together to help the marketing planning process?
- In order to convince the board, illustrate you report with examples from other industries.
- This question is fairly straightforward

Answer

Introduction
How information works to produce better decisions in companies. What decisions will the company need to make and how can research and the database facilitate these decisions.

How information is managed, cover the MkIS briefly.

Define your terms.

What is marketing? What is marketing research? What is database marketing?

Main body
Outline the marketing planning process. You may use one of a number of different frameworks:

- Analysis
- Objectives
- Strategy
- Tactics
- Control.

Under each of these headings, show how research and the database can contribute to decision-making.

Make all points relevant to the business context.

Make sure that you include examples. These can be built-in at each stage of your answer or can be included as a separate section at the end.

Try to cover a range of examples, may be online or business-to-business (b2b) examples. Use your file of examples to inform this section.

Conclusion
Why companies need information.

Constraints on the use of data – ethics and legislation.

Future – where will we be in five years.

Question 2

You have been appointed as marketing manager for the Drama Factory, a small regional arts and entertainments venue. You want to develop a marketing database to facilitate the marketing of the centre, but need to convince the trustees of the centre of its value in order to receive funding.

Write a report for the trustees outlining the process involved in establishing a database for marketing.

How will external suppliers help this process?

What applications will the database facilitate?

Outline answer

Define the marketing database and outline its role in marketing decision-making. Outline the process of setting up the database. Under each heading, discuss the requirements for good practice:

- Business review
- Data audit
- Data strategy, specification and verification
- Data verification
- Hardware/software
- Data capture, maintenance and enhancement
- Management issues – should the database be run in-house/out-of-house
- Applications
- Review.

Discuss the advantages and disadvantages of in-house operation.

Disadvantages

- Cost of hardware and consultancy may be significant
- Speed of development can be slow
- Service standards may be lower than those from an out-of-house provider
- Skills in IT and strategy may be weak
- Specialist processing skills may not be readily available.

Advantages

- Strategic orientation of the business should be assured
- Integration and access is manageable
- Greater control and ownership
- Cost may be lower.

Finally, outline the advantages of data bureaux.

Database bureaux have the following advantages

- Skills and systems are developed and tested
- No fixed costs. You pay for what you get
- Speed. Resources can be allocated to ensure prompt delivery and penalty clauses can be built in
- Performance guarantees can be built into the contract.

Often, there is migration from the bureau into the organization. This means that learning can take place at lower risk. The usual approach is outlined below:

- Set up at the bureau
- Sort out data issues
- Set up updates and enhancements
- Develop internally
- Run the two in parallel
- Import.

Conclude by focusing on the need to establish a business case for a database and establishing the most cost-effective solution.

Applications can be structured around the marketing planning process. This includes analysis, objective setting, segmentation, the development of strategies, campaigns and controls, or as the text identifies find, acquire, develop, keep and reactivate. You should give examples relevant to the context of the question.

Question 3

You are the marketing manager for a company marketing china collectibles. You wish to establish an online service for your products. You wish to recruit a research agency to evaluate the potential of this market. Write a briefing document for the project. Explain how you would choose a short list of agencies to pitch for your business and how you would go about selecting the company to do the work.

Answer

This question asks for a report-type approach. The briefing document outline provides a good structure. You should write the answer as you would lay out a brief in real life, and the use of separate pages for each section, numbered sections and even a contents page and executive summary can show an examiner that you are in control of the paper.

Remember the structure of the briefing document?

- Identification details
- Current business position
- Marketing and business objectives should be laid down and distinguished between
- Research objectives
- How the results will be used
- Outline methodology
- Sample details
- Previous research
- Timings
- Budget
- Deliverables
- Terms and conditions
- Key personnel.

In choosing the agency, the following points should be considered:

- The agency's ability to understand the brief and translate it into a comprehensive proposal
- The compatibility of agency and client teams. Can we work with them?
- The evidence of innovation on the proposal. Has the agency added value?
- Evidence of understanding of the market and the problem facing the organization
- Sound methodology
- Meeting budget and time scales
- Relevant experience
- Professional body memberships.

The way a question like this would be assessed by the examiner is to consider the commercial sense of the content. As a delegate, you would be expected to outline methodology and sampling techniques in the brief.

Question 4

You are working for a small Midlands-based manufacturer of components for the motor industry. Your sales manager has identified a potential new market in the Czech Republic. The company cannot afford to carry out marketing research without establishing the nature of the demand for the product.

You have been asked to produce a preliminary market report from secondary data. There is no syndicated study available. What are the advantages and disadvantages of this approach? How can the disadvantages be overcome?

Answer

Introduction

Define secondary research. Discuss the range of strengths and weaknesses using the following framework:

Strengths

- It is cheap or free of charge
- It may provide an answer to the problem, this will save enormous time and effort
- It can guide or provide direction for primary work
- It can suggest methodologies for data collection
- It can indicate problems with particular methodologies
- It can provide historic or comparative data to enable longitudinal studies.

Weaknesses

- It is not related to the research question and the temptation may be to force the data to fit the question
- It may not be directly comparable
- Data may be incomplete
- It may not be available.

In evaluating secondary data, the following points should be explored:

- The data may have been gathered for a particular purpose.
- Who published the study? Was it a national government? Was it a trade association? What is the nature of the organization? Is the publisher of the data the same as the organization that collected the data.
- For what purpose? Is the study designed to sell a service? Is it designed to counter negative publicity? Is it designed to generate publicity?
- When was the data gathered? Is it relevant?
- How was the data collected? Was the data capture mechanism reliable? Was it a self selecting sample?
- Who collected the data? Are they independent? Are they trained? Are they members of a professional body? What sample was used?
- How reliable is the data?
- Is raw data presented?
- Can I replicate the study? Is the methodology included? Can I test the data for accuracy?
- Is the data comparable?

You may identify other organizations that can help – for example, trade partners, the DTI and the Chambers of Commerce. The use of embassy staff and trade associations may also be mentioned.

Question 5

You work as a marketing manager for a major car dealership. The dealership has 150 sites throughout the UK. Your Customer Satisfaction Scores have been falling recently. You have been to an MRS training course on Mystery Shopping and feel that this technique might help identify the causes for the fall in satisfaction.

Write a report to your director outlining why you feel that this might help.

Discuss the role of mystery shopping in delivering service quality.

What are the benefits and limitations of this technique?

Your report should outline what other research techniques might help uncover the cause of the problem.

Answer

Introduction

Define mystery shopping.

Mystery shopping is defined as 'The use of individuals trained to observe, experience and measure the customer service process, by acting as a prospective customer and undertaking a series of pre-determined tasks' (MRS, 1997).

Discuss this definition

Why is mystery shopping used. The following points form the basis of paragraphs in an essay or sections in a report:

- To act as a diagnostic tool identifying failings and weak points in service delivery
- To encourage and reward staff
- To assess competitors.

Conditions for the delivery of good research should be discussed.

- Mystery shoppers should present facts rather than opinions.
- These should include the shopping environment as well as interactions between the researcher and the staff. The potential for bias must be recognized in all markets.
- There needs to be careful recruitment of mystery shoppers.
- Age, gender and appearance of shoppers may affect the experience.
- Training is very important.
- Data capture and recording needs to be carefully considered.
- Mechanical recording may be desirable.

You should discuss data protection issues.

Other techniques that may help include:

- Focus groups or group discussions with customers
- Group discussions and depth interviews with staff
- Quantitative studies by telephone to customers representing all dealerships to identify if the problem is based in certain areas
- Groups with competitors' customers to identify key success factors in their dealerships.

Question 6

As the marketing research executive of a leading confectionery company, you have been asked to commission qualitative research into the positioning of your leading brand in the market place. You have to select a moderator to facilitate the groups.

What is the role of the moderator in managing focus groups?

Describe the key skills required by a moderator of focus groups.

How would you make your final decision?

Answer

Introduction

Define focus groups and the moderator.

Focus groups: A number of respondents gathered together to generate ideas through the discussion of, and reaction to, specific stimuli. Under the steerage of a moderator, focus groups are often used in exploratory work or when the subject matter involves social activities, habits and status (MRS, 2003).

Moderator: An individual who facilitates but does not influence a group discussion.

The moderator will control the group, keeping the discussion on track and probing for further information when needed.

The moderator will introduce other tasks that may occur within the group.

The main aim of the group is to ensure that the group members discuss the topic amongst themselves; the moderator's touch should be as light as possible.

The moderator will use a range of techniques to control the input of particularly vociferous members and to encourage quieter members of the group to make their contribution.

The moderator manages the timing of the group and ensures that the group is kept to reasonable time limits – normally between 45 minutes and 2 hours.

The moderator will capture information on tape or digitally.

The moderator may take instruction from remote observers of the group.

The moderator may administer the group, recruiting respondents and inviting them to attend. They may also give the respondents refreshments and payment or an incentive.

The moderator may analyse the results of the groups and should therefore understand the context of the research.

You should identify the fact that moderators may be employed by the agency, may be independent or be employed by a fieldwork agency.

Your decision should be based around the fact that moderators should have the following characteristics:

- Highly qualified and experienced in research and, possibly, psychology
- Business and marketing aware. They need to be able to translate respondents' feelings into business advantage for their clients
- Strong communicators – able to relate to a range of people
- Hard to place regionally in terms of socio-economic class

- Socially able, relaxed and friendly, but strong enough to control a room of animated, or conversely, disinterested respondents
- Flexible and quick thinking, with the ability to respond to the unexpected.

Question 7

As an executive of a leading research agency, you are pitching to persuade a client to extend the qualitative work they have carried out on their brands to include quantitative work, using face-to-face interviews.

Write a report to the client outlining the advantages and disadvantages of quantitative research.

What are the advantages and disadvantages of face-to-face interviewing?

How can the disadvantages be countered?

Answer

You should start the report by defining quantitative research as 'research that is undertaken using a structured research approach with a sample of the population to produce quantifiable insights into behaviour motivations and attitudes'.

You can identify the five key characteristics of quantitative data:

1. Data gathering is more structured
2. Research involves larger samples than qualitative research
3. The data gathered can provide answers that will quantify the incidence of particular behaviour motivations and attitudes in the population under consideration
4. Studies can be more easily replicated and direct comparisons can be made between studies
5. Analysis is statistical in nature and will usually be done with the help of computer software.

The answer should then place the idea of face-to-face interviewing in context and defining the term. The alternatives of self completion could be outlined and other methods of interview-assisted survey could be identified and discussed.

The advantages of face-to-face contact methods are many:

- There is greater acceptance of the validity of the research if an interviewer can introduce the reasons for the research and show professional membership cards
- The interview process is more efficient as non eligible respondents can be screened out more effectively
- They improve response rates as the interviewer can answer questions or help with any difficulty in completing the questionnaire
- Personal contact creates a sense of obligation and this can be useful with long surveys. This can reduce the incidence of incomplete or unfinished interviews
- Complexity can be introduced into the survey – for example, the use of show cards or other stimuli material is more easily managed
- Empathy and encouragement can enable deeper consideration of the questions and ensure accuracy of some claims – for example gender and age.

There are some disadvantages:

- Costs, particularly in b2b research, may be high, but this must be offset against a higher response rate
- It can take a considerable amount of time to complete a survey
- Interviewers may be demotivated and may take short cuts to ensure that their quota of completed surveys is made
- Interview bias is a problem. Bias may affect
  - Who is interviewed – interviewers may select those people who want to be interviewed. An Australian researcher used to do all his interviews on the beach at Bondi
  - The way questions are asked. With a negative inflection or a preceding ad libbed comment 'I know this sounds stupid but . . . .'.
  - The way an interviewer responds verbally and visually to an answer. A raised eyebrow or expression of shock is not required!
  - The way an answer is recorded, the interpretation of a response may be biased
- Safety of interviewing staff may be an issue in some areas
- The training and control of field staff is important and adds to costs
- A geographically, dispersed sample, for example regional store mangers, is clearly difficult to administer in this way, and other data collection methods might need to be considered.

Ways to overcome the potential problems are as follows:

- Good briefing
- Training
- Motivation
- Ensuring that the research design is sound
- Making sure that questionnaires are easy to use
- Careful management of the field force
- Using the IQCS
- Using a reputable field force agency
- Back checking completed surveys
- Careful editing
- Ensuring that the data is consistent and complete.

The use of face-to-face methods is dependent on the nature of the research problem and the resources of the business.

Question 8

a. Why is questionnaire design so important in the research process?

b. What is the role of piloting in the questionnaire design process?

Answer

Questionnaires collect data. The quality of data depends on their professional design:

- It is designed to collect relevant data
- To remove bias
- To make data comparable
- To motivate the respondent.

They must be developed in consideration of the research question, the data that is to be gathered, the respondents who will be answering the questions and the method of administering the questionnaire.

Classification questions will ensure that the respondent is part of our sample.

The questionnaire needs to reflect the objectives of the research programme.

The questionnaire must minimize bias through careful wording and phrasing of questions.

A good questionnaire will motivate interviewers and respondents.

The questionnaire and interview time are expensive. It should be efficiently produced to save time and money in the interview process.

Equally, it must be easy to code, edit and analyse.

A questionnaire should be tested in a pilot survey before it is rolled out.

The next stage of the questionnaire is to word the questions. At each stage of the process the researcher should stop and ask 'is the question really necessary?' Each question should be carefully evaluated on its own, in relation to other questions on the questionnaire and in relation to the overall objectives of the study. If the question does not contribute to the overall purpose of the research, it should not be included in the questionnaire.

Piloting or testing the questionnaire is crucial:

- It allows problems to be corrected
- Helps with the coding process
- Improves question sequencing
- Improves wording of questions.

Piloting should be carried out by the staff who will administer the questionnaire, in a comparable environment and with respondents who share the characteristics of the sample.

There are two methods:

1. The debriefing method means the respondents should be asked after completing the questionnaire what their thought processes were as they completed the questionnaires
2. The protocol method allows the respondent to talk through the process of completing the questionnaire.

Question 9

You have been appointed as marketing manager to an online retailer of intimate apparel (underwear). They have succeeded in difficult times to grow their business but have appointed you to look at the marketing research function within the business. Your first piece of research is based on a quota sample. The MD of the business is sceptical.

Produce a report for the MD outlining what quota sampling is.

What benefits does it have? What are its disadvantages and how can these be overcome?

What other sampling techniques may have been considered and why would they have been rejected?

Answer

Define quota sampling:

'A type of non-probability sample where the required number of units with particular characteristics are specified.'

Known characteristics of the population are reproduced in the same proportions as in the sample. Therefore, it is representative of that population. For example, age, sex and social class can be used to select quotas.

Advantages of quota sampling include:

- Speed and cost
- Allows sampling to take place where a sample frame may not be available but key characteristics of the population are known
- Interviewers do not have to interview named individuals – they are screened in or out via a small number of classification questions
- The data when compared to random methods, which are perhaps double the cost, has been proved to be acceptable, provided that the research is managed effectively
- Cost savings may be used to improve the quality of research through increasing sample sizes or using a different method in support of the survey
- Its popularity shows that it works!

Disadvantages include:

- Whilst known characteristics may be distributed in correct proportions, unknown characteristics that may be relevant to the survey may not. Hidden bias may exist that is not discovered.
- Researchers may be biased as to the type of respondents they choose to interview or the location where they choose to carry out the interviews.

Other sampling techniques include:

- Probability sampling
- Simple random sampling
- Systematic sampling
- Stratified random sampling
- Cluster sampling.

Disadvantages:

- It is expensive
- Respondents selected must be interviewed to ensure the integrity of the process. This means that up to three call backs to individuals may be made before classifying a non response
- The cost of pulling together a large sample frame may be prohibitive
- The random selection of a sample means that all members of a national population would have the same chance of being selected.

Non probability sampling includes:

- Convenience sampling
- Judgement or purposive sampling
- Snowball sampling.

These may have been rejected as less reliable than quota sampling or inappropriate to the research programme under consideration.

Question 10

What tasks have to be done before data can be analysed and after surveys have been completed?

Describe the tasks and outline their role in producing effective analysis.

Answer

Data needs to be:

- Entered
- Coded
- Edited
- Cleaned.

Before data analysis can be carried out.

Editing and coding

Before data is processed, it is assessed for completeness and coherence. The editing process involves computer or manual checking of the data to look for respondent or interview errors or inconsistencies. If errors are identified the respondent may be called back. If the questionnaire cannot be rescued then it may be rejected.

Coding is the process that allocates a number to each answer and it is this that allows analysis to take place. As discussed earlier, the coding process may take place as the questionnaire is administered either manually by the interviewer ringing a number on the questionnaire or it may be managed through the computer-assisted methods.

Coding open questions involves using a sample of the completed questionnaires and developing a coding frame or a list of codes for all possible responses to an open question. This process may categorize and group certain diverse responses into a manageable number. This process must be handled carefully to reduce the processing error that might occur.

Data entry

Data entry may be carried out automatically through CAPI, CAWI and CATI systems or may scanned into the computer using optical character recognitions software or they may be entered by hand. After this process, the data will be once again checked or cleaned for key stroke or character recognition problems.

Data tabulations may also be carried out.

Once this is complete, the data can be analysed.

Question 11

List the sections of a research report and briefly outline what goes into each section.

Answer

Title page

This should contain the title of the report. The name and contact details of the agency and the researcher, client details and the date of presentation.

Contents page

This should contain full details of sections, subsections and page numbers. It should include lists of tables and figures. It should make the report navigable. If presenting on the web, the use of hyperlinks which take the browser to the relevant section can be considered.

The executive summary

This should be a short summary of the report and its recommendations. Many say that it should be a one-or two-page summary or it should be a maximum of two pages. There are no hard and fast rules. The summary needs to do a job, i.e. summarizing a report, it also needs to be accessible.

Introduction

The introduction should outline the key objectives of the research, the reasons why the research has been carried out and the constraints that the researchers are working to. It may include profiles and key responsibilities of the researchers.

Situation analysis and problem definition

This section outlines the background to the problem, and reviews business and marketing objectives. It drills down into the problems definition and the detailed objectives for the research programme, reprises the sections of the brief and proposal.

Research methodology and limitations

This section outlines the detailed methodology for the study. It should cover the research method, the data capture mechanism, the topic or discussion guide or questionnaire, the definition of the population of interest, the sampling approach and the method of data analysis. This section should not be too long. Details should be put into the appendices. It should cover sources of error, including sample size.

Findings and analysis

The main body of the report should cover the findings relevant to the objectives. It should be constructed to present a solution to the problem, not on a question-by-question basis. The research data should present data to support a line of arguments, and the focus should be on analysis and insight. Key ideas can be supported by tables or quotes from responders. It may include tables and graphics, and it should be linked by a narrative.

Conclusions and recommendations

This section brings the report to a close. It should present a summary of key findings and recommendations for marketing decisions and future research.

Appendices

This should include all supporting data. It contains material that is relevant to the research but that would be too detailed for the main report. It may include all tables, questionnaires, discussion guides and secondary data. It may be that the appendices are longer than the main report.

Further reading

Baier, M. (1995). *Elements of Direct Marketing.* McGraw Hill.

Bennett, P. (1995). *Dictionary of Marketing Terms.* 2nd edition. American Marketing Association.

Bird, D., Commonsense (2000). *Direct Marketing.* 4th edition, Kogan Page.

Birn, R.J. (2002). *Handbook of International market research techniques.* Kogan Page.

Chaffey et al. (2000). *Internet Marketing.* FT Prentice Hall.

Chisnall, P. (2001). *Marketing research.* 6th edition. McGraw Hill, Chapter: Introduction, pp. 4. (0077097513)

Christopher, M., Payne, A. and Ballantyne, D. (2002). *Relationship marketing; Creating shareholder value.* 3rd edition. Butterworth-Heinemann.

Crouch, S. and Housden, M. (2003). *Marketing Research for Managers.* 3rd edition, Butterworth-Heinemann.

Davidson, H. (1997). *Even More Offensive Marketing.* Penguin.

Gordon, W. (1999). *Goodthinking: A guide to qualitative research.* Admap.

Hilton, S. and Gibbons, G. (2002). *Good business: Your world needs you.* Texere.

Housden, M. and Lewis, K. (1998). *International Marketing.* Kogan Page.

Kinnear, T.C. and Taylor, J.R. (1996). *Marketing research: an applied approach.* 5th edition, McGraw-Hill.

Kotler, P. et al. (1999). *Principles of Marketing.* 2nd European edition, Prentice Hall Europe.

McCorkell, G. (1990). *Advertising That Pulls Response.* McGraw Hill.

McCorkell, G. (2000). *Direct and Database Marketing.* Kogan Page.

McGivern, Y. (2003). *The Practice of Marketing and Social Research.* FT Prentice Hall.

Nash, E. (1995). *Direct Marketing; Strategy, Planning, Execution.* McGraw-Hill.

O'Malley et al. (1999). *Exploring Direct Marketing.* 1st edition.

Payne, A., Christopher, M., Clark, M., Peck, H., (eds.) (1996) *Relationship Marketing for Competitive Advantage.* Butterworth-Heinemann.

Pearson, S. (1996). *Building Brands Directly.* Macmillan.

Peppers, D. and Rogers, M. (1993). *The One To One Future.* Piatkus.

Peppers, D. and Rogers, M. (1997). *Enterprise One To One Currency.* Doubleday.

Pine, B.J. (1993) 'Mass Customisation: The new frontier in business competition' Harvard Business School Press 'Marketing Without Frontiers' Post Office 1997/8.

Proctor, T. (2000). *Essentials of Marketing Research.* 2nd edition, FT Prentice Hall

Reichheld, F. (2001). *The Loyalty Effect: The Hidden Force Behind Growth Profits and Lasting Value.* Harvard Business School Press. (1578516870)

Stone, B. (1997). *'Successful Direct Marketing Methods'.* 6th edition, NTC Business Books.

Tapp, A. (2001). *Principles of Direct and Database Marketing.* FT Prentice Hall.

The IDM (2002). *The Interactive and Direct Marketing Guide.*

Thomas, B. and Housden, M. (2003). *Direct Marketing in Practice.* Butterworth-Heinemann.

Wilson, A. (2003). *Marketing research: an integrated approach.* FT Prentice Hall.

Wright, L.T. and Crimp, M. (2000). *The Marketing Research Process.* 5th edition, FT Prentice Hall.

Journals and Periodicals: Read selectively through a range of journals

Precision Marketing (UK)*

Direct Response (UK)*

Direct Marketing Strategies

Journal of Database Marketing (UK)

Journal of Interactive Marketing (UK)

Net Profit

Harvard Business Review

Research

Journal of Brand Management

Marketing

Marketing Week

Journal of Marketing Management

European Journal of Marketing

Journal of the Marketing Research Society

Admap

International Journal of Advertising

Journal of Database Marketing

Journal of Targeting, Measurement and Analysis

Database Marketing

Direct Marketing (US)

Direct Response

Marketing Direct

Precision Marketing

Journal of Interactive Marketing (US)

New Media Age

Revolution

Net Profit

Loyalty

International Journal of Customer Relationship Management

Customer Loyalty Today

Customer Management

New Marketing Directions (IDM)

Journal of Interactive Marketing

Journal of Direct Marketing

Journal of Database Marketing

Journal of Targeting, Measurement and Analysis

Precision Marketing

Direct Response

Marketing Direct

Revolution

Marketing

Websites: A selection. Use search engines to find your own sites

www.mrs.org.uk	The Market Research Society
www.esomar.nl	Esomar
www.theidm.com	The IDM
www.ama.com	American Marketing Association
www.cim.co.uk	Chartered Institute of Marketing
www.barb.co.uk	British Audience Research Bureau
www.dmis.co.uk	Direct Mail Information Centre
www.dma.org.uk	Direct Marketing Association
www.abc.org.uk	Audit Bureau of Circulations
www.iab.net	Internet Advertising Bureau
www.crm-forum.com	
www.1to1.com	
www.callcentreworld.com	
www.ukonline.gov.uk	
www.statistics.gov.uk	
www.europe.org.uk	
www.europa.eu.int/comm/eurostat/	

www.cec.org.uk	
www.un.org	
www.mrs.org.uk	The Market Research Society
www.managers.org.uk	
www.FT.com.	The Financial Times
www.guardian.co.uk.	The Guardian
www.wsj.com	Wall Street Journal
www.economist.com.	The Economist
www.feer.com	Far Eastern Economic Review
www.carat.co.uk	
www.zenithmedia.co.uk/	
www.totalmedia.co.uk/	
www.acnielsenmms.com/	
www:micromarketing-online.com.	
www.dpr.gov.uk	

appendix 4 debriefings

Unit 2

Activity Debriefing 2.1

You may have come up with the following which are both in the CIM website:

'Marketing is the management process responsible for identifying, anticipating and satisfying customer requirements profitably' (CIM, 2003).

OR

'Marketing is both a concept dedicated to meeting customer requirements and a range of techniques which enables the company to determine those requirements and ensure they are met' (CIM, 2003).

You may have come up with the American Marketing Association's definition:

'Marketing is the process of planning and executing the conception, pricing, promotion and distribution of ideas, goods and services to create exchanges that satisfy individual and organizational objectives' (Bennett, P., 1995).

You may have paraphrased these definitions and have a range of points which may include:

- Customer focus
- Profits
- Customer needs
- Process
- Management
- Satisfaction
- Products.

Don't worry if you can't remember the definition precisely at the moment; however, it may be useful to remember at least one of these definitions. Breaking down definitions into their parts can be useful in that in can unlock a lot of thinking and by expanding on the elements of a definition you can learn a great deal.

Activity Debriefing 2.2

You probably have a long list which might include the following:

- I am thirsty
- I am hot

- I am concerned about the chemical contents of tap water
- I care for my family
- I want a healthy lifestyle
- I am buying packaged water for convenience
- I am going to the gym and need to rehydrate
- I like sparkling water with my meal
- Buying this water says that I am sophisticated
- I like the taste of this brand
- I like the new packaging
- It is cheaper than cola
- I make a better margin on this brand of water
- My staff enjoy discussing business around the water cooler.

You can see that there are a range of needs that are being satisfied. They depend on the type of person, their financial background, their age, their household composition, their life style, whether they are buying for a business or to resell.

Remember Maslow's hierarchy of needs?

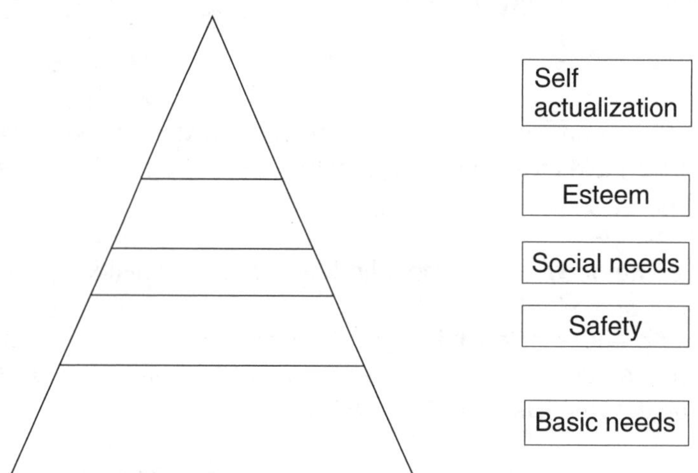

Figure A4.1 Maslow's hierarchy of needs

The basic need, i.e. 'I'm thirsty' is the simplest to understand. The more complex needs emerge from a greater understanding of the way a product or service is consumed. This is the role of research and information.

Activity Debriefing 2.3

The four characteristics are:

1. Generates information to aid marketing decision-making
2. Involves the collection of information
3. Involves the analysis of information
4. Involves the communications and dissemination of information.

We will look at each of these areas in detail as we work through the text.

Activity Debriefing 2.4

A good approach to this question would be to reflect on the marketing planning process. Let's look at this again.

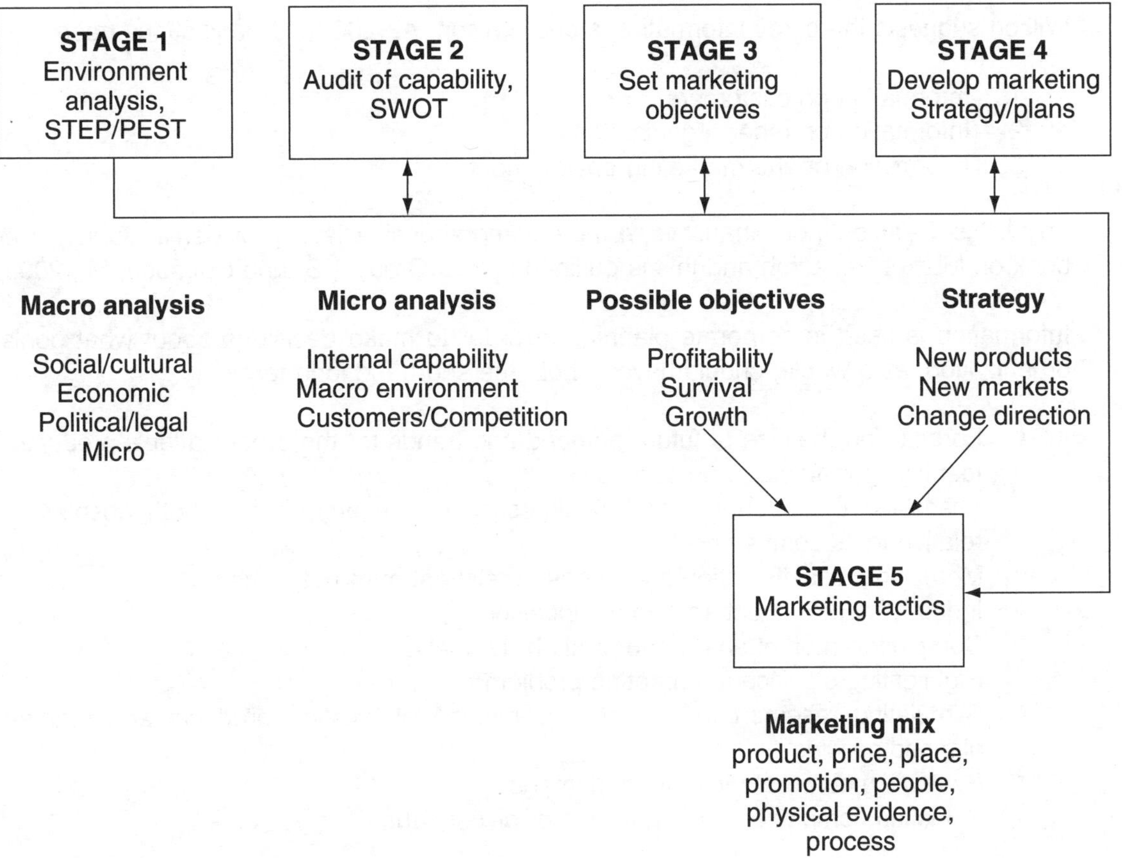

Figure A4.2 The marketing planning process

First of all, research and the database can work also at the corporate level. Research will help determine the nature and scope of the organization, and may be used in developing the mission and values of an organization.

Research and the database will be used significantly in the PEST and SWOT analysis. They will help us understand the current attitudes and opinions of our customers. They will help define our distinctive competence relative to competitive companies. They will help determine future strategies for the business by looking at markets and customers and our brands, products and services. As we drive-in to tactics, research and the database inform the configuration of the marketing mix and help us evaluate its effectiveness. Chisnall talks about this in his book (Chisnall, P., 2001).

He shows that research works at each of four areas of the marketers' responsibilities. These are:

1. **Analysis** – Identify market trends, competitors' activities, customer preferences in existing and potential markets
2. **Planning** – Decide on a range of products and services likely to satisfy identified needs present and emergent

3. **Control** – Check that standards of performance are maintained
4. **Implementation** – Organize development production and distribution of specific products and services.

Of course, the database also works at all these levels.

Wilson suggests three key information areas (Wilson, A., 2003). Organizations need:

1. Information on customers
2. Information on other organizations
3. Information on the marketing environment.

This list is useful but not exhaustive. A more comprehensive list is provided in Sunny Crouch's book on Market Research and this is outlined below (Crouch, S. and Housden, M., 2003):

Information is used in corporate planning in order to make decisions about what goals the organization, as a whole, should have in both the short and long term:

- Forecasting the size of future demand and trends for the organization's products
- Identifying markets to be served
- Assessing the strengths and weaknesses of the organization both absolutely and relative to its competitors
- Measuring dissatisfaction and needs in relevant market segments
- Industry/market structure and composition
- Competitor, market share and profitability analysis
- Highlighting significant marketing problems
- Stimulating research for new or exploitation of existing products and markets by planned policies
- Evaluating corporate identity and image
- Selecting companies for acquisition or divestment.

Market planning

Research and the database are used in market planning to keep the firm in touch with its markets and customers:

- Identifying, measuring and describing key market segments' behaviour and attitudes
- Assessing relative profitability of markets over time
- Analysis and interpretation of general market data
- Placing individual customer transactions, perhaps recorded on a database, in the broader market context
- Analysing business potential of new market areas
- Identifying and evaluating markets for products and new products for markets
- Measuring consumer preferences
- Identifying changes in competitive activity
- Sales forecasting.

Product planning (including packaging and service levels)

Research and the database may be used in making and adapting products to fulfil customer wants more accurately and profitably:

- Generating and screening new product ideas and modifications
- Concept testing
- Product testing and re-testing for acceptance and improvement
- Testing formulation and presentation preferences

- Packaging tests
- Product name tests
- Test marketing
- Comparative testing against competitive products
- Product elimination or product line simplification
- Evaluating perceived service quality.

Promotional planning

Research and the database may be concerned with the selection and effectiveness of persuasive communications. Three main areas are identified below:

Communications planning

- Developing sustainable brand positioning
- Message design and content
- Development of the creative proposition
- Developing effective multimedia communications strategies
- Pre-testing ads
- Post-testing ads, e.g. awareness, comprehension, recall, attitude shifts, brand switching effects
- Advertising weight-of-expenditure tests
- Media planning: evaluation, selection and scheduling
- Advertising effectiveness
- Public relations and publicity effects on awareness/attitude
- Sponsorship effectiveness
- Exhibition effectiveness research
- Direct marketing effectiveness research
- Assessing the impact of integration
- Developing the optimum communications mix.

Sales force planning

- Determining sales areas
- Testing alternative selling techniques and messages
- Setting sales targets
- Evaluating sales performance
- Evaluating sales compensation system
- Making selling operations more productive.

Distribution planning

Research and the database may be concerned with the formulation and effectiveness of distribution policy:

- Channel selection
- Distribution cost analysis
- Wholesaler/retailer margin
- Incentive policy
- Dealer sales levels
- Distribution achievement
- Penetration levels
- Stock checks
- Inventory policy.

Price planning

Research and the database may help as one of the inputs to price selection.

Unit 3

Activity Debriefing 3.1

You probably have a few points of similarity and they may include the following:

- The database may be manual or computerized, but, almost always, today it will be computerized
- It is a source of accurate up to date information or data about our past, present and current customers
- It is relevant to the organization's goals
- Data is collected systematically
- Data is maintained and monitored
- It is used to formulate strategy
- It supports the formulation of marketing objectives of the enterprise.

Activity Debriefing 3.2

So, what do you have? Below are some of the data elements you might have written down. We'll start with consumer markets:

What data should be collected?

Consumer identification data

- Customer reference number
- First name
- Last name
- Title – Mr Mrs Dr, etc.
- Suffixes, e.g. B.A., M.A., Ph.D., M.CIM., etc.
- Date of birth
- Address
- Postcode
- Telephone
- E-mail
- Sales area
- Media sales area
- Fax
- Account number.

Demographic data

- Gender
- Age
- Occupation
- Employment status
- Marital status
- How many children
- What age are the children.

Financial

- Job title
- Income

- What is their credit history and rating?
- Are they a homeowner?
- What is the value of their home?
- Do they own a car?
- Share ownership
- Do they have a credit card?
- What insurance products do they have?

Lifestyle

- Life stage – student, retired, etc.
- Number of holidays per year
- Where do they holiday?
- What leisure interests do they have?
- Media reading
- TV viewing.

Shopping behaviour

- When did they last buy? – Recency
- How often do they buy? – Frequency
- What is the value of their purchases? – Value
- What profit does the customer generate for the business over time? – Lifetime value
- Loyalty scheme member.

Other

- Length of time at current address
- Have they responded before?
- To what campaign?
- Customer service history
- Complaints
- Are they a VIP?
- Data protection issues
- Have they opted out of or into communications?
- Are they a shareholder?

Let's look at business data:

Business identification data

- Company name
- Trading name
- Trading status
- Credit rating
- Contact name or names in the decision-making unit
- Job title
- Areas of responsibility
- Address
- Website address
- Postcode
- Account number
- VAT number
- Region

- Territory
- Salesperson.

Business details

- Size of business
- Turnover
- Employees
- Number of offices
- Head office
- Budget
- Financial year end.

Transaction data

- Account number
- Purchase history
- Recency, frequency and value
- Order size
- Service history
- Response
- Method of acquisition.

Sector

- Standard Industrial Classification code (SIC)
- Type of business.

Key contact

- Contact name
- Job
- Telephone
- Fax
- E-mail.

The differences are immediate. Then so are the similarities. There are standard elements and these are generally the 'golden' fields, that should be completed and maintained for good database marketing. Clearly these include identification data and the fields that cover customers' behaviour. Generally the most important categories here are recency, frequency, amount and product category. The key fields for any database will be different from the next due to the different business contexts and objectives the data supports.

Activity Debriefing 3.4

Data is obtained from a range of sources. Some of these are planned and managed and some are as a result of the day-to-day operation of the business.

Data that comes as a result of the day-to-day activity of the business may include:

- Accounts records
- Sales force reports
- Service records
- Reports from intermediaries

- Customer enquiries or complaints
- Responses to marketing communications
- Guarantee cards.

Any contact with a customer of prospect is an opportunity of data capture. The data strategy must be established in order to ensure that these opportunities are appraised effectively and that relevant data is captured consistently and constantly.

Information that is generated from planned activity include:

- Bought lists
- Industry sector reports
- Primary marketing research
- Competitor analyses
- Responses to exhibitions and public relations events.

Unit 4

Activity Debriefing 4.1

Quite a few things to consider, aren't there. Amongst others you may have:

- Is there a market for whisky-based drinks?
- What is the market worth?
- Who is the target market?
- What are their characteristics?
- What is the reaction of the retail and catering trade?
- How will the competition react?
- What brand strategy should we pursue?
- What shall we call the product?
- How much will it cost to produce?
- What price should we charge?
- How should we promote the product? etc., etc., etc. The list is endless.

Activity Debriefing 4.2

Exploratory Research is intended to develop initial ideas or insights and to provide direction for further research.

Conclusive research covers all other research that is aimed at evaluating alternative courses of action or measuring and monitoring the organization's performance.

Conclusive descriptive research provides answers to the who, what, where, when and how of marketing research. It explains what is happening, not why it is happening.

Descriptive research may be cross-sectional, i.e. involving data collection at a single point of time.

Or, it may be longitudinal involving data collection over time to examine trends.

Conclusive causal research tells us if one variable is related to another. That is, if one variable causes or determines the value of another. For example, drinks and ice cream companies look at the influence of temperature on product sales. A simpler more common approach would be to look at the effect of different creative executions on response rates. This latter example is an example of experimental research or the changing of one variable to observe the effect on another whilst other extraneous variables are kept constant.

Activity Debriefing 4.3

What you came up with on your list might have included the following:

- Advice from colleagues
- Past experience
- Seen their work in the trade press
- Seen a credentials publication
- Size of the business
- Reputation
- Sector-specific skills
- Industry award winners
- Response to marketing activity
- Web searches
- They are local to us
- Recommendation from consultants or business advisors, e.g. business link
- Trade body research.

Trade body research is very useful. As a follow-up to this exercise visit the MRS and ESOMAR websites and try their online research buyer's guide.

www.mrs.org.uk

www.esomar.nl

They are both excellent at identifying potential agencies and their relevant skills base. The Research Buyer's guide of the MRS lists the following for all its members:

- Address and telephone number
- Turnover (Bands)
- Services (all and specialities)
- Key executives/All full members
- Brief description
- MRQSA/BMRA memberships
- Date formed
- Ownership.

Unit 5

Activity Debriefing 5.1

The key point is that the information has generally been gathered to serve some other purpose. It is not directly related to the research problem under consideration. Crouch and Housden point out that it has been gathered at a different time. It may be out of date. In today's fast moving technological market this may be a major factor limiting the use of external data. Wilson's definition also outlines its key strengths. It is maybe cheap or free of charge.

Activity Debriefing 5.2

This is the type of information that you might have found – pretty useful for those contemplating setting up an e-commerce operation.

E-Commerce Inquiry to Business 2000

E-commerce could have a huge impact on the way businesses operate. It has the potential to lead to growth in trade, increase markets, improve efficiency and effectiveness and transform business processes.

Author: Magdalen Williams

Economic Trends, no 572

ISSN: 0013 0400

Download (Pdf file, 39 Kb)

Abstract

E-commerce could have a huge impact on the way businesses operate. It has the potential to lead to growth in trade, increase markets, improve efficiency and effectiveness, and transform business processes. In response, the ONS has developed a package of measures which will help monitor the UK's use of e-commerce.

One strand of the strategy is the E-commerce Inquiry, a new annual survey of UK business which asks about the use of, and attitude to, the Internet and e-commerce. The ONS launched it in January 2001 as part of a European Union (EU) initiative which will provide EU-comparable data on e-commerce later this year.

The UK element was a survey of 9,000 businesses randomly sampled from the Interdepartmental Business Register, stratified by employment size. The sampling methodology ensured wide coverage of the UK economy and the estimates produced cover all sectors except agriculture, fishing, mining, construction and the public sector, and all businesses with employment of 10 or more. The first results were published on 15 May 2001 and indicated that in 2000 there were nearly £57 billion of sales made over the Internet: 2 per cent of total sales by the sectors surveyed.

Published on 1 August 2002 (National Statistics, 2003).

Activity Debriefing 5.3

What is TGI?

The Target Group Index (TGI) is a continuous survey where data collection runs throughout the year so that seasonality does not skew results. TGI yields information on the usage of over 4,000 brands in 500 product areas for those aged 15+. It is updated 4 times a year on a rolling quarterly basis.

What is the sample size?

The survey is based on a sample size of c.25,000 interviews per annum. Results are weighted to match known demographic profiles and re-weighted to the National Readership Survey.

How is data captured?

A self-completion questionnaire is placed with selected respondents at the end of BMRB's Access Omnibus survey.

What are the implications for my business?

TGI data is used to assist the understanding of target markets to aid marketing and advertising decisions. The data helps the users of TGI to optimize their marketing and advertising receipts/expenditures. *Source*: TGI

Activity Debriefing 5.5

Here are the first ten results from Alta Vista

Sponsored Matches About

Marketing Research by Kadence

Kadence uses online surveys to conduct qualitative and quantitative research to provide companies with analysis for strategic decision-making.

International Business Research Limited

We provide top quality, marketing research in industry and commerce. Investigations into customer-related issues and market opportunities are our speciality.

Survey and Marketing Research E-store

United States and worldwide full service or supplier for focus group, Web-based surveys, in-person or telephone interviewing (CATI), mail surveys, data analysis and consultants.

Expertize Search

We help companies to find the right specialist in marketing research. National and international. Free and fast.

Find '**marketing**' at the **AltaVista Jobs Search Centre**

AltaVista found 296,567 results About

PMP Ltd – Prime Marketing Publications (www.pmp.co.uk)

The PMP Group of companies provides a range of services for those responsible for... Consultants' News International Consultants' News **Research**: PMP **Research** Conferences: Conferencepage.com About PMP...
http://www.pmp.co.uk • Refreshed in past 24 hours • Related Pages

More pages from www.pmp.co.uk

The Chartered Institute of Marketing

The Chartered Institute of **Marketing** is the world's largest international **marketing** ... Studying Members access to **Marketing** i-Coach® – an....com Sustainability and **marketing** network launched – Smart:...
http://www.cim.co.uk • Related Pages

More pages from www.cim.co.uk

Index

...What PC? Imark First contact VNU one to one VNU IT directories Accountancyage.com VNUnet.com Network Global Media VNU **Marketing** Solutions VNU News Centre vnu **research** VNU Recruitment Network
http://www.marketing.vnu.co.uk • Related Pages

Welcome to the DMA Website

The Direct **Marketing** Association (DMA) UK is the trade assocation for the direct **marketing**...
http://www.dma.org.uk • Refreshed in past 24 hours • Related Pages

More pages from www.dma.org.uk

International Marketing – Research and Networking

Leading strategy and leadership thinker Rosabeth Moss Kanter spoke with Sarah Powell...... International **Marketing** Companies need to expand...2002 Article of the Month **Marketing** planning and the policy...
'www.managementfirst.com/international_marketing/index.htm • Related Pages

More pages from www.managementfirst.com

eLibrary – Web ads top $10M. (marketing research firm Ernst and Young L.L.P. and the Internet Advertising Bureau of Canada ...

IAB **research** provides ammo to help Canadian Internet advertisers target rapid growth areas TORONTO Revenues from firms purchasing ad space on the Internet in 1997 have reached almost 10 million,...
ask.elibrary.com/getdoc.asp?pubname=Comp...Not%20specified

More pages from ask.elibrary.com

Source: www.altvista.com

And here are the first ten google results:

Category: Business > Marketing > Market Research Suppliers

Sponsored Links

Pay $.01 per New Visitor
Your business in 700 search engines
Over 2 million searches a day
pay-per-search.com
Interest: ■

Marketing Research
Outstanding research service
Quick start. Great rates
www.freshminds.co.uk
Interest: ■

Online Market **Research**
Worldwide Panels (B2C, B2B)
Results in < 48 hours
www.consumer-access.com
Interest: ■

Brand building
Use us to increase your success by successful brand creation
www.customerinterpreter.com
Interest: ■

900,000 **Marketing** Reports
Local-US trends- 15,000 industries
BizMiner Market Research Profiles
www.bizminer.com
Interest: ■

News: CuttingEdgePharma.com: New Pharmaceutical Sales & **Marketing**... – Yahoo News – 18 Mar 2003

Try Google News: Search news for marketing research or browse the latest headlines

Marketing Research Association

. . . **Marketing Research** Association 1344 Silas Deane Hwy., Suite 306 • PO Box 230 • Rocky Hill, CT 06067-0230 Tel: 860-257-4008 • Fax: 860-257-3990 • e-mail . . .

Description: A US national organization of **marketing research** professionals and firms. Find news and events, membershi . . .

Category: Business > Marketing and Advertising > Market Research Suppliers
www.mra-net.org/ – 14k – 19 Mar 2003 – Cached – Similar pages

ESOMAR website

. . . QUALITATIVE **RESEARCH MARKETING** DEMANDS, QUALITATIVE INSIGHTS. . . . MONOGRAPH SERIES.

Volume 10: **Marketing Research** in a .com Environment Editor: Richard Brookes. . . .
www.esomar.nl/ – 47k – 19 Mar 2003 – Cached – Similar pages

Quirk's **Marketing Research** Review [Home] **marketing**, market . . .

The Quirk's **Marketing Research** Review Website is a one-stop source of information on **marketing research**, everything from articles on successful **research** . . .

Description: This online companion to the monthly print publication of the same name includes information and resource ...

Category: Business > Marketing and Advertising > . . . > News and Publications
www.quirks.com/ – 23k – 19 Mar 2003 – Cached – Similar pages

Welcome to PMRS | Professional **Marketing Research** Society

The Professional **Marketing Research** Society is a non-profit organization for **marketing research** professionals engaged in **marketing**, advertising, social and . . .
www.pmrs-aprm.com/ – 5k – Cached – Similar pages

@ResearchInfo.com – FREE **Marketing Research** Resources

The web's most comprehensive site for free market **research** and **marketing research** resources. . . .

www.researchinfo.com/ – 11k – 19 Mar 2003 – Cached – Similar pages

Economists and Market and Survey Researchers

. . . Private industry provided about 9 out of 10 jobs for salaried workers, particularly economic and **marketing research** firms, management consulting firms, banks . . .
www.bls.gov/oco/ocos055.htm – 41k – 19 Mar 2003 – Cached – Similar pages

PJ **MARKETING RESEARCH** – **Marketing Research**, Essays, Research, . . .

. . . Why Should I join PJ **Marketing Research**? . . . Thank you for your interest in PJ **Marketing Research**. Copyright © 1999 PJ **Marketing Research**. All rights reserved.

Description: Get solved **marketing** case studies, listed with classifications.

Category: Business > Marketing and Advertising > Market Research Suppliers
www.pj-marketing.com/ – 14k – Cached – Similar pages

Moved

Deze pagina is verhuisd naar:
www.tilburguniversity.nl/faculties/few/**marketing**/links/journal1.html
Wij verzoeken u uw bookmark of link aan te passen....

Description: Collection of links to academic **marketing** journals. From the Department of **Marketing** at Tilburg University.
Category: News > Magazines and E-zines > Directories
marketing.kub.nl/journal1.htm – 2k – Cached – Similar pages

KnowThis: For **Marketing** Market **Research** Internet Advertising...

...**Marketing** & Advertising, Internet & E-Commerce Intellectual Property Patents, Trademarks & Copyrights Market **Research** Basics of **Marketing Research** General Info...

Description: Resources, references and links specifically for professionals, academics and students involved in...

Category: Business > Marketing and Advertising > Marketing Support Services
www.knowthis.com/ – 24k – 19 Mar 2003 – Cached – Similar pages

NYAMA GreenBook – Home

Market **research**, **marketing**, **research**, advertising, directory, worldwide, focus groups....
What **marketing research** service are you looking for?...
www.greenbook.org/ – 25k – 19 Mar 2003 – Cached – Similar pages

Source: www.google.co.uk

As you can see there are significant differences. It pays to use a range of search engines.

Unit 6

Activity Debriefing 6.1

ACNielsen's services include:

Retail Measurement Services (provides) data on product movement, market share, distribution, price and other market-sensitive information.

Using in-store scanning of product codes and store visits by professional auditors, ACNielsen offers a complete portfolio of sample and census information across the food, household, health and beauty, durables, confectionery and beverage products industries.

Retail Measurement Services help to gauge product penetration, overall product performance, distribution, promotion effectiveness and price sensitivity. Whether long-term strategic planning or tactical decision-making, ACNielsen measures and tracks sales volume, selling price, observed promotion and merchandising execution, encompassing an organization's own brands as well as competitive brands.

Source: www.acnielsen.com

Taylor Nelson Sofres' services include:

Taylor Nelson Sofres Superpanel is GB's leading continuous consumer panel and provides purchasing information on all main grocery markets. The panel was launched in 1991 and now consists of 15,000 households which are demographically and regionally balanced to offer a representative picture of the GB marketplace. Data is collected twice weekly via electronic terminals in the home, with purchases being recorded via home-scanning technology.

Source: www.tnsofres.com/superpanel

Activity Debriefing 6.2

1. Postar
2. Nielsen Net ratingsUS/UK, Netvalue, France, Hitwise (Australia)
3. The NRS is a non-profit-making but commercial organization, which sets out to provide estimates of the number and nature of the people who read UK newspapers and consumer magazines. Currently, the survey publishes data covering some 270 different publications
4. The Audit Bureau of Circulations provides an independent verification of a circulation, attendance or electronic media delivery claim. All titles in ABC membership are audited at least once a year.

Activity Debriefing 6.3

You may have some or all of the following:

- To improve customer service
- To improve store layout
- To improve staffing levels to ensure reduced waiting time at call centres or at service points
- To generate information to inform reward and recognition schemes
- To monitor time spent on any activity, e.g. TV consumption
- To measure the amount of product consumed
- To look at product combinations
- To explore alternative product uses
- To explore product interaction.

Unit 7

Activity Debriefing 7.1

Customer Focus Group Discussion Guide

Below is an outline discussion guide. Each of the sections could have more detail but the framework is correct. A skilled researcher could use this to carry out in the group.

Introduction

Objectives

Rules of the road for focus group research

Introductions: Introduce the person next to you.

5 mins

Customer service generally

Experiences of really good service – why?

Experience of a really bad service – why?

10 mins

The dealership

What was the experience like in the dealership pre-purchase?

10 mins

During the negotiation

10 mins

After sales

10 mins

People

10 mins

Facilities

10 mins

Marketing Collateral

5 mins

Projective technique Dealership CV

10 minutes

Summary

Other issues

Key elements

Thank you and gift

5 mins

Activity Debriefing 7.2

Volvo is interesting; despite the millions spent in advertising Volvo as an exciting car to drive, non-Volvo drivers will invariably describe the Volvo as:

- Male
- Middle class
- Married with children (2.5)
- Two black Labradors and a pair of green wellies; while Volvo owners may present a different view. Try this and see what results you get.

Activity Debriefing 7.3

Exploratory research to define problems

Motivational research to define areas for quantitative research

Attitudes and motivation research

Segmentation studies

Positioning studies

Creative concept testing

Product development and line extensions

Brand and name development

Brand perception studies.

Unit 8

Activity Debriefing 8.1

Sex

The majority are women at the risk of sexism. There are several reasons for this: Part-time work, interview work is flexible and fits around child care responsibilities. Women tend to have better listening skills and find it easier to elicit information from respondents.

Age

The ideal age requirements for entry to consumer interviewing is between 25 and 45 years. In b2b markets, older more experienced interviewers may be required.

Social background

It is useful if the interviewer is not obviously from any social class. It helps if the interviewer has the ability to be 'chameleon-like' so as to be able to fit-in with the respondent. Politically, interviewers should be aware but not activists. It is usual when interviewers are recruited for them to be screened for political activity if they are likely to be employed in asking political questions.

Education

Interviewers should be numerate and literate. Interviewers should have at least GCSE level English and Maths. In certain b2b projects it may be useful to have some business education.

Experience

Some experience of dealing with people and in b2b interviewing experience in the sector under review may be desirable. Training in research interviewing is not vital but those who are not trained will require to be trained under the terms of the MRS's IQCS scheme.

Personality

The ideal researcher is gregarious and outgoing, but not overbearing, and a good listener capable of empathy. They should be capable of multitasking, i.e. listening and recording data simultaneously.

Activity Debriefing 8.2

You may have written down some or all of the following points:

- Prescreening – Calls can be made to respondents prior to sending the questionnaire. This could confirm details and create a sense of expectation and commitment to the process
- Reminder calls or letters to encourage the respondent to reply – These may take place at a specified time after the questionnaire has been sent. Some agencies will send duplicate copies of the research questionnaires
- The covering letter is crucial to introduce the research and the organization carrying out the research. It may contain letter of reference or professional membership symbols.

Wilson (Wilson, A., 2003) suggests that the covering letter should contain:

- the purpose of the research
- assurances of confidentiality
- reasons why they should respond
- the time needed to complete the research
- a number and name for enquiries
- time scales and manner of return
- thanks
- The research may be incentivised. In consumer markets, the use of coupons or vouchers can be used in b2b markets where access to an executive summary of the final report may be offered as an incentive
- Personalize the survey. Postal research response rates tend to be higher when the research is part of an existing relationship. Data collection methods need to reflect the nature of the population under consideration.

Activity Debriefing 8.3

International students can try the same at www.esomar.nl.

Activity Debriefing 8.4

International readers can do the same for their markets at www.esomar.nl.

Unit 10

Activity Debriefing 10.1

You may have several:

The members list of the CIM, MRS or IDM

Members of the institute of directors

Companies house

Subscriber lists to the marketing press

Business directory services such as Kompass

Business-to-business profiling companies like Dunn and Bradstreer

Trade Association in the food and drinks sector

You may have others....

Activity Debriefing 10.2

Probability of selection = 20,000/500.

Probability of selection is 40.

Activity Debriefing 10.3

Remember the formula, and work though the example

$$N = \frac{Z^2\sigma^2}{E^2}$$

$$N = \frac{(2.58 \times 2.58) \times (40.8 \times 40.8)}{5 \times 5}$$

$$N = \frac{6.6564 \times 1664.64}{25}$$

$$N = \frac{11076.514}{25}$$

The sample required is 443.

Play around with the formula. Change the required level of precision and look at the impact on the sample size required.

Unit 11

Activity Debriefing 11.1

Determine the hypotheses:

H_0 The number of responses to each mailing is equal.

H_1 There is a significant difference between the responses to the mailings.

5909 5810 6350 = observed values
6023 = expected value
2.16 7.53 17.75 = observed values – expected values/expected values
27.44 = chi value

At 2 degrees of freedom, alpha value = 5.99.

Chi-value is higher, therefore we can be 95 per cent confident that there is a difference and the null hypothesis should be rejected.

Activity Debriefing 11.2

There are many but you may have come up with some of the following:

Sales volume and variables such as price, level of advertising expenditure, competitive activity, and various consumer variables such as purchase behaviour, income, attitude and so on.

Restaurant	Capacity	Turnover (£100,000)	x^2	y^2	xy
1	210	£1.10	44100	1.199025	229.95
2	80	£0.74	6400	0.540225	58.80
3	80	£0.99	6400	0.97515625	79.00
4	160	£1.14	25600	1.29390625	182.00
5	100	£1.01	10000	1.010025	100.50
6	70	£0.92	4900	0.837225	64.05
7	160	£1.08	25600	1.1664	172.80
8	60	£0.80	3600	0.63600625	47.85
9	300	£1.10	90000	1.199025	328.50
10	200	£1.16	40000	1.334025	231.00
11	150	£1.09	22500	1.18265625	163.13
12	50	£0.68	2500	0.45900625	33.88
13	80	£0.78	6400	0.60450625	62.20
14	150	£1.08	22500	1.16100625	161.63

15	100	£1.12	10000	1.243225	111.50
16	100	£0.90	10000	0.80550625	89.75
17	90	£0.94	8100	0.874225	84.15
18	170	£0.91	28900	0.819025	153.85
19	80	£0.85	6400	0.7225	68.00
20	110	£1.05	12100	1.1025	115.50
Sum	2500	19.375	386000	19.165175	2538.03
Mean	125	£0.97			

R =0.68112

The value of R in this example indicates some association and given that capacity should be a strong indicator of sales in the restaurants, further work may be required.

Activity Debriefing 11.3

Restaurant	Capacity X	Turnover (£100,000) Y	x^2	y^2	xy
1	210	£1.10	44100	1.199025	229.95
2	80	£0.74	6400	0.540225	58.80
3	80	£0.99	6400	0.97515625	79.00
4	160	£1.14	25600	1.29390625	182.00
5	100	£1.01	10000	1.010025	100.50
6	70	£0.92	4900	0.837225	64.05
7	160	£1.08	25600	1.1664	172.80
8	60	£0.80	3600	0.63600625	47.85
9	300	£1.10	90000	1.199025	328.50
10	200	£1.16	40000	1.334025	231.00
11	150	£1.09	22500	1.18265625	163.13
12	50	£0.68	2500	0.45900625	33.88
13	80	£0.78	6400	0.60450625	62.20
14	150	£1.08	22500	1.16100625	161.63
15	100	£1.12	10000	1.243225	111.50
16	100	£0.90	10000	0.80550625	89.75
17	90	£0.94	8100	0.874225	84.15
18	170	£0.91	28900	0.819025	153.85
19	80	£0.85	6400	0.7225	68.00
20	110	£1.05	12100	1.1025	115.50
Sum	2500	19.38	386000	19.165175	2538.03
Mean	125	£0.97			

To calculate the slope

$$B = \frac{2538.03 - 20 \times 125 \times 0.97}{386000 - 20 \times 125^2}$$

$$B = \frac{113.03}{73500}$$

$$b = .0015$$

To calculate the intercept

$$a = 0.97 - 0.0015 \times 125$$
$$a = 0.7825$$

Therefore for every increase in capacity of 7.8, sales should increase by .015 hundred thousand pounds or £1500 per year.

appendix 5 marketing research and information

Aim

The Marketing Research and Information module covers the management of customer information and research projects as part of the marketing process. It provides participants with both the knowledge and the skills to manage marketing information, and the more specialist knowledge and skills required to plan, undertake and present results from market research.

This module is a joint syllabus, shared with the Marketing Research Society.

Related statements of practice

Ac.1 Identify information requirements and manage research projects and the MkIS.

Ac.2 Evaluate and present information for business advantage.

Bc.1 Contribute information and ideas to the strategy process.

Learning outcomes

Participants will be able to:

- Identify appropriate marketing information and marketing research requirements for business decision-making.
- Plan for and manage the acquisition, storage, retrieval and reporting of information on the organization's market and customers.
- Explain the process involved in purchasing market research and the development of effective client–supplier relationships.
- Write a research brief to meet the requirements of an organization to support a specific plan or business decision.
- Develop a research proposal to fulfil a given research brief.
- Evaluate the appropriateness of different qualitative and quantitative research methodologies to meet different research situations.

- Design and plan a research programme.
- Design a questionnaire and discussion guide.
- Interpret quantitative and qualitative data, and present coherent and appropriate recommendations that lead to effective marketing and business decisions.
- Critically evaluate the outcomes and quality of a research project.
- Explain the legal, regulatory, ethical and social responsibilities of organizations involved in gathering, holding and using information.

Knowledge and skill requirements

Element 1: Information and research for decision-making (15 per cent)

1.1 Demonstrate a broad appreciation of the need for information in marketing management and its role in the overall marketing process

1.2 Explain the concept of knowledge management and its importance in a knowledge-based economy

1.3 Explain how organizations determine their marketing information requirements and the key elements of user specifications for information

1.4 Demonstrate an understanding of marketing management support systems and their different formats and components.

Element 2: Customer databases (15 per cent)

2.1 Demonstrate an understanding of the application, the role in customer relationship management (CRM) and the benefits of customer databases

2.2 Describe the process for setting up a database

2.3 Explain how organizations profile customers and prospects

2.4 Explain the principles of data warehouses, data marts and data mining

2.5 Explain the relationship between database marketing and marketing research.

Element 3: Marketing research in context (25 per cent)

3.1 Describe the nature and structure of the market research industry

3.2 Explain the stages of the market research process

3.3 Describe the procedures for selecting a market research supplier

3.4 Identify information requirements to support a specific business decision in an organization and develop a research brief to meet the requirements

3.5 Develop a research proposal to fulfil a given research brief

3.6 Explain the ethical and social responsibilities inherent in the market research task.

Element 4: Research methodologies (30 per cent)

4.1 Explain the uses, benefits and limitations of secondary data

4.2 Recognize the key sources of primary and secondary data

4.3 Describe and compare the various procedures for observing behaviour

4.4 Describe and compare the various methods for collecting qualitative and quantitative data

4.5 Design a questionnaire and discussion guide to meet a project's research objectives

4.6 Explain the theory and processes involved in sampling.

Element 5: Presenting and evaluating information to develop business advantage (15 per cent)

5.1 Demonstrate an ability to use techniques for analysing qualitative and quantitative data

5.2 Write a research report aimed at supporting marketing decisions

5.3 Plan and design an oral presentation of market research results

5.4 Use research and data to produce actionable recommendations for a marketing plan or to support a business decision.

Related key skills for marketers

The syllabus covers the core knowledge and skills for marketing professionals. The 'key skills for marketers' cover the broader business and organizational skills that marketing professionals should also possess. Participants will not be assessed specifically on their ability to perform key skills. However, as professionals working in organizations, they will be expected to demonstrate during assessment in the relevant modules their knowledge, understanding and competence in the areas defined by the key skills. Participants should be encouraged to develop and demonstrate the application of relevant key skills through activities, assignments and discussions during their learning.

- Using ICT and the Internet
- Using financial information and metrics
- Presenting information
- Improving own learning and performance
- Working with others
- Problem-solving
- Applying business law.

Assessment

CIM will normally offer two forms of assessment for this module from which centres may choose: written examination and project-based assessment. CIM may also recognize, or make joint awards for, modules at an equivalent level undertaken with other professional marketing bodies and educational institutions.

Recommended support materials

Core texts

Wilson, A. (2002) *Marketing research: an integrated approach.* London, FT/Prentice Hall.

Dibb, S., Simkin, L., Pride, W. and Ferrell, O. (2000) *Marketing: Concepts and strategies.* 4th European edition, Abingdon, Houghton Mifflin.

Workbooks

CIM (2003) *Marketing research and information companion.* Cookham, Chartered Institute of Marketing.

Housden (2003) *Marketing research and information.* Oxford, Butterworth-Heinemann.

BPP (2003) *Marketing research and information.* London, BPP Publishing.

Supplementary readings

Birn, R.J. (2002) *Handbook of international market research techniques.* London, Kogan Page.

Chisnall, P. (2001) *Marketing research.* 6th edition. Maidenhead, McGraw-Hill.

Christopher, M., Payne, A. and Ballantyne, D. (2002) *Relationship marketing; Creating shareholder value.* 3rd edition. Oxford, Butterworth-Heinemann.

Crouch, S. and Housden, M. (2003) *Marketing research for managers.* 3rd edition. Oxford, Butterworth-Heinemann.

Gordon, W. (1999) *Goodthinking: A guide to qualitative research.* Henley on Thames, Admap.

Hilton, S. and Gibbons, G. (2002) *Good business: Your world needs you.* London, Texere.

Kinnear, T.C. and Taylor, J.R. (1996) *Marketing research: An applied approach.* 5th edition. Maidenhead, McGraw-Hill.

Proctor, T. (2002) *Essentials of marketing research.* 3rd revised edition. Harlow, FT/Prentice Hall. (Due Dec 2002)

Marketing journals

Participants can keep abreast of developments in the academic field of marketing by reference to the main marketing journals, a selection of which are listed in the Appendix to this document.

Press

Participants will be expected to have access to current examples of marketing campaigns and so should be sure to keep up to date with the appropriate marketing and quality daily press. A selection of marketing press titles is given in the Appendix to this document.

Websites

A list of websites that tutors and participants may find useful is shown in the Appendix at the end of this document.

Overview and rationale

Approach

This module aims to provide participants with both the knowledge and the skills to manage customer information and the more specialist knowledge and skills required to plan, undertake and present results from market research. This is a joint CIM and MRS module reflecting the importance of effective gathering, managing and using of customer information to members of both professional bodies.

This module's focus on customer information and market research builds on the Marketing Environment module of the Stage 1 syllabus, which examines the broader elements involved in analysing an organization's marketing environment. Participants are expected to be familiar with the contents of the Marketing Environment module before starting on this module.

The module addresses all of the activities involved in managing a market research project from the initial brief to the completion of the final written report. It integrates the management of this process with the management of an organization's customer databases.

Syllabus content

The balance of weighting allocated to each of the five elements of the syllabus reflects the importance of the area to the achievement of learning and performance outcomes, and the depth and breadth of material to be covered. Although each area may be regarded as a discrete element, there are clear progressions and overlaps in the knowledge and skills base considered, which has important implications for the delivery of the module.

Element 1: Information and research for decision-making (15 per cent)
This element focuses on the importance of information and particularly customer information to marketing, planning and management decisions. It is important that participants understand how research and information integrate with the overall marketing process. Within this, the concept of knowledge management and marketing management support systems should be explored.

Element 2: Customer databases (15 per cent)
Organizations may hold large amounts of information about customers and their behaviour in customer databases. This element looks at the tasks involved in managing and using the information stored in customer databases. It introduces the concepts of data warehouses, data marts and data mining. It also examines the boundaries between database marketing and marketing research. The role of customer databases within CRM should also be explored. This element should link to the Key Skill. 'Applying business law'.

Element 3: Marketing research in context (25 per cent)

This element provides an overview of the market research industry and how it operates as well as its ethical and social responsibilities. It also introduces the various stages of the marketing research process. The material places particular focus on the initial planning of the research and the agency selection process. As such, emphasis should be placed on developing practical skills in writing research briefs and research proposals.

Element 4: Research methodologies (30 per cent)

This element focuses on the methods used in secondary and primary (qualitative and quantitative) data collection. Participants should be able to compare different approaches as well as design a questionnaire and discussion guide. Probability and non-probability sampling theory and processes should also be fully understood.

Element 5: Presenting and evaluating information to develop business advantage (15 per cent)

This element focuses on the evaluation of information (qualitative and quantitative) as well as the communication of information (both verbally and in writing) to assist marketing decision-making. Although participants will not be tested on their ability to undertake statistical analysis, they are expected to show an understanding of various statistical techniques and their outputs. Knowledge and understanding of the communication of results is important in this element. However there is also a large amount of skill development required.

Delivery approach

Although it is expected that learning outcomes should be achieved as discrete goals of attainment, it is also expected that tutors recognize and impart an understanding of the integrated nature of the syllabus content. To achieve this, the continuous assessment could involve the participants undertaking a research project or assessing a case involving a total research project. Practical exercises, such as the development of research briefs, proposals, questionnaires, topic guides and sampling plans, are critical to the development of skills required within this module. It is important that the projects or case studies illustrate the integration of research and information with the marketing process as a whole.

Additional resources

Introduction

Texts to support the individual modules are listed in the syllabus for each module. This Appendix shows a list of marketing journals, press and websites that tutors and participants may find useful in supporting their studies at Stage 2.

Marketing journals

Participants can keep abreast of developments in the academic field of marketing by reference to the main marketing journals.

- *Corporate Reputation Review* – Henry Stewart
- *European Journal of Marketing* – Emerald
- *Harvard Business Review* – Harvard
- *International Journal of Advertising* – WARC
- *International Journal of Corporate Communications* – Emerald

- *International Journal of Market Research* – WARC
- *Journal of Consumer Behaviour An International Review* – Henry Stewart
- *Journal of the Academy of Marketing Science* – Sage Publications
- *Journal of Marketing* – American Marketing Assoc. Pubs Group
- *Journal of Marketing Communications* – Routledge
- *Journal of Marketing Management* – Westburn Pubs Ltd
- *International Journal of Market Research* – NTC Pubs
- *Journal of Product and Brand Management* – Emerald
- *Journal of Services Marketing* – Emerald
- *Marketing Review* – Westburn Pubs Ltd

Press

Participants will be expected to have access to current examples of marketing campaigns and so should be sure to keep up to date with the appropriate marketing and quality daily press, including:

- *Campaign* – Haymarket
- *Internet Business* – Haymarket
- *Marketing* – Haymarket
- *Marketing Business* – Chartered Institute of Marketing
- *Marketing Week* – Centaur
- *Revolution* – Haymarket

Websites

The Chartered Institute of Marketing

www.cim.co.uk	The CIM site with information and access to learning support for participants
www.connectedinmarketing.com	A CIM site providing information on current marketing issues and applications
www.cimvirtualinstitute.com	Full details of all that's new in CIM's educational offer including specimen answers and Hot Topics
www.cimeducator.com	The CIM site for tutors only

Publications online

www.revolution.haynet.com	*Revolution* magazine
www.marketing.haynet.com	*Marketing* magazine
www.FT.com	A wealth of information for cases (now charging)
www.IPA.co.uk	Need to register – communication resources
www.booksites.net	*Financial Times*/Prentice Hall Text websites

Sources of useful information

www.acnielsen.co.uk	AC Nielsen – excellent for research
http://advertising.utexas.edu/world/	Resources for advertising and marketing professionals, participants, and tutors
www.bized.com	Case studies
www.esomar.nl	European Body representing Research Organizations – useful for guidelines on research ethics and approaches
www.dma.org.uk	The Direct Marketing Association

www.eiu.com	The Economist Intelligence Unit
www.euromonitor.com	Euromonitor consumer markets
www.europa.eu.int	The European Commission extensive range of statistics and reports relating to EU and member countries.
www.managementhelp.org/research/research.htm	Part of the 'Free Management Library' – explaining research methods
www.marketresearch.org.uk	The MRS site with information and access to learning support for participants – useful links on ethics and code of conduct
www.oecd.org	OECD statistics and other information relating to member nations including main economic indicators
www.quirks.com	An American source of information on marketing research issues and projects
www.un.org	United Nations publish statistics on member nations
www.worldbank.org	World bank economic, social and natural resource indicators for over 200 countries. Includes over 600 indicators covering GNP per capita, growth, economic statistics, etc.

Case sites

www.bluelagoon.co.uk	Case – SME website address
www.ebay.com	Online auction – buyer behaviour
www.glenfiddich.com	Interesting site for case and branding
www.interflora.co.uk	e-commerce direct ordering
www.moorcroft.co.uk	Good for relationship marketing
www.ribena.co.uk	Excellent targeting and history of comms
www.sothebys.ebay.com	New services offered because of advances in electronic technology

Index